A BRITISH
RIFLE MAN

NAPOLEONIC LIBRARY

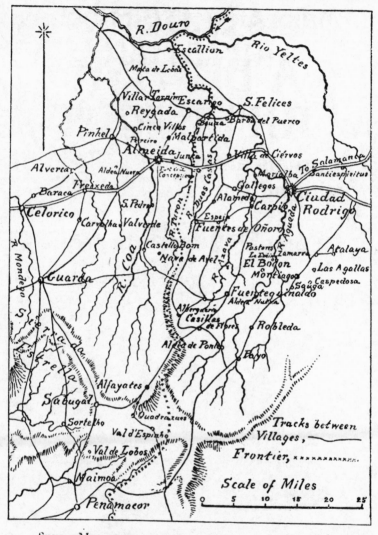

SKETCH-MAP ILLUSTRATIVE OF THE OPERATIONS ON THE COA
AND AGUEDA, 1810-1812.

Major George Simmons

A BRITISH RIFLE MAN

Journals and Correspondence
during the Peninsular War
and the
Campaign of Wellington

Edited, with Introduction, by
LIEUT.-COLONEL WILLOUGHBY VERNER

Greenhill Books, London
Presidio Press, California

Greenhill
Books

This edition of *A British Rifle Man*
first published 1986 by Greenhill Books, Lionel Leventhal Limited,
Park House, 1 Russell Gardens, London NW11 9NN
and
Presidio Press,
31 Pamaron Way, Novato, Ca. 94947, U.S.A.

ISBN 0-947898-33-6

Publishing History
*A British Rifle Man: The Journals and Correspondence
of Major George Simmons, Rifle Brigade, During the
Peninsular War and the Campaign of Waterloo* was first
published in 1899 by A. & C. Black, London. This
edition is reproduced now exactly as the original
edition, complete and unabridged.

Greenhill Books
welcome readers' suggestions for books
that might be added to this Series.
Please write to us if there are titles
which you would like to recommend.

Printed by Antony Rowe Limited,
Chippenham, Wiltshire.

CONTENTS

Contents

SKETCH MAPS

INTRODUCTION

GEORGE SIMMONS, the writer of the following letters
and journals, was born on 2nd May 1785. His
parents resided at Beverley, in Yorkshire. The
family consisted of nine sons and three daughters.

Since some of their names constantly recur in
Simmons's letters, a brief account of them will be
useful. Maud, the second son, obtained a commission in the 34th Foot in 1809. The third,
Joseph, after beginning life as an attorney's clerk,
joined his eldest brother's corps, the 95th Rifles,
as a Volunteer in 1812, and shortly afterwards was
granted a commission in it. All three brothers
served in the Peninsular War. The fourth brother,
John, appears to have been a source of some trouble
to his parents, and eventually ran away from home
and entered the Mercantile Marine. His career
at sea was a brief one. His ship was very soon
attacked and captured by a French privateer, and
he was killed in the engagement. The daughters,
especially the second, Ann, "My dear Ann" of
many a letter, were the object of constant solicitude
to George, and of much good advice and many
anxious forebodings. These details of the family are
rendered necessary by the fact that for some cause or

other the eldest brother appears to have constituted himself as the adviser and protector, and to some extent the supporter, of his parents. His father seems to have been in extremely straitened circumstances, and to have lacked the capability of looking after his family. George was evidently a very steady young fellow, and, realising that his father was unable to fight the battle of life, he set to work and studied medicine with a view to being able to support his parents. In 1805, when Napoleon's threatened invasion had caused all the manhood of England to enrol themselves for the defence of the country, George was given a commission as Assistant-Surgeon in the Royal South Lincolnshire Militia, commanded by Colonel Waldo-Sibthorp, M.P. In this corps he served for nearly four years, and during that time gained the friendship of his Colonel, who subsequently assisted him in various ways.

The Lincoln Militia were quartered in Hythe Barracks in the spring of 1809, as were both Battalions of the 95th Rifles. The latter were in a very shattered condition, having only recently returned from the disastrous campaign of Coruña. In order to fill up their depleted ranks, volunteers were called for from the Militia, and every Militia officer who could induce a hundred men to join the service was granted a commission. No difficulty, however, was experienced in obtaining recruits for " The Rifles," as they were styled. Although a very " young " regiment, having been raised only nine years previously, the peculiar nature of their arm—the rifle—and their exceptionally active em-

ployment, coupled with the fact that they had
already made their name at Copenhagen under
Lord Nelson, at Monte Video, and only recently at
Roliça, Vimeiro, and Coruña, caused many more to
volunteer for service in their ranks than could be
taken.

In the words of Sir William Cope, the historian
of the Rifle Brigade :—

The regiment had already became so famous and
popular, that not only were the deficiencies filled up in a
very short time, but more than a thousand volunteers
presented themselves beyond the numbers required. It was
therefore resolved by the Authorities to add a 3rd Battalion
to the regiment.

George Simmons, partly for reasons already given,
but no doubt also owing to strong military instincts
and a true British desire to "fight the French,"
easily induced a number of his Militiamen to
volunteer for the Rifles, and thereby became entitled to a second-lieutenant's commission himself—
there were no "ensigns" in the Rifles in those days.

It was at this juncture that his friend and bene-
factor, Colonel Sibthorp, unwilling to lose his Assistant-
Surgeon, and doubting the wisdom of his going out
to Portugal amid the circumstances, made use of
influence at the Horse Guards to cause the issue of
the commission to be delayed, trusting that, with
time for reflection, George might be induced to
abandon his project.

Our history opens with a letter from George in
May 1809 to his parents at Beverley, announcing
that he is about to embark at Dover for Portugal with
the 1st Battalion 95th Rifles, and recounting Colonel

Sibthorp's well-meant but inopportune efforts to retain his services in the Militia.

It will be seen that one of his chief reasons for quitting the Militia and joining the Army was " the interests of his family," to whom he hoped to be of use ; he wished " to assist the boys to go to school."

There is something very touching, albeit at the same time painfully incongruous, in worthy George Simmons's unceasing efforts thus to assist his family with small remittances from his hardly-won pay as a subaltern. To us soldiers of the end of the century the idea of a young man seeking a commission with a view to supporting his parents and assisting in the education of his brothers and sisters is so supremely absurd that at first one is inclined to look upon George as a well-meaning visionary. Facts, however, disprove the suspicion. Readers of these letters will learn how throughout the six campaigns in the Peninsula between 1809 and 1814, and also during and after the Waterloo campaign, Lieutenant Simmons, although thrice very severely wounded and put to much expense, managed constantly to remit a portion of his pay, and no inconsiderable portion of good advice as well, to his parents, who were sadly in need of both.

The letters in this volume are truthful accounts, written from many a bivouac and battlefield in Portugal, Spain, France, and Belgium, of the daily experiences of a young British officer taking his part in the great wars which were the main cause of Napoleon's downfall. Only now and then, where George Simmons has alluded to family matters of an entirely private nature, has it been considered desirable to excise the latter. But his views, correct or the reverse, of the military situation of the moment, his opinions of his chiefs and contemporaries, his anxieties about the welfare of his parents, brothers, and sisters, and his unceasing efforts to aid them, all forming as they do an integral part of his daily work, thoughts, and aspirations, have been left absolutely untouched.

To readers unacquainted with military matters it may be explained that these letters and journals claim to possess additional interest, since they are written by an officer who happened to belong to a regiment which saw more fighting in the Peninsula than any other in the British Army.

The Rifles formed part of the famous Light Division which was perpetually in the forefront of the battle, and they were the only regiment of British soldiers armed with the then newly introduced weapon —the rifle—in contradistinction to Brown Bess, the smooth-bore musket carried by the remainder of the Infantry. It is true that certain corps, notably the 5th Battalion of the 60th Royal American Regiment [1] and the Duke of Brunswick Oels' Corps, also were armed with rifles ; but, as these were composed of Germans and other foreigners, and their companies at times distributed among various Brigades, the same interest did not attach to them, nor were they able to take such a leading part in the fighting as the three Battalions of the 95th Rifles, who were present in whole or in part at every great battle in the long and bloody struggle in the Peninsula, save Albuera only.

[1] This Battalion was disbanded in 1818. The present King's Royal Rifle Corps are its representatives.

But although the regiment was composed of three battalions, it never mustered more than seventeen companies in the Peninsula, and at Waterloo only fourteen were present. It took its share not only in the general actions, sieges, and stormings in common with the other regiments, but also was constantly engaged in innumerable "affairs," as they are styled, which caused an unceasing drain on its strength —a drain from which regiments belonging to other Divisions were usually exempt. The reason for this was that the Light Brigade, or, as it was subsequently styled, the Light Division, was used during the campaigns in the Peninsula as a permanent covering or outpost force. Thus in 1810 it acted as a Corps of Observation on the Coa, far in advance of the rest of the army, and took part in the affairs of Barba del Puerco, Gallegos, etc., as well as in the severe fighting at the Combat of the Coa, at which no other troops were engaged. Again, in 1811, Craufurd's Brigade formed the advanced guard in the pursuit of Massena, and hence was constantly in collision with the enemy.

These events are well described by Simmons, and it will be seen that a similar condition of affairs prevailed in the subsequent campaigns of 1812-14. The normal strength of an infantry battalion in the Peninsula was ten companies, and whilst noting that the 95th Rifles had the great advantage of having three battalions in the field, which naturally gave them a greater chance than others of seeing fighting, it is only fair to remember that there were usually only from fifteen to seventeen companies, and *not* thirty, as is commonly supposed.

Several regiments had two battalions serving in the Peninsula, and hence were as strong numerically as the Rifles.

The "Baker" rifle, with which the regiment was armed, was in every sense an arm of precision up to 300 yards, and at ranges of 400 and 500 yards it was possible to hit a mark with it. This alone gave the Riflemen an immense advantage over their comrades armed with smooth-bore muskets, and, as proved by the experiments at Woolwich, it was greatly superior to the rifles of Continental and American manufacture in use at the time.

This rifle was invented by Ezekiel Baker, a London gunmaker, towards the close of the last century, and was the first rifle regularly adopted into the British service. It was tried at Woolwich in February 1800 by order of the Board of Ordnance, and was selected as the arm of the Rifle Corps, then in process of being raised. On this occasion eleven shots out of twelve were placed in a six-foot circular target at 300 yards' distance. The following is a description of the Baker rifle : Weight 9½ lbs., barrel seven-grooved and 30 inches in length, rifling one quarter turn in barrel, bullet spherical, 20 to the pound, charge of powder 84 grains, flint-lock. The ball was placed in the centre of a greased leather patch and rammed home, considerable force being necessary to effect this. At first, wooden mallets were issued to the Riflemen to facilitate the process of ramming home, but these were very shortly discontinued (*circa* 1803). A supply of greased patches was carried in a small box with spring brass lid in the side of the butt of the rifle.

As regards rapidity of fire, the maximum rate at which perfectly steady shots could be taken was reckoned to be one per minute.

This weapon was the one used by the Rifle Corps in their maiden action at Ferrol in 1800, and at the battle of Copenhagen in 1801, where the Riflemen fought under Lord Nelson and were distributed as sharp-shooters among various British ships of the line. It was further used in South America in 1807-8 and throughout the Peninsula campaigns of 1808-14, and also at Waterloo. In 1838 it was supplanted by the percussion-lock Brunswick rifle, having thus been in use in the service for a longer period than has any rifled firearm.

The smooth-bore musket, commonly known as " Brown Bess," was a much heavier and longer weapon, throwing a spherical ball of 14 to the pound, and the uncertainty of its fire is well evidenced by the expression " as random as a common musket," which is to be met with in treatises on rifle-shooting at the beginning of the century. This weapon was in use up to the year 1853. It would not carry straight for 100 yards, and its effective range was barely double that distance. Such was " the musket, that queen of weapons," as it has been styled, with which the British infantry won all its great victories from the time of Marlborough until the conquest of the Punjaub in 1849.

That even greater results were not obtained from the rifle during the Peninsular War is due to the fact that the 95th Riflemen were naturally often compelled to conform to the general movements of large bodies of troops armed with smooth-bores.

Their utility was in consequence frequently unduly circumscribed by the exigencies of the moment.

It was, however, in the affairs of outposts and advanced guards, and on occasions when individual action was both permissible and practicable, that the value of the rifle became most apparent. Thus at the action of Tarbes on March 14, 1814, the three Battalions of the 95th attacked and ousted from an exceptionally strong position a French Division. George Simmons was severely wounded in this fight. An eye-witness belonging to another corps thus describes the attack, and in words which convey a good idea of the methods of Riflemen under such circumstances: "Our Rifles were immediately sent to dislodge the French from the hills on our left, and our Battalion was ordered to support them. Nothing could exceed the manner in which the 95th set about this business. Certainly I never saw such skirmishers as the 95th, now the Rifle Brigade. They could do the work much better and with infinitely *less loss* than any other of our best Light troops. They possessed an individual boldness, a mutual understanding, and a quickness of eye in taking advantage of the ground, which, taken altogether, I never saw equalled. They were, in fact, as much superior to the French Voltigeurs as the latter were to our skirmishers in general. As our regiment was often employed in supporting them, I think I am fairly qualified to speak of their merits." [1]

Unquestionably the most pressing military problem of the present day is how to conduct an attack on troops armed (as all infantry are now) with

[1] *Twelve Years' Military Adventure*, London, 1829.

magazine rifles, which, owing to their flat trajectory
and extraordinary rapidity and precision of fire, are
overwhelming in their effects against favourable
targets up to 2000 yards.

The object-lesson most recently before us is that
of the fight at Khartoum, where the absolute impossi-
bility of masses of men advancing under modern
artillery and rifle fire, although known to students of
war, was practically demonstrated again to the whole
world. The unusually heavy losses experienced by
our troops in the fighting on the Indian Frontier
in 1897 were mostly due to the able manner
in which the Afridis and other tribesmen took
advantage of the ground and worked in unison (as
did the Riflemen at Tarbes and on many another
battlefield) to assist and support one another, and
thus develop their fire so as to obtain the maximum
value from it with the minimum exposure and loss
to themselves. The accounts by officers who served
in that campaign bear a striking resemblance to some
of the instances narrated by George Simmons of the
methods of fighting of the Riflemen during the Peninsular War. Thus the French captain's description in
Chapter V. of the attack of the British Riflemen at
Vimeiro, and the heavy losses he sustained, especially
in officers, is almost an exact repetition of some of the
accounts of the fights in the Tirah Campaign of 1897.

Sir John Kincaid, who served throughout the
Peninsular War, and was adjutant of the 1st Battalion
95th Rifles at Waterloo, says truly that his corps, as
"the Light regiment of the Light Division, fired the
first and last shot in almost every battle, siege, or
skirmish, in which the army was engaged during the

war." But he hastens to add that he considered the
43rd and 52nd Light Infantry *as a part of the Rifles*,
"for they bore a share in everything, and although
the nature of our arm generally gave us more em-
ployment in the way of skirmishing, yet, whenever
it came to a pinch, independent of a suitable mixture
of them among us, we had only to look behind to
see a line in which we might place *a degree of confidence almost equal to our hopes in heaven;* nor
were we ever disappointed. There never was a corps
of Riflemen in the hands of such supporters."

It is notoriously dangerous to prophesy, but I
am presumptuous enough to believe that the difficult
problem of the conduct of attacks in the future will in
all probability be solved by adopting some system based
on the methods originated and carried out so successfully by the first regiment of Riflemen in the British
service during the Peninsular War, of which the
account of their attack on the French position at
Tarbes, given by the author of *Twelve Years' Military
Adventure*, is a good example. It is, of course, an
integral part of the system that the firing line should
be intelligently and effectively supported, so as to
give those committed to the forefront of the battle
that superb *confidence*, both in themselves and in their
comrades behind, so admirably described by Kincaid.

Such confidence can only come from careful training and fellowship in peace time, followed by experience
on active service under fire, and this is precisely what
the celebrated Light Division was fortunate enough to
obtain. For it was largely due to the marvellous
training of the Light Brigade, consisting of these
same three regiments, under Sir John Moore at Shorn-

cliffe during the years 1803 to 1805 that the gallant
Craufurd was able to achieve the splendid results he
did, first with the "Light Brigade," and later with
his famous "Light Division."

But there was another element which should on
no account be ignored, and which unquestionably had
much to do with the successful training under
Moore. On the Rifle Corps being first raised in
1800, the Colonel, Coote Manningham, set to work
to train the officers and men thoroughly in the duties
of Riflemen in the field. In that year he issued
a small book entitled *Regulations for the Rifle
Corps*. The most noticeable point in this is the
great importance he attached to what is known as the
"Company system." Starting with the axiom that
"In a regiment of Riflemen, each company must be
formed upon the principle of being separate from, and
totally independent of, another," the whole of the
book is permeated with the same ideas. Thus it is
laid down that transfers of officers or men from one
company to another are not to be made unless absolutely necessary, since "Riflemen, being liable to act
very independently of each other, and in numerous
small detachments in the field, will feel the comfort
and utility of their own officer, non-commissioned
officers, and comrades with them, and the service
will be benefited by the tie of friendship."

Captains were held responsible for the whole
training of their men, and were directed "to offer
premiums" for those who became good rifle shots.
These were to be styled "marksmen" and to wear
"a green cockade!"

The *Regulations* are of especial interest nowadays,

since they show that as early as the first year of this century there were soldiers, such as Coote Manningham and his second-in-command, Lieutenant-Colonel the Hon. William Stewart (to whom no small share of their compilation is most justly ascribed), who realised the importance of educating the soldier of that day and also in treating him with consideration.

Thus a regimental school was founded and a library provided, periodical examinations were held of the scholars, and lectures on military subjects were given to officers and men. An excellent series of lectures given by Coote Manningham to the 95th Rifles at Shorncliffe in 1803 is still extant.[1]

From the foregoing it will be gathered that the men of the 95th had a thoroughly sound training, based on the soundest of principles — that of the Company in peace and war. This company system was introduced into the 43rd Light Infantry and into the 52nd Light Infantry about 1803. Added to this came the excellent Brigade training under Moore at Shorncliffe. It is amusing to think that the system of " Company " and " Brigade " training has only of recent years been adopted at our chief military school —Aldershot.

It was the outcome of Moore's untiring efforts, on which was engrafted the fiery spirit of Craufurd's remarkable personality, that caused the troops of the Light Division, after the death of their leader at the storming of Ciudad Rodrigo, to maintain their high

---

[1] *Military Lectures delivered to the Officers of the 95th (Rifle) Regiment at Shorncliff Barracks, Kent.* Reprinted recently, as well as Manningham's *Regulations*, by John Bale and Sons, 87 Great Titchfield Street, London, W.

character as skilful and intrepid warriors. So long as
the English language is spoken will Napier's heart-
stirring description of the storming of Badajoz by the
Light Division endure : " How deadly the strife was
at this point may be gathered from this ; the 43rd
and 52nd Regiments of the Light Division lost more
men than the seven regiments of the Third Division
engaged at the castle ! . . . Who shall do justice to the
bravery of the British soldiers ? to the noble emula-
tion of the officers ? Who shall measure out the
glory of . . . O'Hare of the Rifles, who perished
on the breach at the head of the stormers, and with
him nearly all the volunteers for that desperate
service ? Who shall describe . . . the martial fury
of that desperate Rifleman who, in his resolution to
win, thrust himself beneath the chained sword-blades,
and there suffered the enemy to dash his head to
pieces with the ends of their muskets ? Who can
sufficiently honour . . . the resolution of Ferguson
of the 43rd, who, having at Rodrigo received two
deep wounds, was here, with his hurts still open,
leading the stormers of his regiment, the third time
a volunteer, and the third time wounded ? "

It is a significant fact, and not very complimentary to the intelligence of the military
authorities of the period, that the 95th were not
granted several so-called " Honours " (or names of
battles) to wear on their appointments, albeit they
were present and took an active share in them.
Notable among these is " Pyrenees," in which region
the Rifles lost 15 officers and 264 non-commissioned
officers and men, killed and wounded. A full account
of the heavy fighting at this time will be found in

George Simmons's letters. In 1849, when the long-deferred medal for the great war was at last issued, no fewer than 294 men of the Rifle Brigade were granted the clasp for "Pyrenees," although to this day the regiment does not carry the "Honour" on its appointments.

The vast difference between a corps, for technical reasons (such, for example, as the Colonel having been granted the gold medal for having commanded his regiment in a fight), being given an "Honour," and its having been present and performed gallant service at the same engagement, is best illustrated by the remarkable fact that in 1849 no fewer than *three thousand four hundred and sixty-nine clasps* for Peninsula battles and sieges were issued to survivors of the 95th—a far greater number than were granted to any other regiment, and over *twenty-four times as many* as were issued to some which to this day carry more Peninsula Honours.

As regards the compilation of this volume, the original journals are contained in three small pocket-books, in paper covers, measuring only a few inches square and weighing $\frac{3}{4}$ oz., 1 oz., and 2 oz. respectively. These were carried by George Simmons in his head-dress throughout the wars, and hence he was always able to make notes from day to day of events as they occurred. These small books form the framework, so to speak, of the more voluminous journals, which were evidently written subsequently, when more time was available for such a purpose.

The journal which is now published is chiefly taken from the latter, but all dates, etc., have been verified from the smaller books. Concurrently with the journal, a series of letters to his parents from the seat of war, covering the whole period between May 1809 and September 1815, are here reproduced without alteration, save and except in the orthography of proper names and of Spanish and French towns, etc.

When possible, the signature of officers concerned, as given in the " Pay Lists and Muster Rolls " at the Record Office, has been adopted in rendering their names. Certain Spanish names, the spelling of which, although notoriously wrong, has been consecrated by usage, have been retained in the form most familiar to Englishmen.

No little difficulty was experienced in locating many of the places mentioned by Simmons, whose rendering of Spanish names was at times very erratic. This, however, is excusable when it is remembered that the whole British army, from the Duke downwards, habitually ignored the most elementary rules of orthography in the Spanish language. Sir William Napier himself was one of the greatest offenders in this way. To this day about half a dozen of the names of great battles in Spain and Portugal worn as " Honours " by regiments on their Colours are incorrectly spelt !

No two atlases agree as to Spanish spelling, but I was fortunate in obtaining a very fair Spanish map, entitled " Mapa Civil y Militar de España y Portugal," by Dauty and Malo, published in 1857, which I have taken as the basis of the rough sketch maps which illustrate these pages.

Even this, however, is at places difficult to follow nowadays, owing to changes in names of places.

Thus the town at the junction of the rivers Tagus and Zezere known as " Punhete " in 1809, and shown as such in 1857, is marked as " Constança " in more modern atlases.

A very clear map of the Peninsula, published in 1810 in London (which no doubt was largely used during the subsequent campaigns), is so utterly at variance with this Spanish map, not only in the spelling of names, but also in the position of towns and the course of rivers, that it is practically useless.

A word of explanation as to the title. When the Corps was first raised, Riflemen—being at the time a novelty—were styled Rifle Men. In one of the earliest " Clothing Warrants " of the regiment they are described as " the Regiment of Rifle Men."

George Simmons in his journals and letters adopted this form of spelling, and hence it has been retained as characteristic of the fashion of that period.

WILLOUGHBY VERNER,
Lieut.-Colonel.

ROYAL MILITARY COLLEGE,
   SANDHURST, *March* 1899.

OPORTO

TRAS OS MONTE

River Douro

Lamego

BEIRA

R. Vel.

R. Agueda

Barbo

R. Coa

Pinhel

Almeida

Vill

Trancoso

Vizeu

Celarico

Bataco

Freixeda

Fuentes de Onoro

Galleg

R. Azava

Alde

Sa da Caramula

R. Mondego

Sampu

Pinheiro

Moimenta da Serra

Vendas novas

S. Payo

Vª Cortez

Pinhancos

Mello

Maceira

Guarda

Foya

Busaco

Galizes

Sierra da Estrella

Sabugal

Alfayates

Lofran

Sobreira

Ponte de Murcella

R. Alva

Sortelho

Maimon

S. Fe 7ª Cl

Coimbra

Foz de Aronce

R. Ceira

Penamacor

Moraleja

Mondego Bay

Figueira

Condeixa

Casal Nova

Miranda do Corvo

Lousa

Atalaya

Pedrogao

Bemposta

S. Miguel d'Acha

R. Ponsul

R. At

Redinha

Alca

Estalos de Cima

Pombal

R. Soure

R. Nabao

R. Zezere

R. Ocreza

Lousa

Ladoeir

Zibreira

Zarza la I

Castello Branco

Leyria

Aldea da Cruz

Sarnadas

Ourem

Thomar

Villa Velha

River Tagus

Berlengas

Carvalhos

Torres novas

Colegao

Parnes

Punhete

Abrantes

Gaveao

Apalhao

Niza

Salorino

del Alcantara

Valencia

Arroyo d

Obidos

Roliça

Bemposta

Aldea de Mata

Manvão

Castello de Vide

Portalegre

Vimiero

Torres Vedras

(Lines)

Alenquer

Sobral

Arruda

Monchique

Bucellas

Cintra

Mafra

Belem

Lumiar

LISBON

Cataxa

Vejle

Almeyrim

Santarem

Juncos

Villa nova

Castanheira

Villa Franca

Alhandra

Alverca

Rio Mayor

R. Soura

Vallada

Crato

Ponte de Souro

Pedrosa

ALENTEJO

R. Cayo

R. Alvega

Arronhes

Campo Mayor

Albuquerque

Estromoz

ELVAS

BADAJOZ

Talavera R

River

Albu

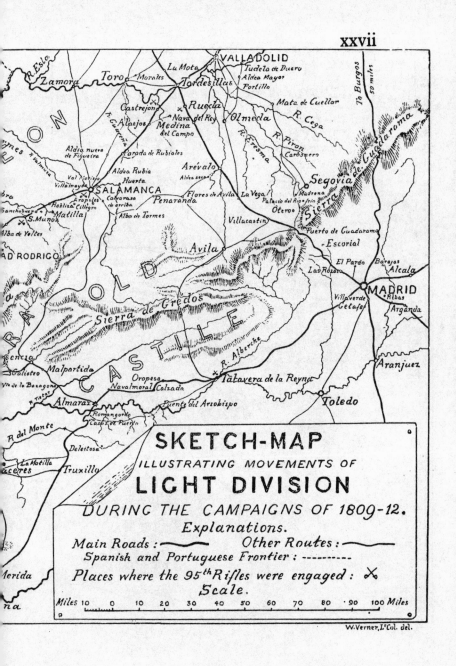

SKETCH-MAP
ILLUSTRATING MOVEMENTS OF
LIGHT DIVISION
DURING THE CAMPAIGNS OF 1809-12.
Explanations.
Main Roads : Other Routes :
Spanish and Portuguese Frontier : ----------
Places where the 95th Rifles were engaged : ✕
Scale.

Miles 10   0   10   20   30   40   50   60   70   80   ·90   100 Miles

W. Verner, L'Col. del.

SKETCH-MAP

ILLUSTRATING MOVEMENTS OF

LIGHT DIVISION

DURING THE CAMPAIGNS OF 1813-14.

Explanations.

Main Roads: ⎯⎯⎯⎯   Other Routes: ⎯⎯⎯

Spanish and French Frontier : ------------

Places where the 95th Rifles were engaged : ✕

Scale.

10 0 10 20 30 40 50 60 70 80 90 100 Miles

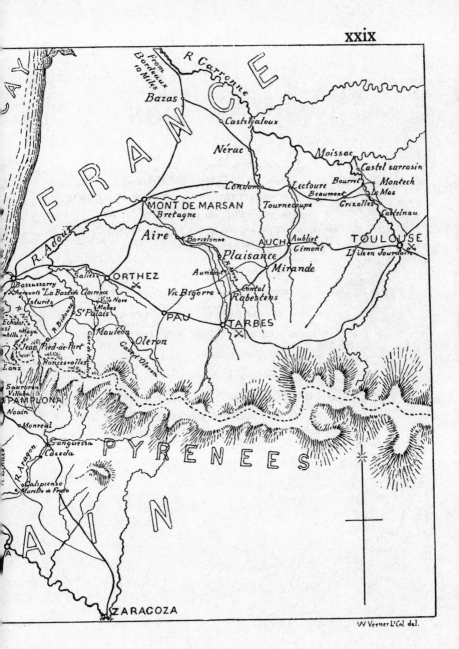

FRANCE

SPAIN

PYRENEES

R Garonne

From Bordeaux 10 Miles

Bazas

Casteljaloux

Nérac

Moissac

Castel sarrasin

Condom

Lectoure

Bourret

Montech

Beaumont

Le Mas

MONT DE MARSAN

Bretagne

Tournecoupe

Grizolles

Castelnau

Aire

Barcelonne

AUCH

Aubliet

TOULOUSE

Plaisance

Gimont

L'isle en Jourdain

R Adour

Mirande

Auriébat

Bassussarry

Salies

ORTHEZ

Vic Bigorre

Rabestens

Arcanyts

La Bastide

Cairence

Ville Nove

Mabes

Isturitz

S'Palais

PAU

Cantal

Echalar

R Bidoux

Maye

TARBES

Mauleon

S'Jean Pied-de-Port

Oloron

Gave de Mauleon

Gave d'Oloron

Roncesvalles

Lanz

Saurrurers

Villaba

PAMPLONA

Noain

Monreal

Sanguessa

Caseda

R Aragon

Calipienzo

Murillo de Frutn

ZARAGOZA

W. Verner L'Col del.

To

GENERAL HIS ROYAL HIGHNESS

THE DUKE OF CONNAUGHT AND STRATHEARN,

COLONEL-IN-CHIEF OF THE RIFLE BRIGADE,

FORMERLY (1803-1816) STYLED THE 95TH RIFLES AND

(1800-1802) THE RIFLE CORPS,

THIS VOLUME

IN WHICH A BRITISH RIFLE MAN RECOUNTS HIS PERSONAL

KNOWLEDGE OF MANY OF THE DEEDS THAT HAVE

MADE THE NAME OF THE REGIMENT

SO FAMOUS

IS (BY PERMISSION) DEDICATED

BY HIS MOST HUMBLE AND OBEDIENT SERVANT

WILLOUGHBY VERNER,

LIEUTENANT-COLONEL, LATE OF THE RIFLE BRIGADE.

A British Rifle Man

COMMENCEMENT OF THE PENINSULAR WAR
CAMPAIGN OF 1808

THE Peninsular War commenced in the year 1808, on 1st
August of which year Major-General Sir Arthur Wellesley
disembarked at Mondego Bay and marched on Lisbon, at that
time occupied by a French army under Marshal Junot. The
latter sent General Laborde with a Division to oppose Wellesley's
advance, and on 15th August the first skirmish took place at
Obidos. On this occasion the 95th Rifles had an officer killed
(Lieut. Bunbury), the first British officer who fell in the
Peninsular War. On 17th August, Wellesley defeated Laborde
at the battle of Roliça, and four days later he met and defeated
Junot at the battle of Vimeiro. Then followed the Convention
of Cintra, under the terms of which Junot was permitted to
embark his army of 25,000 men at Lisbon and the French
evacuated Portugal.

The British Government now sent out strong reinforcements
to the Peninsula, and appointed Sir John Moore to the chief
command. Moore's forces concentrated in the vicinity of
Salamanca, and then advanced to engage Soult, who was holding
the line of the Carrion river. Meanwhile the Spanish armies
had been defeated at all points, and the French army, commanded
by Napoleon in person and numbering over 100,000 men, was
set at liberty to attack Moore, whose forces only amounted to
25,000 men. In spite of these appalling odds, Moore conducted

an admirable retreat, and at Rueda, Sahagun, Benavente, and Mayorga his cavalry obtained brilliant successes over the French.

On 1st January 1809 Napoleon entered Astorga, only to find that he was too late to destroy the English army, which had evaded his blow and was in retreat on Vigo and Coruña. Leaving Soult to continue the pursuit, the Emperor now returned to France.

Moore carried out his retirement in a masterly manner; at Caçabelos, Constantin, and Lugo he checked his pursuers and inflicted heavy losses on their advancing columns. The retreat terminated with the battle of Coruña, fought on 16th January 1809, when the gallant Moore was killed, but not before he had heavily defeated the French and thus secured the embarkation of his forces.

CAMPAIGN OF 1809

The French army in Spain was ordered by Napoleon to reoccupy Portugal, and Marshal Soult was directed to march, *via* Oporto, on Lisbon, Marshal Ney to hold Galicia, and Marshal Victor to invade Portugal south of the Tagus.

The British Government sent out Sir Arthur Wellesley to Portugal with strong reinforcements. Wellesley marched on Oporto and seized the passage of the Douro on 12th May, and drove Soult back into Galicia. Victor meanwhile had reached Talavera de la Reyna on the Tagus, and was supported by King Joseph and Marshal Jourdan.

Wellesley now advanced and joined the Spanish General Cuesta near Talavera. Victor thereupon fell back, and, Cuesta following him up alone, was severely handled by King Joseph and driven back behind the Alberche river.

The French army, under King Joseph with Jourdan and Victor, now advanced and crossed the Alberche, and, after several sharp combats, the battle of Talavera was fought on 28th July. After a desperate struggle, the French were finally driven back at all points, and early on the following morning retired across the Alberche.

On the same day, the Light Division under General Craufurd, consisting of the 43rd and 52nd Light Infantry and the 1st Battalion 95th Rifles, reached the field and immediately took up the outposts. This Division, after a march of 20 miles, was in bivouac at Malpartida, when Craufurd received a report that the British were hard pressed at Talavera. He at once started "with a resolution not to halt until he reached the field of battle. . . . The troops pressed on with impetuous speed, and, leaving only seventeen stragglers behind, in twenty-six hours crossed the field of battle, a strong compact body, having during that time marched 62 English miles in the hottest season of the year, each man carrying from fifty to sixty pounds weight." [1]

Soult being joined by Ney, Mortier, and Kellermann, now moved against Wellesley's line of communications, and the latter, leaving Cuesta to watch King Joseph on the Alberche, marched to oppose him. Cuesta, however, abandoned his post and fell back on Wellesley, closely pursued by Victor. At the same time the English General learned that Soult, having received reinforcements, had now a force of over 53,000 as against his 17,000 British troops ; and he was in consequence forced to recross the Tagus at Puente del Arzobispo and retire on Portugal.

Thus ended the campaign of 1809, during which the British losses amounted to over 3500 ; and, owing to the hopeless conduct of both the Spanish Government and the Spanish generals, all the advantages which should have accrued to the British, from the successful operations on the Douro in May and the victory of Talavera in July, were rendered nugatory, and the French, in the words of Napier, were left with "all the credit of the campaign."

[1] Napier's *History of the War in the Peninsula*, vol. ii. p. 407.

CHAPTER I

LETTER No. I

To his Parents, from Hythe and Dover, dated 21st May 1809

Announces the embarkation of the 1st Battalion 95th Rifles—Colonel Sibthorp endeavours to dissuade him from going out, but fails.

Journal—25th May–17th July 1809

Embarkation at Dover, the voyage out, landing at Lisbon—The Rifles are posted to Major-General Craufurd's Brigade, and march to join Sir Arthur Wellesley, who is moving against Marshal Victor on the line of the Tagus—Halt at Castello Branco.

LETTER No. II

To his Parents, from Castello Branco, dated 18th July 1809

Describes landing at Lisbon—His opinion of Portuguese manners and morals—Account of the advance and nature of the country traversed—Conduct of the French to the Portuguese.

Letter No. I

Hythe, 21st May 1809.

My dear Parents — The long-wished-for day has come at last. I am this morning marching, with as fine a body of men as ever left England, for Dover, where we embark. I believe a very great army will accompany us. Our destination is a profound secret, and as I am not inquisitive, it gives me little concern; I daresay I shall soon enough see some diversion. The rumour goes, Austria or Portugal. Our men are in very high spirits, and we have a most excellent band of music and thirty bugle-horns, which through every country village strikes up the old tune, "Over the hills and far away." This, my dear parents, is the happiest moment of my life; and I hope, if I come where there is an opportunity of showing courage, your son will not disgrace the name of a British soldier.

Col. Sibthorp arrived here the other day, and directly sent to speak to me. I waited upon him, and told him it was impossible for me to recall what I had stated to the men who had done me the honour of preferring to be with me and the regiment I was pleased to sanction, to any others. When he found me inflexible, he then felt extremely hurt at frustrating my views; and, to make up for putting a stop to me being gazetted, he immediately wrote to the Commander-in-Chief and begged to recommend me as a very deserving young man, and stated exactly the reasons which induced him to endeavour to stop

1809 me entering the Line ; he also hoped he would take into consideration the manner I had acted in procuring, entirely through my own exertions, the number of men for His Majesty's service, and have my commission antedated. He said I deserved great credit for my resolution in not being dissuaded from my project, as I had determined to follow the profession of a soldier ; and my conduct in his regiment hurt him exceedingly to lose me, but he hoped I should meet with friends wherever I went, and his friendship he should always be proud of showing me at all times. He sent for me to breakfast with him, and before I came away presented me with twenty-five guineas, which just came at a time when I should have been obliged to borrow to equip myself for service. The Colonel recommended me very strongly to the notice of Colonel Beckwith, whom I now have the honour to serve under, and from whom I have received every mark of esteem, with a promise to do me every kindness in his power. I felt some anxiety at leaving my brother officers, who vied with each other in showing their friendship and kindness on all occasions. My Captain gave me an elegant sabre, and another gave me a large cloak—Rifle Men being generally obliged to sleep in the fields (on service), and their cloaks are their beds upon all occasions. I never shall experience more friendship from any set of men. Some will say, pray why do you leave them when you can be so happy (this was my late Colonel's observation), but my reasons I cannot explain to every one. I am confident there would have been little chance of promoting the interests of my family as I was situated ; and as a soldier, with perseverance, I must in time have promotion, which 1809 will soon enable me to be of use to my family ; and at all times it will be my greatest pleasure and pride to take care that the boys go regularly to a good school, and I have no doubt of seeing them one day men of some experience through my interposition.

I have left two large boxes in the stores of the 1st Battalion 95th Regiment at Hythe Barracks. One, which I brought out of Yorkshire with me, is filled with clothes and linen ; the other with my bed and bedstead. If I should not return to England again, I think it would be worth your while to have them home, as they would pay the carriage and they could come by sea.

You would see by the newspapers, if you did not hear from me, you may always know where the Regiment was stationed. I deem it necessary to give this notice for fear of mistakes, as, if I happened to be popped off, in my last moments it would be a comfort to me to think I had left you all I was in possession of. Should you not procure my boxes by that means, write to Captain Platt of the Royal South Lincoln Regiment of Militia, there stationed, and you will at all times be enabled to find out ; he will soon forward them to you. Do not laugh at my giving such strict injunctions, as I like to do everything concerning myself methodically, and then I have nothing to fear.

Maud,[1] I daresay, will be in this Expedition ; if not it may be some time before we meet. As most likely you will have his address, write and tell him I am gone. As soon as I arrive at our destination I shall

[1] George Simmons' second brother in 34th Regiment.—Ed.

1809 take the earliest opportunity of letting you have the particular occurrences which may befall me. Until then, farewell.

I have in the Navy a friend who, I expect, will soon be made Captain ; and have, if that takes place, a chance to procure a berth for my brothers. Make them good scholars, I have not the least doubt of soon taking them off your hands. I hope you will obey this command, and read this part to Joseph and John, which, if they wish one day to shine in the world, they will now strive to pay every attention.

I have left in my box some letters from Colonel Sibthorp, which I shall feel pleasure another day to read to you, as it is impossible to express the fatherly and friendly manner he has at all times condescended to address me with. Being in such a hurry to embark, it is with some difficulty I have time to address you at all, and I had almost forgotten to mention my dear Ann, who, I hope, will forgive me, and not attribute it to my neglect. My blessing to the children ; and, if it pleases God to spare my life, I hope on my return to see you all. My best wishes to uncle, aunt, and friends.—I am affectionately yours,   GEORGE SIMMONS.

Dover, May 25th   Do not mention my letters, I beg of you. It was a most beautiful sight to see us embark, and the lovely creatures cheering the men as they passed.

Journal—25th May–15th July 1809

May 25th   The 1st Battalion 95th Regiment had been under orders to embark at a moment's notice for some days.

The order arrived last night, and at two o'clock this 1809 morning the Battalion was formed in the Barrack Square, consisting of 1000 as fine young fellows as were ever collected to fight their country's battles. For my part, my heart was as light as a feather when we marched off; and, if I may judge from appearances, every person had the same feelings. We entered Dover about six o'clock and marched through it. The windows were crowded with inhabitants; some greeted us, but in general the women seemed sorry to see us depart, knowing well that numbers must never return to their native land again.

The Battalion embarked in three transports, *Fortune*, *Malabar*, and *Laurel*, and sailed immediately for the Downs, where we came to anchor. The 1st Battalion 43rd and 52nd Light Infantry joined us here, which with ourselves formed a Light Brigade, under the command of Major-General Robert Craufurd, who took post on board the *Nymph* frigate, 44 guns, commanded by the Honourable Captain Percy, and also the *Kangaroo* sloop of war under his command. Foul winds and sometimes very stormy until 3rd June.   June

The Commodore hoisted the signal for sailing at daylight. The fleet got under weigh towards evening and stood down the Channel.

Saw the Isle of Wight at daylight; we neared it 4th and anchored at St. Helens.

The weather very squally. The fleet weighed and 5th moved close to Cowes, where we were detained by contrary winds for six days.

The wind seeming to become favourable, the fleet 11th was put once more into motion, but proving a

1809 false alarm, we brought up opposite Yarmouth, and
June were again detained with foul winds until the 18th.

18th   Yesterday a boat upset coming to our ship, the
Fortune, from the Commodore's, and a young midshipman and one sailor met with a watery grave.
The midshipman was coming to invite Captain
Pakenham to dinner.   Our fleet sailed now in good
earnest with a fair wind, passed the Needles, and bid
adieu to the shores of Old England.

24th   Saw land ahead at daybreak, which was found to
be Cabo Prior, near Coruña in Spain ; weathered
Cape Finisterre.   At noon the Commodore chased
a strange sail ; it proved to be a Spanish brig, and
being a friend she was allowed to proceed.

25th   Sailed along the coast of Portugal, passed the
mouth of the Douro at 4 P.M.

26th   The *Kangaroo* took her departure for England.

27th   Passed through the inner passage of the Berlengas,
having previously taken on board a Portuguese pilot.
The Berlengas are a cluster of small rocky islands ;
on the largest of them the Portuguese have established a battery.   '

28th   Saw the Rock of Lisbon at daybreak.   It is a
bold mountain, whose sombre front overhangs the sea.
About noon we entered the Tagus, and our fleet
came to anchor close to Lisbon, which from the sea
appeared a most magnificent place indeed.   On landing the charm ceased, as the streets are exceedingly
filthy.   The quays are built of stone, and very good
along the river.

The Citadel is on a commanding eminence in the
town, from whence in every direction you may observe
churches, monasteries, convents, etc.   The most

magnificent church is that of S. Roche.   The French, 1809
under Junot, robbed this church of many valuables,
but the priests were fortunate enough to save some
things by hiding them from the grasp of these rapa-
cious plunderers.   We remained on board for four
days waiting for orders.

A number of Portuguese and transport boats
came alongside each ship for the purpose of conveying
us up the Tagus.   The tide began to flow about
midnight ; we entered the boats and proceeded up the
river.   The boats were crowded with men and we
rowed on slowly up the river, anxious for the approach
of day, which at last arrived.   The men were tugging
at the oars all day, and occasionally the boats ran
upon banks of sand.

At dusk we arrived at the village of Vallada, July
where we halted, and for the first time in my life I 3rd
was treated with a bivouac.   Hungry, wet, and cold,
and without any covering, we lay down by the side
of the river.   I put one hand in my pocket and the
other in my bosom, and lay shivering and thinking
of the glorious life of a soldier until I fell fast asleep.

We fell in at daylight.   I found the dew had wet 4th
me through, but the sun soon made his appearance
and dried me.

Marched into the town of Santarem, and halted
two days until the whole of the Brigade and the
baggage animals purchased in Lisbon arrived.   The
town is surrounded with hills that are covered with
innumerable olive-trees, a great source of wealth to
the inhabitants.   The place has a most respectable
appearance, the ground very fertile, and plenty of
wine, grapes, oranges, and vegetables of every descrip-

1809 tion in the greatest abundance. I made my way immediately with many hungry fellows to a *bodéga*. Breakfast was instantly produced, but the quantity of each article did not at all agree with our ideas of a breakfast, so that we were continually calling out for more of this thing and the other in broken Portuguese, which bothered the landlord so much that he took to his heels and we saw no more of him. I got a billet upon a blacksmith, and found his family very kind. They brought me fruit, wine, and cakes, but, as I do not understand one word of the language properly, everything was done by signs.

July I went on guard as supernumerary with Lieutenant
5th Macleod at a convent. At night I had lain down on a marble slab near the men, when a monk requested me to rise and follow him. He led me upstairs and into a large apartment, where a number of his brotherhood were assembled, and soon had the table filled with rich food, plenty of fruits, and good wines in abundance. I passed a few hours very agreeably with these hospitable monks, who all appeared, from their roundity of body, to pay more attention to feeding than praying.

7th This morning at daylight I left the hospitable blacksmith, who filled my calabash with wine and my haversack with food. I slung these across my shoulder and marched to Golegão, which is a small town on the banks of the Tagus.

8th Marched to Punhete and Tancos. The former town stands on the junction of the Zezere and Tagus, and the latter on the Tagus. In the river is an island with an old castle in ruins named Almorel; I paid it a visit.

A bridge of boats enabled us to pass the Zezere 1809 near Punhete.

A short sultry march brought us to Abrantes, July which being an hospital station, there was no room 9th for us in the town. We crossed the river over a bridge of boats, and took up our bivouac.

Abrantes is a town of some importance, with a citadel and fortifications round it. Marshal Junot took his title as Duke of Abrantes from it.

Marched to Gavião ; weather exceedingly hot.   11th

Marched over an uninteresting and hilly country 12th to Niza, which has a wall all round it in ruins, and the remains of an old Moorish castle in tolerable preservation. One observes on entering the town that several storks have built their nests near the gateway, which the inhabitants seem to be very careful of preserving, as they say that good luck attends those who are fortunate enough to be honoured by these birds building their nests in their grounds or upon their houses.

Marched to Villa Velha, and crossed the Tagus 13th over a bridge of boats, and bivouacked upon the opposite bank. The scenery at this place is very bold and romantic indeed, particularly by the pass. The country round has a barren appearance, except that portion covered with the gum cistus. The village is poor and miserable enough.

Marched to Sarnadas, a miserable place.   14th

Marched to Castello Branco ; halted two days in 15th this town, which has many good houses in it. The Bishop's house and gardens are superior to any other. The small river Ocreza runs close to the town.

LETTER No. II

CASTELLO BRANCO, 18*th July* 1809.

MY DEAR PARENTS—After experiencing a very favourable voyage, we came in sight of Lisbon on the 27th of June, and cast anchor before the town on the 28th. We received orders not to disembark the troops immediately. I therefore went on shore with a party of our officers. I must confess I felt much disappointed with the place, as a stranger seeing the town at a distance would conceive it a beautiful city ; but on a nearer view you find out all its imperfections. Elegantly-built houses, without windows or curtains for them, and as dirty as possible ; some few exceptions to this, I allow. The people in general are dirty in the extreme, their houses never whitewashed, and, stink worse than an English pig-sty. All the nastiness is thrown out of windows in the evening, and, having no scavengers to sweep the streets, you may judge the state of them in some measure; and in hot weather it is very offensive to the nose of an Englishman. I went to see several churches, which afforded me some amusement and excited my pity, to see a people, through ignorance and gross superstition, duped by a set of worthless priests under the plea of religion. I dined at an English hotel, and afterwards went to the opera. The dancing was too indelicate to give pleasure ; at least I felt it so, and blessed my stars I was an Englishman. The Portuguese ladies seemed to enjoy the performance with great rapture, which must make a Briton turn from them with disgust, and

awake in the soul those refined sentiments for delicacy 1809
and virtue which characterise our British dames;
and at all public entertainments a man possessing
any degree of feeling for the honour of the sex, must
be disgusted with such immodest performances.

As I have very few moments to spare, I must
endeavour to dedicate all my leisure time to re-
cruiting myself for the next day's march. On the
30th of June our Regiment, the 43rd and 52nd, disembarked into flat-bottomed boats about nine o'clock
in the evening and sailed up the Tagus. As the wind
was not very favourable, we were obliged to be
continually rowing; I frequently took a spell with
them. We landed at Vallada, about 90 miles from
Lisbon, on the evening of the 1st of July, and
directly formed in divisions. Marched about 10
miles up the country; halted upon a common; each
man took his greatcoat and contentedly lay down;
and for the first time in my life I slept very comfortably upon the ground. After sleeping three hours,
the bugles sounded. We again commenced our march
to Santarem, a large town situated in the interior of
Portugal. I was tired, but curiosity led me all over
the town, and, wandering from one place to another,
I found myself in a nunnery. The girls said I was
a Portuguese, as I was very much tanned by the sun
(the officers joke me frequently upon the same
subject). After amusing myself at the gratings with
the nuns, and receiving some little presents, I left
them and went to a convent of friars. I supped
with the grand priest; several monks were also
present. I then went to the play, came home to my
lodgings about half-past eleven o'clock, lay down

1809 till half-past one, and was upon the road marching at two. We continue marching every day in this manner, halting occasionally for half an hour, so that we manage to get to our destined place about eleven o'clock in the forenoon, which is generally upon a piece of ground shaded with trees. There we rest till one or two the next morning and start as before. I never enjoyed better health, and no difficulty appears a hardship ; my feet never blister, and I am always ready to commence the march with the first, and sleep as well upon the ground with a stone for my pillow as upon a bed of down. The weather is intolerably hot, and some men have died from the heat of the sun when marching. Our men, generally speaking, are healthy.

This country in some parts which we have passed through abounds with grapes, peaches, oranges, lemons, and fruits of every kind. The country we are at present in yields very little, being a continued series of immense mountains, which are difficult in ascending. We are often troubled to procure water ; I always make a practice of carrying a supply for myself, also provisions in my haversack for two or three days' support, so am very seldom at a loss. Wine is very cheap, but bad.

The French have carried away or eaten up all before them, and we often pass through villages entirely deserted by the poor unfortunate people. Sights of this kind will become habitual as we enter Spain ; from the rapid progress we make, in a few days we shall pass the frontiers of Portugal.

The French in some towns in Spain have murdered numbers of the inhabitants, and plundered the rest of every movable that was worth their taking—in short, 1809 their conduct has been barbarous in the extreme. Sir Arthur Wellesley, we hear, is rapidly advancing towards Madrid, and we are endeavouring to join him as soon as possible. It will be a little time before we have a general engagement unless the French make an advance and meet us. At present their army occupies a very strong position about forty miles from Madrid and in our line of march. It is supposed we shall give them battle as soon as we come up with them. The army has great confidence in Sir Arthur Wellesley, and are exceedingly anxious for the day of battle. I am a young soldier, but hope I shall do my duty when put to the trial. My Colonel has ever treated me with every mark of respect, and has put me into a company under the patronage of an old warrior, whose bravery has often been shown to the regiment. I have not had an opportunity of writing to Maud. I expect he will soon be here. I hope he has managed to surmount all the difficulties he had to encounter. A few years will put us, I hope, above a repetition of the same, as, if I live, we will be together. Endeavour to give the boys at home a liberal education, and I can soon provide for them as gentlemen.

My love to my dear mother. I hope she will not make herself unhappy on my account. If I am fortunate in the service I have embarked in, my greatest earthly pleasure will be to let my family reap the benefits. I only pray my father will strain every nerve to educate them, and the rest, leave to me. My love to my dear sisters Ann and Betsy. I hope Ann is now a comfort to her mother. I do not

1809 forget her.   Should I return, I will endeavour to come
and spend a few months with you.   My respects to
Uncle and Aunt and friends.—I remain, with every
good wish, your dutiful son,   GEO. SIMMONS.

As I am continually on the move I cannot inform
you where to direct for me, but if you have nothing
of moment to impart you need not write ; or should
you write, direct as follows : Lt. Simmons, 1st Batt.
95th or Rifle Regiment, Spain or elsewhere.   I
particularly charge my father not to expose my
letters to any one.

CHAPTER II

Journal—18th July–10th December 1809

Advance of the Light Division—The forced march on Talavera
—Arrival on the field of Talavera—Marshal Cuesta
abandons his position at Talavera, and at same time Marshal
Soult threatens the British line of retreat—Sir Arthur
Wellesley is forced to retire—The retreat to Portugal—
Simmons loses General Craufurd's private canteen cart—
Wrath of General Craufurd—Cantoned at Campo Mayor—
Simmons gets typhus fever—Great sickness amongst British
troops.

LETTER No. III

*To his Parents, from Campo Mayor, dated
September* 1809

The forced march on Talavera—Scene on the battlefield—
French dead and French prisoners—Kindness of French to
English prisoners— Return to Portugal — Meeting with
brother Maud—Forecasts as to his future military career—
Messages to his family.

LETTER No. IV

*To his Parents, from Campo Mayor, dated
29th October* 1809

Life in cantonments—Movements of the French—Vanity and
incapacity of the Spanish officers—Opinion of the army of
Lord Wellington—A letter from brother Maud—Advice to
his parents and messages to his sister.

Journal—11th–31st December 1809

The Light Division ordered to form a Corps of Observation on
the Coa—March from Campo Mayor to Coimbra *en route*
for the Coa.

1809   *Journal—18th July–10th December* 1809
July
18th   Marched to Ladocir.

19th   Marched to Zibreira, a tolerable village close to
the Spanish frontier. Country hilly.

20th   Entered Spain by crossing the river Herjas, which
takes its name from the Castle of Herjas ; it runs
close to the walls, and is the boundary between Spain
and Portugal for some considerable distance. Halted
at Zarza la Mayor.

21st   Moraleja.

22nd   Marched to Coria, which is a nice little city surrounded by a wall, and stands upon a plain. The river
Alagon runs close to it. The cathedral is a fine
building. I went into it and heard some sacred music
played upon the organ by a blind man. The people
since we entered Spain are much cleaner in their
persons and houses than the Portuguese, but the Portuguese are more hospitable and attentive to our wants.

24th   Marched to Galisteo, a town strongly situated and
walled all round, upon the Alagon.

25th   Marched to Malpartida and saw at a distance the
Gata mountains with their summits covered with
snow.

26th   Marched to the river Tietar and crossed by a bridge
of boats ; the day exceedingly hot and the column
much fatigued. Arrived at Venta de Bazagona.

27th   Marched to Navalmoral. Heat very oppressive.

Marched very early to the town of Calzada, 1809 where an express arrived from Sir Arthur Wellesley July directing the Brigade to make the least possible delay 28th in joining the army.   The Brigade, after a short rest, marched to Oropesa, where it halted four hours to cook, having marched under a scorching sun.   We again commenced the march all night in very deep and sandy roads, and arrived early upon the field of battle at Talavera de la Reyna this morning, 29th completing thirty miles during the night, having marched sixty-two English miles in twenty-six hours.[1] The Brigade was aware that the British army was engaged with the enemy.   Every one amongst us was anxious to participate if possible in the glorious cause, but we only arrived in time enough to see the dead and the wounded, which was a novel sight to me, and affected me exceedingly.   I almost wished myself well out of the scrape I had voluntarily entered into, but we had little time to reflect, as the Brigade was ordered to take up the chain of advance posts on the Alberche, which runs into the Tagus above Talavera. On the 27th the British and Spanish armies in position were attacked partially, but the French were obliged to retire back to their position.   The Duke de Belluno, Marshal Victor, made a general attack with all his forces this morning (28th) upon the British, but Sir Arthur Wellesley repulsed the enemy at all points. King Joseph was with the French.   The Spaniards under General Cuesta occupied the right of the position and the enclosures, but *Johnny* knew very well if he could dislodge John Bull, the Spaniards would soon

[1] Napier also gives these figures, but Simmons in his letter to his parents has a somewhat different version.   See p. 31.—ED.

1809 leave him in possession of the field. During this
sanguinary action numbers of the soldiers fell wounded
amongst the long grass and fields of standing corn,
which was set on fire from the bursting of shells.
Many of these men were frightfully burnt, not being
able to move away, and others literally burnt to death.

July   We were employed all this day in collecting the
30th dead bodies and putting them into large heaps mixed
with faggots and burning them. The stench from
so many dead bodies was volatile and offensive beyond
conception, as the heat of the weather was very great.
Some little firing took place between the outposts.

31st   Continued burning the dead as before. Talavera
is a good-sized town upon the right bank of the
Tagus, over which there is a well-built stone bridge.
It is about fourteen leagues from Madrid.

In consequence of the Light Brigade having arrived,
the enemy have not shown a disposition to repeat their
attack.

August   At daybreak the enemy's piquets were gone, leaving
1st a number of fires to deceive us. Patrols crossed
the Alberche.

3rd   The British army fell back to Oropesa, as the
Spanish general, Cuesta, had undertaken to keep the
French in check at Talavera whilst Sir Arthur
Wellesley made this movement to bring Marshal Soult
to action, who had passed the Sierra de Gata, and had
arrived at Plasencia with an army under his command.

4th   The Spanish general was menaced with an attack
by Marshal Victor; the Spaniard, *butt* uppermost
—that is, his musket carried in the opposite way
from other folk's—making the best of his way in
the most irregular and unsoldier-like manner out

of the reach of the French army. Our astonishment 1809 and vexation were beyond conception, knowing that the sick and wounded Englishmen had fallen (through the cowardice of the Spaniards) into the hands of the enemy, and also that our army was now placed in a most critical situation between the two French armies. The only retreat open was by the bridge at Puente del Arzobispo ; we passed it ; the advanced guard of Soult's army, consisting of cavalry, was close to it.

The bridge was secured by a body of infantry, and we had now the river between us. The British army at the battle of Talavera numbered about 20,000, and lost 6000 killed, wounded, and prisoners. The French, who were 45,000 strong, had 10,000 killed, wounded, and prisoners, and lost twenty pieces of cannon. The Spanish army of about 30,000 lost nothing of consequence sufficient to comment upon.

The French army was supplied by the villagers with a number of articles, while our army was nearly starving, although there was no want of money in our camp, but our Spanish friends infested every road for miles and robbed the peasantry who were bringing bread and vegetables to us for sale, so that they were completely prevented from rendering us any assistance. I rode several miles from our camp in search of bread, and luckily bought some from a peasant who had plenty hidden in his house, and would have gladly brought to our camp but durst not, from the dread of being robbed by the Spanish soldiers. Colonel Donkin's Brigade, consisting of the 45th, 87th, 88th, and five companies of the 60th (5th Battalion) and our Brigade, formed the 3rd Division under Brig.-General Craufurd.

1809   Marched in the middle of the night, and continued
August marching for fourteen hours, the weather very hot
5th   and no water to be obtained, as the rivulets in our
        course were all dried up. The soldiers were very
        much fatigued. Bivouacked on a barren hill near
        no human habitation.

6th   A very tiresome march over a wild country to
        the village of Casas del Puerto and Romangordo.
        Colonel Donkin's Brigade in bivouac at the former,
        and ours at or near the latter village, posting piquets
        on the bank of the Tagus and at the broken bridge
        of Almaraz. Marshal Soult's advanced posts were
        on the opposite bank of the river. Our Brigade
        moved every evening after sunset near the river, and
        there remained all night with our arms ready in case
        the enemy should attempt to ford the river.

        This was a nasty damp place, and the exhalations
        from the vegetable matter which was corrupting from
        the heat of the sun, and the half-dried swamps that
        were swarming with vermin, laid the foundation of
        disease amongst our men. We called the place we
        occupied by day *Dough boy Hill* ; a more appropriate
        name for it would have been *Starvation Hill*, as a
        small quantity of goat's flesh and a little coarse pea-
        flour was all we obtained here daily. The flour was
        made up into little cakes by each individual and put
        upon a thin stone over a fire until sufficiently done.

20th   We marched from this abominable place of
        starvation and misery at midnight, passed through
        Deleitosa, and, some distance farther, bivouacked in
        a large forest of cork trees and on the banks of the
        Rio del Monte. The men in making fires, set fire to
        the long grass, which grows luxuriantly, and, from

the dryness of the season, is a thing almost impossible 1809
to prevent. We fell in, in a great hurry. Some part of
the forest trees took fire also, but the ground was
cleared of the grass near us, and the danger ceased.

At sunset we moved a short distance and August
bivouacked.   21st

Marched over a plain country to near La Matilla. 22nd
Bivouacked on the banks of the river Almonte. At
a short distance passed Truxillo, celebrated as the
birthplace of Pizarro.

Marched to Caceres. Halted in an olive grove 23rd
until the evening, and then moved a short distance
for the night. This place has the appearance of
being wealthy. The inhabitants were more kind to the
soldiers as we passed than I had witnessed since my
arrival in Spain, the women offering bread and milk
to them. We observed several large convents. One
in particular attracted our notice, being perched on
the top of a high rock.

Marched to Arroyo del Puerco, the day being 24th
very hot indeed and the men exceedingly fatigued.
Rested in the shade under the trees during the
meridian heat; moved two leagues in the evening
and bivouacked.

Marched to Salorino, a very hot and harassing 25th
day's toil.

Marched to Valencia de Alcantara, which is a 26th
frontier town (fortified as far as the citadel goes)
and walled round.

Halted.   27th

The Division moved to the banks of a river named 28th
Sever, and bivouacked.

Passed the frontier between Spain and Portugal. 29th

General Craufurd put the provost-marshal under
arrest and ordered him to be marched a prisoner
with the provost guard. It was my duty on this
occasion to be put in charge of this guard. I had
several delinquents also in charge. I was ordered
to pick up all stragglers and to take care that no
baggage was left by me upon the road. The only
baggage I found was the General's light cart filled
with wine and eatables. I tried every means to make
the mules draw this load, but without effect. A
soldier of my party volunteered to mount the first
mule, and with the slings of the rifles we laid on
handsomely on both sides of the stubborn animals.
We at last started them, but they set off with the
greatest fury, away went my rifleman, and luckily he
was not hurt. The road happened to be very steep, so
that the animals could not avoid increasing their pace
every moment. The cart was dashed to pieces, and
the mules were also sadly injured. We passed a
curious town situated on a very high rocky hill, called
Marvão. It is the Portuguese barrier, and lies opposite
Valencia de Alcantara. On entering Castello de Vide
I proceeded first to lodge the prisoners in a secure
place, and then to inform the General how well I had
endeavoured to perform his orders. He had a party
at dinner, and was expecting his light cart every
moment with its contents in the best possible order.
When I related the sad catastrophe he became nearly
furious, and directed me to march up the prisoners
to their respective regiments, to obtain drummers,
and in the front of each regiment to flog the
culprits—in fact, to become a provost-marshal for
the occasion. I was highly indignant at such usage

for having exerted myself zealously to serve him. 1809
I went with my party to Colonel Beckwith, and
made him acquainted with the instructions I had
received from the General. He admonished the
stragglers for having left the line of march, and told
them to go and join their regiments and not transgress
again. He took the responsibility off my shoulders,
and I went to my corps. I heard no more of this
business, but this General Officer never forgave me.

We were bivouacked among large chestnut trees
for three days, the weather extremely sultry ; we then
were indulged with quarters in the town for five days.

The Division marched to Portalegre, in Alentejo. Sept.
The town is large and populous. It has several 7th
convents in it. I visited them, but did not find the
nuns either beautiful or great devotees ; they seemed
to like a good joke and nonsense as well as most
folks. The regiments under General Lightburn
passed us to join the army, viz. 2nd Battalion 5th
Foot, 1st Battalion 11th, 2nd Battalion 34th, 39th,
42nd and 57th. My brother visited me here. I gave
him my watch. He slept at my quarters.

Marched to Arronches, a walled town near the 10th
rivers Alegrete and Caya.

Marched into Campo Mayor, and remained there 11th
three months. Our General treated us occasionally
with a field day. Numbers of the finest men in the
Division were carried off by disease, typhus fever
being alarmingly prevalent through the greater part
of the British army. Headquarters at Badajoz.
The cavalry in advance at Merida and Albuquerque.
Estremoz and adjacent towns and villages were filled
with our troops.

The river Guadiana passes for a great way through a flat country, whose banks in the rainy season are overflowed ; consequently when the river diminishes from dryness and the heat of the weather, its banks become impregnated with myriads of vermin and also with vegetable matter in a state of putrefaction. In every stagnant pool these exhalations poison the surrounding atmosphere with pestilential vapours. The people of the country leave it for some months at this season, and a common observation among them is that strangers who come here at this season seldom leave it again, *i.e.* they die.   The town of Campo Mayor is fortified, and has also a citadel.   It stands on a plain abounding with corn.   At about the distance of a league a small river named the Caya flows. This river forms the boundary line between the two countries.   Campo Mayor was besieged by the Spaniards in 1801, and fell in nineteen days.   I got a bad typhus fever here, and the priest wanted to confess me and save me from everlasting perdition ! I recovered very slowly until the order for leaving this part of the country arrived.   In a few days, even on the line of march, I became well.   My brother, in the 34th Regiment, also suffered from the effects of this contagion.

Badajoz is the frontier Spanish fortification, and is of much more importance, being very strong and upon the left bank of the Guadiana, over which is a fine strong Roman bridge in good preservation, 700 paces long and 14 wide.   This place is the capital of Estremadura, and a Bishop's See.   Fort San Christoval is an outwork upon the right bank of the river, and commands the town.   Elvas is

a fortified town of Portugal, of considerable import- 1809
ance, and about four leagues from Badajoz. It Sept.-
is placed upon a rising piece of ground about a 10th
league from the Guadiana, and has two outworks to
support the town. Fort de Lippe is placed upon a
high hill and justly called a masterpiece in fortification.
The other fort, Santa Lucia, stands upon a smaller
hill, and communicates with the town by a covered
way. Elvas is supplied with water by an aqueduct.
The water is brought a considerable distance. If the
place was invested regularly the aqueduct might easily
be destroyed, which would be a most serious inconvenience to the inhabitants. The general hospital
was at this place. Above 4000 British soldiers were
buried here during our stay in cantonments.

Albuquerque is a walled town of Spain, about
three leagues from Campo Mayor. It has a fort
situated upon a hill close to the town. This place
gives the title to a Duke, who possesses many
privileges and an extensive range of forests, in which
are plenty of wild boars and wolves, hunted frequently
by those who are fond of such amusement.

Letter No. III

Campo Mayor, Portugal,
September 1809.

Dear Parents—My last letter was written at
Castello Branco, which I hope you received. I must
now enter into a long detail of proceedings, the
result of which has not proved of any service to
England or Spain as yet, and I am afraid there is
no likelihood our services in this quarter ever will,

1809 unless we have a sufficient disposable force to cope
with the French, who are much more numerous than
we expected. I will now bid adieu to the land of
plenty, a land well according with the Scripture
phrase—flowing with milk and honey.

We very soon passed the frontiers of Portugal
and entered Spain by forced marches, generally of
twenty English miles by day and sometimes much
more, the weather extremely hot and sultry and the
roads very bad. Sometimes we met with stupendous
mountains, whose summits were enveloped in the
clouds ; the villages in general were deserted by the
unfortunate inhabitants, and houses, churches, and
everything they possessed were one entire scene of ruin ;
some towns were completely burnt to the ground,
even the corn-fields (of this year's produce) were
generally laid waste by fire wherever the French had
been. We daily experienced great hardships from
want of a proper supply of bread and food of every
kind. Sometimes with difficulty we got a little, when
every man endeavoured to get as much as possible for
himself, and I generally was not backward in contriving
to satisfy the cravings of a hungry stomach, as well as
the oldest soldier among them. From such fatiguing
marches, and often bad food and water, by day
exposed to burning sun, and by night to the heavy
dews, sleeping generally upon the ground, you will
not wonder at the men becoming unhealthy, which
daily obliged men to fall out on the march. Even the
strongest in outward appearance would lie down, or
rather fall down, and say positively they could not go
any farther. The officers of our regiment—most of
them rode on horses or mules—did not experience the

fatigues so materially. As I had no money to spare, I 1809
was obliged to walk, and, God knows, if illness had
intervened or I had not been able to march, my case
would have been dismal ; but, thank the Almighty,
He has blessed me with an excellent constitution, and
all the hardships I have met with have not made the
least impression upon me. A little John Bull-like,
when hunger stared me in the face I put on a
sorrowful countenance, but by some means or
other a sheep or pig came in my way and I soon
turned butcher. No sooner dead than roasted or
grilled. I assure you I have dined thus many times
and felt much more real content and pleasure than at
a sumptuous feast. We now and then met with fields
of corn, and if the men were allowed to halt, they
soon filled their haversacks with ears, and boiled it
when they arrived at the end of the march.

An express arrived from Sir Arthur Wellesley
desiring the Brigade would lose no time in making
a speedy junction with the Grand Army, and the
last twenty-four hours' march is almost unparalleled
by any soldiers after the fatigues we had already
experienced. I had only six ounces of mouldy bread
and some bad water, which I got by the road occasionally
in passing, to support me for twenty-four hours, in
which time we marched fifty-two miles, resting three
hours on the ground. We certainly should have
found a much greater difficulty in accomplishing it
had we not met several wounded British officers
riding from the field of action, who told us what was
passing when they left. Every man seemed anxious
to push on, and all were in high spirits, hoping soon
to be on the field of battle and to assist their brave

1809 countrymen. The cannons distinctly sounding on
our ears as we came near. I forgot to say that the
dastardly Spaniards were running in all directions,
the field being covered with the panic-struck. They
received many a hearty curse as they passed us.
After all our efforts, we arrived on the field of battle
just soon enough to be too late. The horrid sights
were beyond anything I could have imagined.
Thousands dead and dying in every direction, horses,
men, French and English, in whole lines who had
cut each other down, and, I am sorry to say, the
Spaniards butchering the wounded Frenchmen at
every opportunity, and stripping them naked, which
gave admission to the attacks of myriads of pernici-
ous flies and the heat of a burning sun. You may
be sure everything was done on our part and the
commanding officer's to put a stop to such horrid
brutality and give assistance, but the ground being
covered for at least five miles with dead and dying,
and we expecting another attack, the army was
drawn up in a line ready to receive the enemy. Our
regiment was posted in front of the army, but' the
French thought proper to have no more of it at the
present, and retreated about three miles and beyond
a river, which secured their front.

The French are very fine tall men, well dressed
and accoutred. I saw a colonel surrounded by
his Grenadiers who had fallen by coming to the
charge with an English regiment, whose desperate
courage and strength of arm no troops in the world
can cope with in that sort of warfare. I have not
time or room to dwell longer upon this subject ;
some other time it possibly may be in my power to

give a clearer account. The papers, I have no doubt, 1809 will explain the business, and also inform you how, from superior force, we were obliged to waive all advantage gained by the gallant action at Talavera. The French followed us, the wounded were all taken prisoners, and, I am happy to say, used very well. The French are a brave and generous enemy, and their humanity to the English prisoners is generous to the extreme.

We have once more arrived in Portugal, after a tedious march and under the continual expectation of having a battle with the French army, sometimes being only two miles distant from them, and frequently on piquet within gunshot of each other, though as yet I have never had the honour of being fired at.

I must not boast, we shall have enough of it before long, I daresay, as it is believed the French are concentrating their forces, and will come to see us shortly in a friendly way. The Spanish officers in general are traitors or cowards, and of course the men will not fight when their leaders set off. The Portuguese fight better.

I saw my brother some days back ; he has not been out of Portugal. Of course the hardships experienced have been trivial. He is plump and hearty. I walked over a mountainous country above twenty miles to shake hands with him once again. Stayed two days. He marched one way. I returned, and had on my arrival to commence instantly another march. We again met at Portalegre on 17th September, and I gave him a good dinner, wine, grapes, etc. (having once more got into the land of plenty). He slept with me,

3

1809 and marched at three o'clock in the morning. He would change sashes with me. He is a fine spirited boy, enjoys good health and bears fatigue well. I gave him all the advice in my power, and it will give me pleasure if it is of service. He is now very economical. I believe his regiment will go to the East Indies from here. If I escape from Portugal with a whole skin I think of going to the West Indies for promotion. As I have commenced to soldier, I must fight for promotion as a soldier, and everything I have yet seen are trifles compared to what I have often experienced in England. Oh! father, when the mind is at ease, a fig for the body! Danger is merely ideal to a man of spirit.

I am sincerely the friend and well-wisher of your family. As this may not arrive, I have not written the regiment. Do not let this letter be seen or talked about as any of mine. Right or wrong, I have no time to read this epistle, and as it is the scrawl of a few moments, you must excuse the diction ; we cannot write when we please. My love to my dear Ann. It is a lucky thing I did not fold the letter up in my hurry. My blessing for her.

Take care of the boys—I mean their learning. I had nearly bought my mother a snuff-box, but the difference of six shillings in the bargain occurs. I shall be able to bring or send one possibly, should things stand square with me, in a little time. God bless her. I never lie down on the ground to take my night's repose without praying for the welfare of my dear parents and family. Something strikes me in my reveries that I am yet to comfort and cherish them when age shall put it out of their power.

CAMPO MAYOR, 29*th October* 1809.

MY DEAR PARENTS—I hope by this time you will 1809 have received my letters. If so, the present state of affairs is not altogether foreign to you. The Brigade has been stationed here about six weeks, which has made my lank and sunburnt countenance return nearly to its pristine appearance. In my last letters I observed that from the commencement of campaigning I had not felt ill except from starvation. My good landlady and I being upon excellent terms, she indulges me to excess in dainty dishes and a good bed. I had forgotten that there was a great difference in being always exposed to the weather (I mean the sun) and now seldom. One day, being intolerably hot, I exposed myself as usual, and have had a very severe attack of ague, which has returned three times, and obliged me to put my medical skill to the test after the above severe battles. I drove my enemy from his intrenched position, and he has never since dared to resume the attack, so have proved the best general. I regularly rise with the sun, and go to exercise every morning. I pay that attention to my present profession which another day (if not suddenly stopped in my course) may be attended with success. I thought I merited it in the profession which necessity and great disappointments obliged me to relinquish. Col. Sibthorp's last words were, "Simmons, you give me much uneasiness at leaving my regiment, and I feel for your future welfare,

1809 and you may have greater hardships than it is possible to conceive." I instantly said, as I had pledged my honour to his men, I hope he could not for a moment entertain so mean an opinion of me or think me a weathercock. He then could say no more, but parted with me with as much affection as a near relation—I mean a parent. I hope you will not for a moment conceive I mean to feel regret at relinquishing the medical profession ; far otherwise. I am as happy as my present situation will admit of, and, thank the Almighty, have no reason as yet to be to the contrary. A soldier thinks of nothing that has passed by ; it is only the present time that concerns him ; he is a careless and thoughtless being. I wish I could say he was a little more prepared for a speedy exit into a future state.

I will now endeavour to give you a slight sketch of the present state of affairs. Our men are exceedingly unhealthy, and the hospitals are crowded. Several officers of other regiments have died suddenly, and numbers of men also have died from the effects of fatigue in our march from Talavera.

The French, from the best reports I can learn, have 30,000 men at and near Almaraz and Puente del Arzobispo. Another French force of 100,000 men are concentrating and collecting near Madrid. The whole of our army is not more than 25,000 men, so some day shortly we shall have hard fighting and hard running. We laugh heartily at the bombast which you are gagged with, and seem to swallow, relating to the brave Spaniards. John Bull will soon be in another way of thinking. The Spaniards are as much afraid of the French as a child is of the rod.

If you refer back to a paper giving an account of our 1809 unforeseen retreat over (using the words expressed in a French bulletin) an impassable mountain, you will see in how dastardly a manner the grand and illustrious Spaniards set off and left us no other resource than the above retreat. Otherwise we were in the highest spirits in expectation of breakfasting in a day or two with Marshal Soult at Plasencia. You can well conceive the consternation at the sight of General Cuesta's army. Our gallant commander, Lord Wellington, I am sorry to perceive, has already enemies at home ; they are illiberal rascals that can think only of puffing forth such falsities. The old adage, " Great men have many enemies." I may confidently say that every soldier entertains the highest opinion of his Lordship, and if we face the French, where there is any possibility for a general to lead on his army with credit to himself, he certainly is the man to perform it.

I am sorry to find our army in Flushing has not succeeded in the grand attack intended upon Antwerp and carrying off the fleet. I some days back wrote to Maud ; the Brigade he is attached to is stationed about five leagues from this place, Torre Mayor in Spain. He sings out bitterly at the scarcity of provisions. He is in good spirits, I am happy to say, much respected by his brother officers, and I am under no apprehension of him ever forfeiting their good opinion. I have put him upon an economical plan of paying for every article as he procures it, or go without it. He informs me he owes the tailor of the regiment he left £10. I have not the least doubt as soon as I return to England to be able to settle that business.

1809 The young rogue took a fancy to my watch (I forfeited to Joseph in town). I hope to purchase him a better some other day. He must forgive me. He gave me my knapsack for shirts and stockings. (I lost my own. I took it from the back of a Frenchman at Talavera who had paid the debt of nature by the bayonet, and it has proved very serviceable.) While writing this, I have this moment received a letter from him. He writes in high spirits and enjoys good health ; he informs me of a shocking accident which happened to a poor boy. Being on guard, the boy attracted his notice, and was playing and amusing himself with his antic tricks when a man passed through the guard-room leading a mule (a restive one). He was carrying a loaded musket also, which, coming in contact with the horse's side, discharged its contents. Maud had the luck to escape, but the poor boy was shot, and expired instantly.

His words struck me rather forcibly on the occasion, which were to this effect : " The Spaniards came in numbers to the spot, and from the howling of the men and women, whose *concord* and *discord*, will give me the blue devils before the morning." I have written to-day and begged in his next he will explain the latter sentence. I expect him here soon to spend a day or two. I remain, with every good wish to my dear friends— with me my brother also joins in duty and love— yours sincerely,

G. & M. SIMMONS.

I beg you will answer this as soon as possible, as

my brother is, as well as myself, anxious to hear 1809 from you. *Do not show my letters.*

My brother informs me Joseph is with an attorney at Hull. I hope, if he likes his situation, in a few years I shall be enabled to assist him. Pay great attention to all your children's learning ; make them good scholars, and they will have little to apprehend. I hope Joseph is a good boy. My dear mother, I am sometimes afraid, thinks too much of her grace-less boy. I know I am not deserving any better name. I hope yet at some future day to be a comfort to her. I assure you the welfare of my family is always uppermost in my mind. I hope my sister is well and happy. I beg she will ever be upon her guard in forming new friends or acquaintances, as we see every day the misfortunes young women are subject to by such connections. I have too high an opinion of my dear sister to think she will do so. I am con-vinced her prudence and good sense, with the advice of the best of mothers, will be her guard from forming connections with imprudent people. Give her this advice. I bought a shawl here for five dollars, rather a whimsical thing, which I hope to send you, at least when I return to England ; we have some idea of coming back, you see.

Write soon. I am particularly anxious to hear from you, as is also my brother. Direct to me, Lieut. Simmons, 1st Battalion, 95th or Rifle Regiment, Grand Army, Portugal (or elsewhere).

1809   This day we have been stationed at Campo Mayor
Dec. three months, and are now ordered to prepare for
11th a march. I am recovering from fever. The con-
valescent and sick are ordered to be sent to Elvas,
but I am allowed to proceed, by my own wish,
with my regiment.

12th   Marched to Arronches and halted.

16th   Marched to Portalegre, where the Brigade assembled,
consisting of 1st Battalions 43rd and 52nd, and ours,
the 95th or Rifle Men. I was in the same company
I commenced my military career with, and being the
junior officer, I consequently got the last choice of
quarters, which too frequently was a dirty floor with
my blanket only. Captain O'Hare did not show me
much kindness, but the change of air improved my
health daily.

18th   Marched to Crato, the officers of the company,
viz. five, billeted upon the house of a priest, who
gave us all beds and sold us one of the finest turkeys
I ever saw, and also some excellent wine, which he
partook of. I enjoyed myself so much this day and
slept so well that in the morning I felt myself as
well as ever, and from that moment shook off the
villainous effects of disease. The weather cool and
refreshing.

19th   Marched to Ponto do Souro, a village situated in
a pleasant valley, through which the river Souro runs
its course. The neighbouring country is well covered
with wood.

20th   Marched to the town of Abrantes.

Marched to Punhete.

Marched to Thomar, a large town which is observed at a considerable distance, being built upon a most prominent hill, at the bottom of which flows the river Nabão.

Marched and crossed a ridge of mountains to Ourem. Aldea da Cruz and adjacent villages being very small and only calculated to lodge a few companies in each of them.

Marched to Leyria, where the company's officers were billeted together again ; we got excellent white wine and good mattrasses. My Captain, having enjoyed the wine very much, pulled off his boots, placed them near the fire and a soldier took them away. Captain Mitchell of ours was in the street just as the man left the house ; something struck him at the moment that the soldier was about no good, so he ordered him to come into the room where we were. On opening his greatcoat, Peter O'Hare's boots fell to the ground. This man was tried and flogged. My Captain had the command of the detachment when the sentence of the court-martial was put into execution. He gave the man every lash, and recommended the buglers to lay it on lustily and save the fellow from the gallows. This was the first punishment I had witnessed.

Marched to Pombal, on the Soure.

Marched to Condeixa, upon the same stream as yesterday.

To Coimbra, a large commercial city upon the north bank of the Mondego. This city we entered by passing over a long bridge of many arches. The gardens are supplied with the most delicious oranges

1809
Dec.
22nd
23rd

24th

25th

27th

28th

29th

1809 in every stage of growth upon the same tree; and plenty of grapes and other fruits, which we were allowed to eat at pleasure. I visited several of the convents, and met with great kindness from the nuns, who gave any British officer who visited their convents sweetmeats and fruits in abundance, and to particular favourites little purses to keep as tokens of regard.

CAMPAIGN OF 1810

Viscount Wellington arranged for the defence of Portugal by massing the Anglo-Portuguese army at two points—the first, under his own command, on the Mondego, and the second, under General Hill, on the Tagus. He also issued orders for the construction of the Lines of Torres Vedras. The Light Division under General Craufurd was pushed forward to the Agueda as a Corps of Observation.

Massena, with a mobile force of 65,000 men, now threatened Portugal, having captured the fortress of Ciudad Rodrigo, defended by the Spaniards.

The first fight of the campaign was on 10th March, when General Férey endeavoured to surprise the Light Division by a night attack on the bridge of Barba del Puerco; this was held by the 95th Rifles, who drove back the French with heavy loss.

Craufurd maintained his position on the Agueda for four months after this, but in July, Ney with 30,000 troops advanced on Almeida, and Craufurd elected to stand and fight him with the Coa River behind him, and being vigorously attacked by overwhelming forces, withdrew with great difficulty and with heavy loss. The fortress of Almeida shortly afterwards fell into the hands of the French, and Massena advanced on the line of the Mondego with the object of driving the British army out of the country. Wellington, however, barred his advance at Busaco, and a sanguinary battle was fought, in which the French were worsted. Massena, finding he could not force the position at Busaco, manœuvred to his right and threatened Wellington's line of retreat, and the latter fell back to his prepared defences of Torres Vedras.

CHAPTER III

Campaign of 1810

Journal—1st January–27th February 1810

March from Coimbra to the Coa—The Light Division placed in cantonments in advance of the Coa—A company of Rifle Men, sent out to reconnoitre, find the French advanced posts in possession of Barba del Puerco.

Letter No. V

To his Parents, from Villar Torpin, dated 28th February 1810

Suffers from fever and ague—Description of Coimbra, its museum, monasteries, and nunneries—Reflections on the superstition and bigotry of the Portuguese—Miserable condition and poverty of the inhabitants—Description of cantonments occupied—Conduct of the French—Rumours as to the impending campaign and confidence in Lord Wellington—Severe lecture to his father and good advice to the family all round.

Journal—4th March–30th April

Advance from Reygada to the Agueda—The Rifles on outpost duty on the Agueda, with one company on piquet at the

Bridge of Barba del Puerco—The French, who occupy
the opposite bank, make a night attack in force and
endeavour to seize the bridge—Desperate fight, in which the
French are repulsed—Complimentary order issued by
Brigadier-General Craufurd to the Rifles by order of Lord
Wellington in consequence of their gallant behaviour on
this occasion—Dispositions of the Light Brigade on the
river Azava—Captain Ross's troop of Horse Artillery
attached—The Rifles on piquet and 1st King's German
Hussars on vedette duty on the Azava—Formation of the
celebrated " Light Division "—The 1st and 3rd Portuguese
Caçadores attached to it.

Letter No. VI

To his Father, from Villar de Ciérvos, dated 30th April 1810

Describes the events of the preceding two months—The
mountainous country and defile of the Agueda—Position
held at Barba del Puerco—Disposition of the Rifle Men on
piquet at the bridge on 19th March—The French attack
—Death of Lieutenant Mercer—Captain O'Hare brings up
the support—Sharp hand-to-hand fighting at the bridge—
Colonel Beckwith arrives with three companies of the
Reserve—The Rifle Men fix swords and charge—Retreat of
the French—The losses on both sides—Strength of the
French column of attack—Captain O'Hare's commenda-
tion of Simmons' behaviour.

Campaign of 1810

Journal—1st January–27th February 1810

Began the year rather roughly by a long day's
march over bad and mountainous roads to the

1810
Jan.
1st

1810 wretched village of Ponte de Murcella. The Alva
runs near it, and falls into the Mondego some
distance from the village.

Jan.   Marched to Galizes and adjacent villages ; the
2nd country mountainous and poor.

3rd   Marched to Pinhancos and San Marinha, near the
foot of the extensive ridge of mountains named the
Mountains of the Stars (Sierra da Estrella). This
chain is the highest in Portugal, and continues to the
southern part of Estremadura.

4th   Marched to Celorico.

5th   Pinhel. On our arrival here were informed that
the French had a body of men in San Felices, and
that their piquets were upon the river Agueda, and
that strong parties of Frenchmen occasionally passed
the river and entered Portugal to plunder or levy
contributions. The headquarters of the Brigade
remained here.

7th   The Rifle Men were ordered to proceed across the
Coa to the villages of Cinco Villas, Villar Torpin,
and Reygada, two leagues in advance of Pinhel.
Cinco Villas is half a league nearer Pinhel, and stands
close to the Coa, with a strong stone bridge over it.

17th   Marched and occupied the villages of Figueira,
Mata de Lobas, and Escallion, close to the river
Douro. The rest of the Brigade marched from
Pinhel, taking up a line on our right. The
banks of the Douro are extremely rocky, wild, and
romantic—in short, the country all round, with few
exceptions, is wild and stony. We have had a heavy
fall of snow, in which I observed innumerable prints
of wolves. I endeavoured to track them, but without
success.

Retired to Valverde Pereiro, in consequence of some information our Brigade received about the enemy.

Returned to our cantonments and continued very quiet until this day, when a company of Rifle Men were ordered to the Spanish village of Bouza. A party was sent forward to feel the enemy. It crossed the river Duas Casas, and proceeded to Barba del Puerco, which was found in the enemy's possession. The party fell back upon Bouza and the enemy followed and fired a few long shots, but did not cross the river. Two companies of Rifle Men now occupied Bouza, and two companies as a support at Escarigo, on the Turon. The Duas Casas rises near Castello Bom, on the Portuguese frontier; it passes between Bouza and Barba del Puerco, after which it falls into the Agueda.

LETTER No. V

VILLAR TORPIN, 28th February 1810.

DEAR PARENTS—Your epistle came to hand a few days back, which gave me infinite pleasure and gratification.

I have for some time been in expectation of receiving a letter from Maud. I suppose he is not well informed where I am stationed. He had a severe illness in the neighbourhood of Badajoz, and wrote for advice, which he since informs me was of service, and before he marched he had quite recovered. At the same time I was expected hourly to bid a final adieu to this world. Judge what a situation to give advice to a bed-ridden brother. However, I hinted nothing

1810 relative to myself, and endeavoured to write in good spirits, which at that period had good effect.

From fatigues my ague again revisited me, and continued daily for some time, and at last terminated in a fever very prevalent through the army at that period, and which confined me entirely to bed for three weeks. But from the kind attention of my good landlady, who was continually watching over me, I surprised numbers and deceived the grim King of Terrors. As soon as I was able to move I went to a very healthy spot in Spain, and improving daily (in a wonderful manner) speedily recovered. Since that time I have traversed nearly the whole of Portugal, and seen most of the best towns through the country, marching four, five, and six leagues per diem, sometimes sleeping and living in the grandest houses in the country, and at others in the most wretched hovels not as good as an English pig-sty. Our present situation is about 300 miles march from Campo Mayor, and half of our way was over stupendous mountains—in short, it was beyond anything I could have conceived, and has highly compensated me for my labour. I spared no pains in visiting all the churches and monasteries and castles in my way, which were curious and frequently very interesting. At Coimbra, an exceeding good town, and possessed of several rich convents, with a beautiful church and museum of curiosities, two stuffed crocodiles attracted my notice much, being 30 feet long, also tigers and a variety of different beasts of prey in a high state of preservation. At the convent of Santa Clara the nuns presented several of the British officers with sweetmeats, which were very nice.

The friars and nuns at all the convents I have 1810
visited behaved with the greatest politeness. It
often excited my pity for so many poor unfortunate
women, who might have lived in the world and
proved an ornament to Society, but, alas! doomed
by their parents from superstitious bigotry to be
secluded from the world and live entombed in a vile
prison, like common felons or miscreants, not fit to be
at large. The monks and priests of different orders
live and prey upon the vitals (if I may use the
expression) of the people; they endeavour to keep up
that superstitious bigotry, which enables them to
exercise their extortions to the greatest degree upon
the deluded and infatuated multitude. The most
miserable hovels in the country must have six or
eight painted images, dressed out in the most
whimsical and fantastic manner, imitating Jesus
Christ, etc., a variety of saints more calculated to
excite laughter than convey any idea of the Deity.
It is through these wooden dolls they worship the
Almighty, but it is my opinion one half of them
worship the images or saints they stick up. At a
certain hour in the day, sometimes twice or thrice, a
bell rings, the people off with their hats and chatter
over a little prayer, which, if their conscience pricks
them, or they have committed a slight irregularity,
they repeat ten or a dozen times and feel perfectly
satisfied. Our present quarters are truly miserable;
on all sides stupendous mountains; the people
wretched in the extreme, clothes hardly sufficient to
cover themselves, and positively not a degree above
savages—I mean as to their method of living. Of a
morning they will turn out of their wretched cabins

4

1810 and are to be seen sitting in rows upon the ground in the sun picking lice off themselves and out of each other's heads ; they do not mind, or endeavour to hide themselves from your view. At first it disgusted me, but from habit I stand by and joke them about the number they have killed, which they take in great good-humour, and tell you, so many that they could not keep account !

Their houses are built of rough stone, generally 7 or 8 feet high (some exceptions to this rule), with no outlet for smoke ; the fire is made by the wall side, and consists generally of mountain heather or broom, which produces a most intolerable smoke, and gives a person who is not well seasoned, a copious flow of tears. The family sit on the ground round it ; the house is entirely enveloped in smoke, and every side of the wall is like a chimney, which they never take pains to sweep clean. The people never wash themselves, and seldom comb their heads. The women have an immense quantity of long black hair, and never wear bonnets, and seldom shoes and stockings. Garlic, oil, and dark brown bread of Indian corn and rye is principally their food ; they certainly stared to see us eat beef, pork, etc., in such quantities, and drink wine so freely.

These are the people we have the honour of living with at present in the mountains on the north frontier of Portugal. Our regiment occupies this position to preserve the left flank of the army from a sudden attack. The other day the French menaced us, but retired. They are at present in great force in the vicinity of San Felices, three leagues from us ; they make sad havoc among the cattle in the vicinity, killing and wasting all they cannot carry away, and 1810 breaking everything in the houses of the unfortunate inhabitants, and what is worse than all, they knock down all idols in the churches ; this shocked the people more than all the rest put together. Things are daily drawing to a crisis. Spain is lost, I firmly believe. Whenever the French show themselves the Spaniards are panic-struck. The French are, it is supposed, forming two grand armies to attack us, and we daily expect to retire in order to concentrate our little army. It is rumoured that the Portuguese have refused to march to attack the French near Badajoz, who are besieging that town. If this is the case we shall soon retire upon Lisbon, but let it be as it may, I have great confidence in Lord Wellington, who is able to extricate us if difficulties have to be surmounted, and highly competent to command Britons in the field and lead them off with glory. In a few weeks you will have great news on this head, depend upon it.

The only thing I at present want is a supply of clothes. The lying out at night in the fields for months together soon puts your raiment in disorder. I am nearly in rags.

We have been in the habit of procuring excellent wine latterly at 6d. per quart. We live well now and then. John Bull likes good feeding, and none better than myself.

I think that if we should soon leave Portugal and not have a battle, in all probability we may go up the Mediterranean, as the regiment is not at present very strong.

The newspapers will direct you as to everything. I think the move must certainly take place. If so,

1810 you will hear from me possibly next in England. My love to my aunt, uncle, etc.—I remain your ever affectionate son,   G. SIMMONS.

Journal—4th March–30th April 1810

1810
March
4th

Marched from Reygada to Escarigo. Halted. The enemy finding us so near, did not like to continue at Barba del Puerco, and withdrew across the river. We occupied it immediately. The rain fell violently, and as the Duas Casas had no bridge and was in our rear, and was frequently so swollen as to be rendered impassable, our Brigadier ordered the post to be evacuated.

AFFAIR OF BARBA DEL PUERCO

11th

On the 11th, with four companies of Rifle Men, we again occupied this post, having our company posted on piquet near the most formidable passes I ever beheld. The French were also posted opposite us. The river Agueda, which rises in the great Spanish mountains named Sierra de Gata, and runs furiously in the bottom of this deep chasm over rugged rocks, causing a continued noise, separated us. At the bottom of the zig-zag pass is the bridge over the river, 100 yards long and 5 yards wide. San Felices, in which the advance of the French army were lodged under the command of General Baron de Férey, is about half a league from the pass. We remained quietly here until the night of the 19th inst., being upon outlying piquet with Captain O'Hare's Company. Early in the evening I crossed the bridge to find a paper left there (in the piquet house) for me to fetch from the French side, and

had just returned from visiting the advanced 1810
double sentry and made my report to Lieutenant
Mercer, when a tremendous firing commenced.
Mercer immediately ordered the men to fall in and
move forward to our alarm post, which was on the
edge of the rocky chasm. The night being dark and
stormy, with rain occasionally, caused the river
to make more noise in its passage over the rocky bed
than usual, and completely prevented our advanced
sentinels hearing the approach of the enemy. Also
from the obscurity of the night, it was not possible to
see any object, so that the enemy passed the bridge
so rapidly that only one sentinel fired before they were
both knocked down. Two men, Maher and M'Can,
were taken at the bridge. However, this gave the
alarm, and a small party stationed amongst the rocks
kept up a fire. The sergeant being shot through the
mouth and the enemy being so numerous, they
could not impede their progress. In a moment,
after the arrival of the main body of the piquet, the
French were literally scrambling up the rocky ground
within ten yards of us. We commenced firing at
each other very spiritedly. Their drums beat a
charge, and the French attempted to dislodge us
without effect. My friend, Lieutenant Mercer, who
was putting on his spectacles, received a musket ball
through his head, and fell dead close to my feet.
Several were now falling, and the moon for a few
minutes shone brightly, then disappeared, and again
at intervals let us see each other. We profited by this
circumstance, as their belts were white and over their
greatcoats, so that where they crossed upon the breast,
combined with the glare of the breast-plate, gave a

1810 grand mark for our rifles. Our men being in dark
dresses, and, from their small number, obliged to keep
close together, the ground also being exceedingly
rugged, were all favourable circumstances. We fought
in this way for at least half an hour against fearful odds,
when Lieutenant-Colonel Beckwith brought up the
three reserve companies from the village, who soon decided the affair. The enemy was driven in the greatest
confusion back over frightful precipices, leaving two
officers killed and a number of men wounded.

About 9 o'clock in the evening, Captain O'Hare had
been taken unwell, and as there was no idea of an
attack, he went home to bed. Lieutenant Cowan was
sent for him when the firing commenced. They arrived after poor Mercer was killed, so the command of
the piquet devolved upon me for a quarter of an hour.
Thus I had the honour to command for some time after
poor Mercer was killed and until O'Hare returned.
I merely mention this circumstance as it was the first
time I had been in a fight, but the gallantry displayed
by the *varmint* fellows that were with me left no
doubt on my mind that we should have resisted all
these attempts to dislodge us until the reserves came
up. A young Frenchman that was taken, fired into
Colonel Beckwith's face. A Rifle Man was just going
to blow his brains out, when the Colonel stopped
him, saying, " Let him alone ; I daresay the boy has
a mother. Knock the thing out of his hand, that he
may do no more mischief with it, and give him a
kick on the bottom and send him to the rear."
The next morning the boy was given a hearty breakfast at the Colonel's house. On being questioned
about firing so wantonly, he said he was in such

agitation that he was not aware his finger was upon 1810 the trigger of his gun. The ball went through the Colonel's cap peak, which, being turned up, made it take a slanting direction; it passed through and grazed the top of his head. Six hundred volunteers were chosen by the French general to attempt the annihilation of our party, and fifteen hundred more were formed to support the attack in case of success. A number of men kept up a fire from the enemy's side of the river during the time the soldiers were passing the ravine.

A body of Spaniards under a captain was stationed on our right. We had a corporal and file with them, merely to give us intelligence if necessary. When the firing commenced the Spaniards became very uneasy; the officer wished our corporal to leave his post; he said he was determined to wait until the enemy overpowered him, so the noble Castilian and his forces started off. Two French officers, a Light Infantry captain and a subaltern, and seventeen men lay stretched upon the rough ground. We afterwards heard from a deserter that the colonel who led the attack was shot through the mouth and his jaw broken. He was making a great noise before, but this circumstance made him so quiet that a child might have played with him. Several other officers were wounded and a number of men who were carried off during the affray, Lieutenant Mercer killed, seventeen of our men killed and wounded. Fairfoot was of the party taken; Betts, the sergeant, wounded in the jaw; O'Gallagher wounded and died; William David, his skull blown off and his *dura mater* exposed. A French sergeant was wounded through the knee, and

1810 afterwards I assisted Surgeon Burke to remove his leg. This being the first affair of the outposts, and it having resulted in the total discomfiture of the enemy in his midnight attack, the following Complimentary Order was issued on the occasion :—

DIVISION ORDERS

Brigadier-General Craufurd has it in command from the Commander-in-Chief to assure Lieutenant-Colonel Beckwith and the officers of the 95th Regiment who were engaged at Barba del Puerco that their conduct in this affair has augmented the confidence he has in the troops when opposed to the enemy in any situation. Brigadier-General Craufurd feels peculiar pleasure in noticing the first affair in which any part of the Light Brigade were engaged during the present campaign. That British troops should defeat a superior number of the enemy is nothing new, but the action reflects honour on Lieutenant-Colonel Beckwith and the Regiment, inasmuch that it was of a sort that Rifle Men of other Armies would shun. In other Armies the Rifle is considered ill calculated for close action with an enemy armed with Musket and Bayonet, but the 95th Regiment has proved that the Rifle in the hands of a British soldier is a fully efficient weapon to enable him to defeat the French in the closest fight in whatever manner they may be armed.

(Signed) T. GRAHAM, D.A.G.

This night gave me a good opinion of myself. I fought alone for some time with fearful odds, my

friend dead at my feet. I had been often joked 1810
and told, " Would you not like to be at home again ? "
After this night I was considered a soldier fit to face
the devil in any shape.

Another attack being expected from the enemy, March
two more companies of Rifle Men marched in, also 21st
two of the 52nd and one of the 43rd Light Infantry.

This post being frequently cut off in rainy weather 23rd
by a river which ran in our rear becoming so swollen
that it was impossible to ford it for days together,
our General withdrew us, and sent a piquet of the
1st German Hussars as a look-out post ; we moved
into Villar de Ciérvos. A few days before we left
the post of Barba del Puerco a deserter wanted to
come to us, but the river ran so furiously that he durst
not cross it. Some Spaniards who were hiding from
the French observed him, and did not know his
wishes, but seeing this Frenchman without arms and
unsupported, deliberately stoned him to death, several
of us looking on without the power of doing the unfortunate man any service.

A battalion of French Infantry and a squadron April
of Dragoons marched from San Felices and proceeded 6th
to the ford of Valdespina. The infantry formed
up whilst the cavalry foraged and plundered the
small villages, after which the whole returned to San
Felices, followed by a party of 1st German Hussars.

Our battalion marched from Villar de Ciérvos to 8th
Val de la Mula, Val de la Cuellar, and Malpartida.
The former villages stand on the Turon below the
hill of Fort Concepçion ; San Pedro and Valermosa
were occupied by the 43rd Regiment.

This day two of our companies were divided and 11th

1810 the Battalion formed into eight companies instead of ten. The staff of the two companies were ordered to proceed to the depôt in England. Captain Ross's troop of Horse Artillery was also attached to the Light Brigade.

April 21st General Craufurd reviewed the Brigade on the heights of Fort Concepçion, after which the following change of quarters took place : 43rd relieved the 52nd at the outposts, 95th occupied the villages vacated by the 43rd, 52nd marched into the cantonments vacated by the 95th. The enemy are making their appearance in the vicinity of Ciudad Rodrigo in considerable force ; it is a strongly fortified Spanish town upon the Agueda.

29th The enemy have invested the town in very large force. Four companies of Rifle Men marched to Espeja and four into Gallegos ; these villages are about a league apart and three from Ciudad Rodrigo. The enemy sent a reconnoitring party, which, after making its observations, returned by the ford below.

30th Two companies of Rifle Men were now posted as piquets above, about two miles in front, upon the river Azava, at the bridge of Marialba and the forts. A vedette of the German Hussars was posted on the other side of the river in our front upon a commanding height in the village of Carpio ; from his station he could overlook all between him and Ciudad Rodrigo. Two companies of Rifle Men left Gallegos for Espeja, to admit the 1st and 3rd Caçadores, who are to be attached to us, into the village. The Division is now to be called *Light* in future. These Portuguese soldiers are dressed in brown and are Light Infantry.

Letter No. VI

Villar de Ciérvos, Spain,
30th April 1810.

Dear Father—You will wonder, I suppose, at my sending one letter after another in this way, as I wrote you so recently from Reygada in Portugal.

I had the other day a long letter from my friend Maud. I answered it the following day. He is in high health. I gave him all my news, ending the letter, as usual, with advice. He has been stationed for some time at Portalegre in Portugal, an exceeding good town, while I have been traversing the country for months, not staying more than a day or two in a place, and sleeping in tents or churches. For the last two months back we have been stationed so near the enemy we durst not take off our shoes. The weather has all along been very bad, continually raining or snowing. I am in hopes it will soon clear up. The other day I was posted on a bleak rock from four o'clock in the morning till one after noon before I was relieved, and got famously ducked ; but I derived this advantage—it gave me a keen appetite for my breakfast, which my servant has provided for me in style— four eggs, roast fowl, and plenty of tea. We have no certainty as to meals, sometimes we dine at two o'clock, and other times at ten at night. In our company we have three mules and an ass to carry our provisions and wine, which, when we move about, we carry in deer skins.

This day I marched four leagues under a continuous torrent of rain. I am now under tolerable shelter, sitting drying my trousers over a fire of wood upon

1810 the ground, and am in a very ill-humour, having burnt the leather which encircles the bottoms. I have my jacket off and a blanket round me until my jacket and shirt are dried. I am so much accustomed to get wet I think little about it. For some time the French had been stationed about eight leagues from us, but lately they made a move and menaced Ciudad Rodrigo, but not having sufficient cannon, they were obliged to retire for the present. I saw a fine puff in the English papers treating upon the bravery of the garrison (how John Bull is gagged!) Depend upon it the French have much greater influence with the Spaniards than the English. All the Spanish soldiers I have seen look more like banditti than soldiers.

We always know when the French are near—they, the Spaniards, run away in every direction. Our soldiery hate to see them.

The Portuguese are much superior in appearance. We shall soon try their composition in the first battle. The enemy marched to San Felices, which caused us to advance upon Bouza (our regiment only). The other part of the Light Brigade continued in the rear, occupying villages, waiting ready to advance in case we required their assistance.

The French the next day had the impudence to pass the bridge and come to Barba del Puerco, about four English miles from us. A peasant came in the same evening and gave information, stating they demanded rations for 1000 men; 300 men were in the town. The next morning three companies of us moved to attack them at daylight, but they thought it prudent to retire and not wait till the bread was baked, so we had hot bread for breakfast.

Between Barba del Puerco and San Felices is an 1810 immense chain of mountains, which divides in the middle and forms a deep chasm, the bottom of which is the bed of the river Agueda, which, in the rainy season, runs with incredible violence. It receives a great quantity of water from the rocky and rugged sides of the mountains, which are for above half a mile nearly perpendicular ; here is also a bridge about ninety yards across.

The way to this bridge is very bad, being a zig-zag pathway called the pass of San Felices. The water dashing against the rugged sides of this river and the great depth of the chasm make the appearance to a stranger wonderfully terrific. These were the mountains we had to guard and place our sentries in the different intricate pathways, and to post them in the dark in order to deceive our enemy and take them off before daylight. One night at twelve o'clock I went to visit the sentries, when, missing my way, owing to the excessive darkness of the night, I travelled until daylight. The French had a piquet of seventy men on the opposite side of the mountain on a level with ours. On this side we for some time were in the habit of looking at each other with only about half a mile in a direct line between us. They now and then tried to pick some of our men off, but their shots never took effect. On the 19th of March the company I belonged to had the post of honour for the night, and about eight o'clock in the evening I went with my captain (Captain O'Hare) to post the sentries. After placing a sergeant and twelve men about fifty yards from the bridge, we posted a double sentry behind a rock about fifteen yards

1810 from it, which, in case the French passed it, were to fire and retire back to the twelve men and endeavour to maintain their ground until the company came to their assistance. I crawled over the bridge to the French side to see if I could see their sentries or observe if any of them were coming near the bridge, but saw nothing and returned up the mountain to the tent pitched for the convenience of the officers for lying in between the hours of going their rounds.

The remainder of the company were in a little church lying round a wood fire until their turn for duty at half-past eleven o'clock. The other lieutenant returned and pronounced all quiet. At twelve o'clock we heard several shots fired. We directly fell in the remainder of the company and marched towards the bridge. We soon met a man coming with information that the French were passing the bridge in great force. We marched forward and found them forming in line, with drums beating and yelling furiously. They fired to the amount of five hundred rounds, the balls whistling over our heads. Our gallant Commander ordered us not to let the men fire until we came within fifteen yards of them. The French fired another volley. We still moved on as silent as possible, fired, and gave them an English huzza. The men opposed to us were a little staggered. We again loaded and came breast to breast. Lieutenant Mercer called, " Simmons," and rushed on towards a stone several had got behind, while he drove others in front. Our men were shooting them in every direction, when an unlucky ball passed through poor Mercer's head just as he was saying, " Our brave fellows fight like Britons."

At this moment three or four fell wounded near

him. A French officer I had the satisfaction to see fall 1810
also. A fine young fellow put his rifle to the officer's
throat and shot him dead, crying out, " Revenge the
death of Mr. Mercer." He instantly received seven
shots in his body. At this time the enemy were
surrounding us in every direction. Captain O'Hare
called out, " We will never retire. Here we will stand.
They shall not pass but over my body." The shots
flew round us as thick as hailstones, and they were
advancing upon us, but we kept up a terrible fire.
The moon showed sufficiently to let us see their
numbers. I saw French officers beating their men
with their swords to make them try to drive us from
the rocks we occupied, and several letting their
muskets fall and clapping their hands upon their
sides or arms when they had received a wound and
scampering. Just at this serious crisis, I saw the three
companies coming to our assistance—the pleasantest
sight I ever beheld. We set up a most furious
shout. The French soon knew the reason. Our
companies fixed swords and came on like lions, the
Colonel at their head, the French scampering off in
the greatest dismay, throwing down their arms and
running down the precipices and carrying off their
killed and wounded, as they generally endeavour to do,
in order that the number they lose should not be well
ascertained by their enemies. Our gallant Colonel
received a musket ball through his cap. The French,
luckily for us, fired very high, or, from their great
superiority, they must have destroyed every man of
our company before the other three came to our
assistance. We had only 43 men opposed to over
500 for half an hour. When we disembarked in this

1810 country first we had 100 rank and file.   In the morning we found our loss to be one officer and five men killed, seven men badly wounded.   The other three companies lost two killed and eight wounded.   We found twelve Frenchmen and two officers killed.   Some of them had six or seven wounds.   We also picked up five poor fellows most desperately wounded and caught three prisoners.

The next day we learnt from a spy that the French colonel, who headed the storming party, received a shot through his jaw, and that they dragged away nearly 100 killed and wounded.   The French that attacked us were Grenadiers and Light Infantry, to the amount of 600, picked from 3000 men who had volunteered for the occasion.   They also had among the rocks on their side, 1500 men, who kept up a fire merely to deceive us, and ready to pass the bridge as soon as the storming party had gained their point.   So confident was their General (Baron de Férey) of success that he ordered them as soon as they got to the town to bring up all the English wounded and take care of them, and not use the prisoners ill.   This man had all along been fighting with Spaniards, and thought we should fight like them.   It is not likely, I think, from the present appearance of things in general, that we shall stay much longer.   We expect the French will soon bring ten to one against us, and of course we must retire, after some hard fighting, for 250 miles before we get to Lisbon and embark to come home.   I consider myself very lucky in not receiving a scratch, being exposed so long to the enemy's fire.   I now know what it is to meet the enemy in the field, and am confident I shall always do my duty when opposed to the foes of

my country. My captain was pleased to say my conduct had given him the greatest satisfaction. He is a
very brave man, and has fought in twenty actions in
different parts of the world.[1] I hope shortly to give
you an account of something more decisive, should
they come on by daylight. I hope you will stick by
the regiment I ordered for Charles. I send this
account of the battle only for your information, knowing it will please you, but do not wish it to be made
known ; the man who passes himself off to the world
only shows his weakness. My love to the best of
mothers. I hope yet to meet and tell her personally
of the hairbreadth escapes and dangers I have passed.
My love to my dear Ann and all the family. My
respects to my uncle and aunt. I wrote a long letter
to Colonel Sibthorp the other day. I remain your
ever affectionate son, GEO. SIMMONS.

You must pay the postage to Falmouth, I believe,
or inquire at the post office, or it is ten to one I ever
receive your letters.

Direct when you write, Lieutenant Simmons, 1st
Battalion, 95th or Rifle Regiment, Lord Wellington's
Army, Portugal.

[1] Peter O'Hare joined the Rifle Corps (from the 69th Foot)
on its first formation in 1800, and fought with it at Monte
Video, Buenos Ayres (severely wounded), Roliça, Vimeiro,
Coruña, The Coa, Busaco, Fuentes de Oñoro, and the Storming
of Ciudad Rodrigo. He was slain at the Storming of Badajoz
when leading the Forlorn Hope.—ED.

CHAPTER IV

Journal—7th May–8th August 1810

The Light Division are posted as a Corps of Observation on the
Portuguese frontier with General Picton's Division (3rd)
in support—The French invest Ciudad Rodrigo and open
fire on the fortress—The Light Division constantly on the
alert owing to rumoured movements of French—Don
Julian Sanchez, the Spanish guerrilla chieftain—French
cavalry reconnaissances on the Azava—The Light
Division occupy the high ground at Gallegos—Advance
of the French in force—Combat between a 14th Light
Dragoon and a *Grénadier à Cheval*—The *Grénadiers à
Cheval* act as " mounted infantry " and occupy Alameda—
" A body of men of this description at the end of a day's
march would be unpleasant neighbours "—Two companies
of Rifles occupy Fort Concepçion—The French capture
Ciudad Rodrigo after a forty days' siege—The Rifles march
to Barquilla—Skirmish near Barquilla—A squadron of the
14th Light Dragoons charges the French cavalry and takes
many prisoners—Colonel Talbot charges the French
infantry, but is slain and his Dragoons driven off—The
French make good their retreat—The Light Division retire
on Almeida—Massena advances against it—Results of the
fall of Ciudad Rodrigo—Boastful utterances of the French,
who announce their intention of driving the " Leopard "
into the sea at Lisbon—Blowing up of Fort Concepçion
—The Light Division retire from Almeida, leaving it
garrisoned—The Combat of the Coa—Position occupied
by the Light Division—The French advance to the attack

—Conduct of their officers in leading on their men—The Rifles fall back on the bridge—Charged by French Hussars—The 43rd Light Infantry check the advance of the latter—General Craufurd orders the Rifles to retire from a hill covering the passage—The retreat of the 52nd is thereby imperilled—Colonel Beckwith, with the Rifles, recaptures the hill " in style," but with heavy loss—Simmons severely wounded—Napier assists him until wounded himself—Simmons is carried off by the Rifle Men—Stratagem of the French to effect a crossing—The Rifle Men tricked—The French attempt to storm the bridge, but are defeated—A flag of truce—Compliments by French officers on the stand made by the Light Division—Losses of the Division—Simmons conveyed in a bullock cart to Pinhel—Severe nature of his wound—Moved to Celorico with Lieutenants Reilly, Pratt, and Harry Smith—Death of Lieutenant Reilly—Shocking condition of wounded owing to sun and flies—The Portuguese bullock-drivers desert—Adventures on the road to the Mondego—Embark in boats on the Mondego—Sad death of Lieutenant Pratt—Arrival at Coimbra—Sails for Lisbon—Arrival at Lisbon—Simmons is billeted comfortably and nursed by his servant, Rifleman Short.

LETTER No. VII

To his Parents, from Lisbon, dated 10th August 1810

Describes advance of Massena in July and many incidents of the Combat of the Coa and of his journey to Lisbon—His arrangements in case of death—General good advice to his parents, brothers, and sisters—Expectation of speedy recovery—Unabated confidence in Lord Wellington.

Journal—7th May–8th August 1810

The Light Division assembled for the inspection of General Craufurd.

1810
May
7th

1810   The Division occupied the following villages, Gallegos, Espeja, Nava de Avel (a Portuguese village), and Fuentes de Oñoro on the Duas Casas ; Headquarters of the British army, Celorico. The 3rd Division, under the command of General Picton, being in support to the Light at Pinhel, and the rest of the army at Vizeu, Trancoso, and adjacent towns and villages considerably in the rear of us.

The enemy has remained very quiet in consequence of the weather being rainy. Several Germans, Swiss, and Italians have deserted from the French, and occasionally Frenchmen, who all speak with horror of prolonging the war in Spain, as they dare not individually leave their camp. The Spanish guerrillas lay in wait to destroy them, and have become so impudent of late, that they have even attacked convoys of considerable force.

June   The French have begun throwing up works
1st   before Ciudad Rodrigo, and have completely invested it.

6th   The French made an attack on the suburbs, but the Spaniards drove the assailants back. Heavy cannonading from the town.

15th   The French opened a battery upon the town, and kept up a heavy fire during the day.

16th   The enemy's cavalry made a reconnaissance and skirmished with some German Hussars stationed at Carpio, and retired.

17th   A heavy fire kept up against the enemy's battery from the town.

19th   The Light Division assembled at Gallegos, being the nearest point toward Rodrigo, and as the enemy's fire is increasing daily before the besieged town, our

General has concentrated his Division so that we may be ready to fight or retire according to circumstances. From the frequent alarms we receive, as one body or other of Frenchmen are continually falling in and moving, we are becoming very active, and can move off with all our baggage in a quarter of an hour at any time. The Spaniards are astonished at us remaining idle, as they term it, and allowing the French to invest their town, consequently they have no high opinion of our valour. The young women, with whom we joke and talk, make no scruple in calling us cowards, and say if we fought as well as we eat and drink wine, we should be fine fellows indeed. These observations are very galling, and people who are not conversant with military movements might easily imagine we do not attack the enemy from fear. We know that it would be impossible to give the least assistance to the besieged, only being in advance of our army as a Corps of Observation. I often feel distressed that we cannot do the place any service. From our piquets we can see the enemy's cannon playing upon the town and the garrison returning it. Although the place is so closely invested, a guerrilla chief named Julian Sanchez and his orderly man, a South American, frequently dash through their outposts and go to the Governor with communications from our General, and return in the same way to us. They possess determined bravery and know every pathway about the place. Don Julian Sanchez has put to death many Frenchmen in personal conflicts on different occasions, and from his appearance, I have no doubt his bottle-holder could also play his part handsomely if put to such an extremity.

1810
June
24th

The French cavalry came on this morning in force, waited a while, retired, then returned and drove in our cavalry piquets from Carpio and Marialba over the Azava. Our Division formed close column in front of Gallegos. This appeared to be merely a reconnaissance, as the enemy retired and our cavalry reoccupied their posts as before. Some alteration had taken place, by bringing up a few companies from the rear, which probably induced the French to suppose that our army was moving to the front to raise the siege of Rodrigo.

For three or four days the firing on both sides has been very slack. The French have been working hard and approach the town much closer.

25th

At daybreak the French unmasked a battery and commenced a heavy fire upon the town, which was returned with much spirit. About 10 A.M. a tremendous explosion took place in the enemy's lines, caused by a shell falling into a field magazine. Some time after this the enemy moved a strong force of cavalry and some infantry towards us. We were compelled to retire our cavalry piquet from Carpio ; our advanced posts are now at the ford over the Azava (called the Carpio ford) and at the bridge of Marialba, and the ford of Molino dos Flores over the Agueda, which is at the junction with the Azava. Two squadrons of the 16th Dragoons joined us.

26th

The enemy threw a great number of shells into the town. During this day an oil magazine was consumed by fire. Our Commander-in-Chief visited the outposts.

27th

The enemy have two pontoon bridges over the Agueda, one above and the other below Rodrigo,

and have now a large force of cavalry and infantry 1810
on its left bank in order to, if possible, cut off all
communication between us and the garrison. The
Governor contrived to send a letter by an old man to
Lord Wellington. The firing of cannon on both
sides very briskly kept up, and there was occasionally during the night some musketry; we found
that the French had attempted, under the cover of
night, to take the town by storm, but were repulsed.

The cannonade continued during this day in the June
most lively way, much to our annoyance that we 28th
could not drive the rascals from before the town.

The cannonade continued last night and this day. 29th

The Division marched into camp into a wood near 30th
Alameda. In the evening before dark we formed
sections, and opening out very considerably so as to
make it appear at a distance that a very large body
of men were upon the march, we returned to
Gallegos. A barricade of carts had been placed upon
the bridge of Marialba to prevent the enemy crossing
suddenly. We brought up a gun and fired at them
to clear the way.

Our Brigadier drew up the Division in rank entire July
upon the high ground in the rear of Gallegos to 3rd
watch the enemy and make him fancy we were
much stronger in force. The 14th Dragoons joined
us.

At daylight the enemy, in considerable force, 4th
advanced; our piquets retired. The Division formed
line between Gallegos and Alameda upon the high
ground. Our Horse Artillery fired shrapnel and round
shot at the enemy's columns of cavalry as they
approached us, and the 3rd Caçadores fired a volley

1810 as soon as they perceived the French, without doing any mischief. This sort of thing was excusable, being young soldiers. We are in hope that time may accustom them to judge their distance better.

I saw a Light Dragoon attack a French Horse Grenadier and trounce him handsomely. The man's helmet was nearly all brass, with large bars across in various ways; he had literally cut through this and also the man's head most severely and brought him in a prisoner. Our General sent the cap home as a present to some of his friends to show with what strength the Englishman had dealt his blows upon the Frenchman's head.

The French infantry and artillery were now advancing in great force, so it was deemed prudent to retire, which we did in good order over the Duas Casas by the bridge in rear of Alameda. The prisoners informed us that Marshal Junot's corps was all employed to make us fight or retreat. I was much amused by the dexterity displayed by a body of French Dragoons (Grénadiers à Cheval) who passed through Alameda and dismounted, leaving their horses in line under the charge of some of their men. They then trotted off in their big jack boots and large hairy caps as Light Infantry to skirmish with us. As we had got the high ground across the river, and they could neither check nor impede our progress, they returned to their horses and became Dragoons again. A body of men of this description at the end of a hard day's march would be unpleasant neighbours. The enemy did not attempt to cross the Duas Casas; the Division moved into Val de la Mula. Two

companies of Rifle Men were put into Fort Con- 1810
cepçion for the purpose of assisting the Engineers in
guarding the different communications with mines, as
the angles were to be destroyed when the French
advanced. The company which I was in, was on this
duty, and curiosity led me to explore some places
underground. I found in a corner of a large place
that had on some occasion been made a depôt for
provisions a cask of brandy and three casks of fine
biscuit. This was quite a God-send to us all. The
cavalry remained at Castillejo and Aldea del Obispo
on the Duas Casas.

Ciudad Rodrigo fell into the hands of the French July
at seven o'clock P.M. Its Governor made a noble 10th
defence indeed ; the enemy's trenches were open before
the place for forty days.

Seven companies of Rifle Men marched at mid- 11th
night, with two companies of the 52nd, to near Barquilla and lay down. The enemy had a piquet of
cavalry and infantry in advance of Villar de Ciérvos,
but withdrew them after dark and reoccupied the post
at daylight. The Dragoons came on very cautiously,
placed a vedette, and formed up upon a steep hill ;
the infantry, amounting to sixty or seventy men, were
in the flat below. Major Butler, with a squadron of
the 14th Dragoons, attacked the French cavalry and
brought in one captain, one subaltern, and thirty-four
privates prisoners, many of whom were a good deal
hacked and cut about the head. The French infantry
were attacked by Colonel Talbot, though it was pretty
evident that they would have had to surrender without
firing a shot had he waited. He charged with a
squadron of the 14th and fell dead amongst them, as

1810 also his Quartermaster ; thirty men were killed and
wounded and twenty horses. During this sad affair
we were not allowed to show ourselves, although a
few infantry would have compelled them to lay down
their arms. Our *wise* General had the 14th, 16th,
and German Hussars all to assist, also Horse Artillery and seven companies of infantry, but let this small
party of Frenchmen slip through our fingers so
shamefully. The French officer who commanded the
party deserved great credit for the bravery he displayed,
and most extraordinary good luck attended him.

July 12th   The enemy entered Fuentes de Oñoro.

15th   The Division assembled at its alarm post in consequence of the enemy being in motion near Villar de
Ciérvos. I forgot to observe that yesterday we fell
back upon the village of Junça, a little way from
Almeïda, and placed in a very rugged and rocky
ground near the banks of the Coa. Almeïda is the
frontier fortification of Portugal, and is commanded by
Colonel Cox, a British officer. The garrison consists of
3000 men, well appointed, and possessing every requisite to sustain a siege. In consequence of Ciudad
Rodrigo having fallen, the enemy began to concentrate
an immense force of every arm for the invasion of
Portugal under the command of one of Napoleon's
favourite Generals, Marshal Massena, Prince of Essling
and Duke of Rivoli. Almeïda now was the only im-
pediment which could for a moment prevent the
French army from bringing their whole force against
the British, the latter consisting of not more than
25,000 men altogether. As these Gasconaders, under
their different Generals, had carried their victorious
arms through the greater part of the Continent, too

frequently through intrigue and treachery, such 1810
vaunting soldiers had great contempt for us for pre-
suming to enter the lists with them.   Their Generals
published bills, telling the Portuguese that they
would not stop until they had driven the frightened
Leopards at the point of the bayonet into the sea at
Lisbon.   This "nation of shopkeepers and general
disturbers of all nations" should be made a most awful
example of to deter others from opposing them !

Our infantry piquets were upon the high road to July
Val de la Mula, upon a plain, the cavalry piquets upon 20th
the Duas Casas, and a few men with the Engineer
officer left in Fort Concepçion, ready to blow it up
at any moment when required.

At daylight Fort Concepçion exploded and made 21st
a tremendous noise.   I was lying under a tree in a
sound sleep.   I sprang up, thinking the French army
had got into the camp, and seized my sword, which
hung upon a bough of the tree, and proceeded to our
alarm post.   I found the same effect produced by
the noise upon the whole of us, and the only feeling
we had was to sell our lives at as dear a rate as
possible.   When the cause was known, and that the
enemy had not driven in our outposts, we fell out
and took our breakfast.

I was on outlying piquet.   I fully expected to be 22nd
attacked this morning, as several peasantry told us
that large bodies of men were concentrating close to
us, and all the villages were filled with what was now
called the Army of Portugal, amounting at least to
100,000 men, many of whom had been in a number
of Napoleon's great battles.

Lieutenant Uniacke and Lieutenant M'Cullock 23rd

1810 relieved us this morning. Spent a jovial evening with Lieutenants Pratt and Beckwith in Almeida. About eight o'clock an officer told us that he had orders to clear the town of every person that was not to be employed in the siege, and regretted that we could not be allowed to remain longer within its walls. We drank success to their defence of the fortress, and that many Frenchmen might bite the dust before the place, shook him by the hand, and departed. We had scarcely left the town when the rain began to fall in torrents ; the thunder and lightning of that night was the most tremendously grand I ever beheld either before or since. The Division, officers and men, had no shelter from this inclement night ; as to lying down, it was nearly impossible, for the water ran in gutters amongst the rocks. I sat upon a stone like a drowned rat, looking at the heavens and amusing myself with their brilliancy and longing for the morning, which came at last, and the rain ceased. Our next consideration was to set the men to work to clean their arms and look after their ammunition. Our cavalry outposts since the fall of Fort Concepçion had been on the Turon.

COMBAT OF THE COA

July 24th A little after daybreak the enemy advanced against our piquets and drove them in. The Division was put into position, the left upon Almeida and the right in rugged ground upon the Coa, which river was running furiously in its course ; several companies of Rifle Men and the 43rd Light Infantry were placed behind stone walls. The enemy now advanced in vast bodies. The whole plain in our front was 1810 covered with horse and foot advancing towards us. The enemy's infantry formed line and, with an innumerable multitude of skirmishers, attacked us fiercely ; we repulsed them ; they came on again, yelling, with drums beating, frequently the drummers leading, often in front of the line, French officers like mountebanks running forward and placing their hats upon their swords, and capering about like madmen, saying, as they turned to their men, " Come on, children of our country. The first that advances, Napoleon will recompense him." Numbers returned to the attack. We kept up a very brisk fire. Several guns began to play upon us, and as the force kept increasing every moment in our front, and columns of infantry were also moving upon our right flank, we were ordered to retire half the company. Captain O'Hare's retired, and the remainder, under Lieutenant Johnston, still remained fighting for a few moments longer. I was with this party. We moved from the field into the road, our men falling all round us, when a body of Hussars in bearskin caps and light-coloured pelisses got amongst the few remaining Rifle Men and began to sabre them. Several attempted to cut me down, but I avoided their kind intentions by stepping on one side. I had a large cloak rolled up and strapped across my body ; my haversack was filled with little necessary articles for immediate use ; thus I got clear off. A volley was now fired by a party of the 43rd under Captain Wells, which brought several of the Hussars to the ground. In the scuffle I took to my heels and ran to the 43rd, Wells calling out, " Mind the Rifle Man !

1810 Do not hit him, for heaven's sake." As I was compelled to run into their fire to escape, he seized me
by the hand and was delighted beyond measure at my
escape.   The road to a small bridge across the Coa,
which the Division would have to retire over, was
very bad and rocky.   Our gallant fellows disputed
manfully every inch of ground and retired towards
the river.   Every place we left was covered with the
enemy's Light Infantry in ten times our number.   As
we got near the river the enemy made several attempts
to cut us off.   General Craufurd ordered a number
of Rifle Men who had occupied a place that prevented
the French from stopping our retreat over the bridge
to evacuate it before half the 52nd, who were on the
right, had filed over.   The enemy directly brought
up their infantry to this hill, which commanded the
bridge, and kept up a terrible fire.   Colonel Beckwith,
a most gallant and clever soldier, saw this frightful mistake and ordered us to retake the wall and hill instantly,
which we did in good style, but suffered severely in
men and officers.   Lieutenant Harry Smith, Lieutenant Thomas Smith, and Lieutenant Pratt were
wounded, and I was shot through the thigh close
to the wall, which caused me to fall with great force.
Being wounded in this way was quite a new thing to
me.   For a few moments I could not collect my ideas,
and was feeling about my arms and body for a
wound, until my eye caught the stream of blood
rushing through the hole in my trousers, and my leg
and thigh appeared so heavy that I could not move
it.   Captain Napier took off his neckerchief and
gave it to a sergeant, who put it round my thigh
and twisted it tight with a ramrod, to stop the bleeding.

The firing was so severe that the sergeant, on finishing 1810 the job for me, fell with a shot through the head. Captain Napier[1] was also about the same time wounded in the side. The Division had now nearly got over the bridge ; some men put me into a blanket and carried me off. Our General had placed himself some distance from the fight to observe the enemy's movements. I passed him in the blanket. The General had still in his remembrance the loss of his light cart. He told the men this was no time to be taking away wounded officers, and ordered them back. They observed, " This is an officer of ours, and we must see him in safety before we leave him." The last party of our men retired over the bridge and occupied it. The ground was very rugged and rocky close to the bridge, so that Rifle Men were placed behind every stone, and two companies of the 43rd hid themselves and were ready to support our men. Several Frenchmen held up calabashes as much as to say, " Let us get some water to drink." Our men allowed some of the enemy to get water, and did not fire upon them, but the cunning rogues made lodgments between the stones, and when their party was ready to storm the bridge, they commenced firing upon our men.

A number of French officers and some drummers headed the storming party. Our fellows allowed them to come close to the bridge. Some officers got over before they fell, but few went back to tell the tale, either men or officers. They attempted to force the bridge several times before the evening, and

[1] William Napier, 43rd Light Infantry, the author of *History of the War in the Peninsula.*—ED.

1810 finding it impossible to effect their purpose, they made a signal to cease firing. An officer came forward waving a white handkerchief and requested to be allowed to remove their wounded, as the bridge and its vicinity were covered with their killed and wounded. This request was granted. The officer said he had heard of the English fighting well, but he could not have supposed men would have fought against such fearful odds. He complimented our men much upon their gallantry, and observed what a pity it was we were enemies. During this day it rained occasionally, and towards evening more so, which made the arms frequently miss fire. After dark the Light Division marched to Carvalha.

A party of the 1st Hussars, under Colonel Arentschildt,[1] was upon the road. He paid me the most kind attention and ordered an Hussar to dismount. I was placed upon the horse, and was taken on it to the church of Alverca, where I found a number of poor fellows as bad, and some worse wounded, laid in every direction upon the stone floors. A poor fellow, who died some time after I entered, begged of me to lie upon a paillasse beside him, as I was upon the bare stones ; he divided it with me.[2] In the evening I was

[1] Colonel Arentschildt, of the 1st German Hussars, was very kind to me and put me upon a horse, sending two Hussars to accompany me. He thought I was dying. The tears trickled down the veteran's face. God bless his memory.—G. S.

[2] This soldier belonged to the 43rd Light Infantry. I was on the ground, and very ill from loss of blood ; he had been placed on a paillasse of straw and was dying, but his noble nature would not allow him to die in peace when he saw an officer so humbled as to be laid near him on the bare stones. I have experienced many such kindnesses from soldiers, and indeed if I had not, I should not be alive to tell the tale.—G. S.

put upon a car drawn by bullocks—the most clumsy 1810 machine possible. Here now commenced my misfortunes. The car proceeded, with me upon it, to Pinhel, suffering the most severe torture from the jolting motion to my poor limb, sustained at almost every movement. I was lodged in the Bishop's house, and Colonel Pakenham behaved very kindly to me. I now became anxious to know the nature of my wounds. My trousers and drawers were cut up the side ; the latter article of dress was literally glued to my thigh ; in fact, I had bled so profusely that it had steeped my shirt, which stuck to my skin most unpleasantly. I found the ball had passed through the sartorius muscle and close to the main artery, directly through my thigh, partially injuring the bone. The surgeon who visited me shook his head and looked serious, recommending a tourniquet to be put round my thigh, and in case of a sudden effusion of blood to stop it by tightening the ligature until assistance was procured. A spent ball had also hit the calf of my leg, but the skin was not broken.

Put into an English spring waggon with Lieutenants July Reilly, Pratt, and Smith. The springs of this machine 25th were very strong, and the rough ground we passed over made them dance us up and down in an awful manner. Bad as the movement of the bullock car was, this was ten times worse, if possible. I felt happy when I was put under cover for the night upon the ground floor of a dilapidated house at Baraca with a little straw and my blanket. [1] My thigh and leg were frightfully

[1] This night I was so reckless of life, thinking the artery injured, that some fool gave me a bottle of strong wine, which I drank off at a draught. It was very wicked of me.—G. S.

1810 swollen, and also the lower part of my body. My ration bread I directed my faithful servant, Henry Short, to make into a large poultice, which was soon done. I then dressed the wound of Lieutenant Coane, who was shot in the side; he was in the same company as myself.

July 26th Poor Reilly this morning told me it was useless tormenting himself by taking another day's journey, as he felt he could not live many hours (the ball had gone directly through the lower part of his body); he shook me by the hand and regretted our parting. As the wounded were obliged to proceed daily to the rear or fall into the hands of the enemy, I was obliged to leave him in this unfortunate manner.

At daylight we proceeded to Celorico, which place we reached, after suffering indescribable torture, in the evening. Here I learned our loss more particularly, a sergeant having come to take charge of us. Captain Creagh, shot through the lower part of his body, died the night of the action; Lieutenant M'Leod shot through the heart, eight officers wounded, and Lieutenant M'Cullock taken prisoner.[1]

[1] Lieutenant-Colonel Beckwith and the Battalion were particularly thanked in Lord Wellington's despatches for their gallant conduct on this trying day, and indeed nothing could exceed the devoted gallantry displayed by every one. The Light Division lost in killed and wounded on this day 27 officers and 336 men; 53 Rifle Men were made prisoner; many of these were also wounded. The French loss must have been very considerable from the immense numbers in the field.—G. S.

Napier puts the French loss as "above a thousand."

The losses of the 95th Rifles during this fight were 1 officer, 1 sergeant, and 10 Rifle Men killed, and 9 officers, 1 sergeant, and 54 Rifle Men wounded. Of the wounded officers, three died within a few days of the fight, and many of the wounded Rifle Men also succumbed to their injuries.—Ed.

This morning we found the Portuguese muleteers 1810
had disappeared and left the spring waggon without July
the mules, so we were all put upon bullock cars once 27th
again. These were easier to ride upon, so I was
pleased with the change. I had the intelligence that
Reilly breathed his last towards evening yesterday.
Several of our poor fellows died from the rough
usage they suffered, and several soldiers who had
neglected to cover their wounds now became one
frightful mass of maggots all over the surface,
which really made me tremble to see them dressed.
The flies and mosquitoes followed us in myriads.
We had no means of keeping off the swarms of insects,
and the slow pace that the bullocks went, made us
feel the vertical rays of the sun with redoubled force.
We had some salt meat as rations, which, in the feverish
state of our existence, we turned from with disgust ; we
very seldom got bread, generally biscuit, and that full
of worms or mouldy ; we were hurried away daily to
the rear as fast as possible in order that our army, if
pressed by the enemy, should not have us on the
line of its march to impede its progress to the rear.
Halted for the night at Villa Cortez.

Villa Cortez to Pinhancos. 28th

On this day's journey to Galizes I had very nearly 29th
finished my military career. As the bullocks were
dragging me along through a pass between two steep
hills, a Portuguese who had three loaded mules behind
each other and tied together, was also travelling along
a sort of sheep path several yards above me. The
last mule, when just over my car, stumbled and down
he came, dragging the rest with him ; he fell very
heavily upon the car close to me ; how he did not

1810 injure me I cannot account for, but so it was. It alarmed me, and consequently increased my circulation, which gave me more pain than usual in my wounded thigh for the rest of the way.

July   Arrived at San Payo, where the bullock-driver
30th took my food and my servant's, and departed with his bullocks also.

I sent to the *juiz de fore* to request him to procure me two bullocks. He told me the people would not obey him now, but directed me to send my servant armed and to take the first two bullocks he could find. Short soon brought two and yoked them. I could not get a driver, so my servant marched in front of them with a *rivo* (that is, a long pole with a sharp piece of iron at the end), for the purpose of goading the bullocks (to make them move on), over his shoulder. I had by accident got a paillasse under me filled with straw, which made me more comfortable. My servant, not knowing how to manage these animals properly, and the flies teasing them exceedingly, they became quite unmanageable. He attempted to stop the car, but was knocked over, and the car passed over him. The animals became furious. In this perilous situation I was carried along most violently, when the animals started on one side of the road, which gave the car a considerable jerk and landed me and the paillasse upon the only soft piece of ground for a distance round. All the rest was rough and rugged ground mixed with granite rock. I was in great alarm, but thankful to the Almighty for having preserved me so miraculously. The bullocks soon stopped among the thick underwood, from the resistance it made to their further

progress. I now had another danger to encounter. 1810
Two men with guns had been observed occasionally
by myself and servant skulking among the trees and
keeping at some distance. It struck me that these
fellows were following us with the intention of
attempting to take the bullocks, and, waiting a
favourable opportunity, I made my servant load his
rifle, and though I could not stir, I had my sword
drawn by my side, but being bundled out of the car
had bothered all my previous arrangements for
defence, and these men went directly towards the bullocks. Short soon made his appearance, and was glad
to see I had not suffered much. He picked up his
rifle upon the road, which, with every other article,
had been thrown out of the car. At this moment
two British Artillerymen who had lost their way came
up. I told my situation in a few words to them,
and now desired them to assist my servant in taking
prisoner one of the Portuguese, in order that I might
proceed under the management of a proper driver.
This was soon done, but the fellow had not calculated
upon being embargoed into my service in so rough a
manner, and became very sulky. The bullocks were
again put to rights and I was replaced upon the car.
The driver did not pay attention to the road, so
that I was jolted over large stones, which made
me suffer extremely. My man Short observed his
carelessness and gave him a good drubbing, which
had a very good effect, and we jogged on afterwards
quietly. My thigh was very painful from the shock
I received when thrown out, when I arrived in the
evening.

My thigh felt very painful, and I commenced my July
31st

1810 journey with great reluctance. My friend Pratt came and endeavoured to cheer up my spirits, telling me our miseries would end with this day's march, as we should then embark and go much easier in boats, and when we got to Lisbon we should be able to make up for all our miseries. The road on our approach to the Mondego was very narrow and down a very steep mountain ; the least deviation on the part of the bullocks would have precipitated me some hundred feet. I was convinced that the driver had no good-will towards me ; I was perfectly helpless, but not quite at his mercy. My servant drew his sword and told him that if any accident happened to me he would bury it up to the hilt in his bosom, and from what I know of his character he would have fulfilled his promise. I must say I breathed much more freely when we arrived on the banks of the Mondego near Lofrece. Tents were supplied, and we encamped for the night. Here now my miseries and suffering from travelling ceased.

Several of the poor soldiers died upon the road. Each individual could not be supplied with a car, consequently the poor fellows suffered more. On two occasions I took one of them on the same car with me, and I found sad inconvenience long before the day's journey was finished. Soldiers in general are like children, and must be directed as such ; although they were frequently told if they exposed their wounds, the flies would deposit their eggs upon them, still they took no notice, and there was no officer present to enforce this command, so their wounds became completely alive with myriads of large maggots, the sight of which made me really

shudder again.   Oil was found the best thing to 1810
take them away, as when applied it killed them,
obstructing their breathing.   We now got everything
to eat we could have wished for : fruits, vegetables,
bread, milk, and eggs.   We had been generally
living upon salt rations and bad biscuit.   The people
were afraid of the advance of the French army
on our line of march, and most of them had
retired to fastnesses in the mountains, taking away
every article they could collect for their future
support.

My poor friend Pratt was brought into the boat Aug.
a corpse !   We had embarked in boats upon the 1st
Mondego River and were proceeding to Coimbra.
Pratt went ashore to get some milk for our breakfast,
as we rested, to give the rowers breathing time.   I
suppose the exertion he used, the day being very hot,
had assisted to remove the slough in the wound in his
throat, the carotid artery being injured ; he died
instantly from one gush of blood.   The ball had
entered his jaw, taken a transverse direction, and gone
out near the base of the neck.   When he drank a
quantity of anything, the fluid ran down his bosom,
so that the gullet was also partially divided.   It was
a sad sight to see him brought back to us in this way.
He was wrapped up in a blanket and laid in the boat
beside us.   Thus finished the life of as a noble a
fellow and as worthy a man as I ever met with.   In
the afternoon we arrived at Coimbra.   Crowds of
people came to the wharf from curiosity.   One young
gentleman entered the boat and began to remove the
blankets to show my wound to some ladies that were
close to the wharf.   It vexed me so that I doubled

1810 my fist, and as he leaned over me I gave him a blow which sent him on his back ; he made the best possible use of his legs to get out. An order from the Commandant came to direct us to proceed immediately to Figueira. We begged and entreated to go on shore, as we were literally naked. We did not wait for any reply, but requested some soldiers to take us into houses. Four men of the company I belonged to, who had gone to the rear sick, took me upon a door to a silversmith. He received me very reluctantly into his house, but we soon became good friends. Afterwards I sent out and purchased some shirts, tea and sugar, got plenty of bread to poultice my thigh, and in comparison was in paradise. Pratt was decently interred.

Aug. 2nd Embarked in a boat and rowed down the river to Figueira. I was laid down upon the shore, for some time sadly annoyed by the Portuguese wanting to uncover my wound. They came close, then began to pity me, and at the same time tried cautiously to get the blanket off little by little. I was heartily glad when a boat came for me to remove me from these tormentors, who, I have no doubt, thought their noisy way of showing me how they appreciated my misfortunes was the greatest display of kindness, and that such patriotism was due to their allies, the English. I was carefully handled by the sailors, and taken into the ship much more easily than I expected—the *Nestor* transport. She lay outside the bar. I found Capt. Mitchell, Lieuts. Smith and Thos. Smith, also Lieuts. Cowan and M'Diarmid of the 43rd Regiment, and all the wounded men on board.

7th The wind and weather proved favourable. We

arrived safe in the Tagus. I was put upon a board and 1810 taken to the Golden Lion. We had beds upon the floor. Those who were wounded so as not to be able to sit up, remained in them. I ordered a good dinner, but the landlord began to remonstrate with us upon the danger of taking much food in our present condition. All my friends were of the same opinion as myself, namely, that we had been starved long enough and ought now to enjoy ourselves. I do not think I ever was more happy. An occasional twitch in my leg and thigh merely came at intervals to remind me that I must not expect happiness without some alloy in this world.

In the General Orders of the 6th the Light Division is to be formed into two Brigades : 1st Brigade under Colonel Beckwith, 43rd Regiment, right wing of 95th (Rifle Men), and 3rd Portuguese Caçadores; 2nd Brigade to consist of the 52nd, left wing of 95th, and 1st Caçadores, under Lieut.-Col. Barclay.

I found this morning that my bill was a very large Aug. one, which induced me immediately to take measures to 8th live at a cheaper rate, so I got a billet at No. 26 Rua de Buenos Ayres. My servant, and a most faithful one he was, took great care of me and enabled me to live very well under my income, which made me as easy and comfortable as a forlorn bed-ridden person could be in a strange land, without a friend (except my servant) to beguile my lonely hours; particularly after leading so active a life made it much more irksome.

With the fall of Almeida, the enemy were in possession of the two frontier fortifications, in

1810 which their stores could be deposited in safety. Marshal Massena's whole attention was now turned to the subjugation of Portugal, which could only be effected by first expelling the English from the country.

The enemy, having concentrated his whole force and supplied his magazines with every requisite for his advance, endeavoured to bring Lord Wellington to action as speedily as possible, and pushed forward more rapidly than the Commander-in-Chief would allow. The Battle of Busaco[1] was fought on 27th September, and terminated gloriously for the British and Portuguese arms.

Letter No. VII

Lisbon, 10th *August* 1810.

MY DEAR PARENTS—When this letter comes to hand, which I hope no unforeseen accident may prevent, it will be a means of quieting your troubles on my account. I am out of danger. I know my dear mother's affection for her graceless son. An earlier opportunity did not present itself, which you will be convinced of in the sequel.

For some time, as usual, the Light Brigade had been continually in sight of the army under the command of General Massena, numbering about

---

[1] I regret as a soldier I was not in the battle, but I could not help it, being unable to crawl, from my wounds in the thigh and leg. I was at that time so ambitious of being in the fight that I really wept at not being there.—G. S.

80,000, frequently partially engaged in skirmishing, 1810 which we took little notice of, being so much in the habit of it.

About the 14th of July the enemy advanced, feeling their way toward Almeida. We retired, fighting, to the right of Almeida, and took up a position, having the town on our left flank, or rather in front, and here we waited the further advance of the enemy.

On the evening of the 23rd of July, on coming off piquet, and having a mind to go once more into Almeida, a friend of mine accompanied me. After taking coffee we returned to our encampment. It began to rain most violently, attended with the most vivid lightning I ever beheld, thundering also most terribly. This would have been of little consequence, but having to sleep among the rocks without any covering from the weather, we of course were soon wet through.

On the appearance of day (about 4 o'clock A.M.) the enemy began to advance and fight with our piquets. Our Brigade immediately took up their position in the grape gardens behind walls and rocks, ready to receive them. After smoking two pipes I damned them to my Captain for not coming on faster, who laughingly said, "Stop, my boy, do not let us be in a hurry; there is time enough before night to get a broken head." Soon after this observation the French appeared in great numbers, some singing, others screaming and howling like wild beasts, their drums also beating in every direction. Our company was ordered to advance with three companies of the 43rd Light Infantry. We soon came

1810 very near the enemy, who kept up a most desperate fire. We returned a steady fire. They now advanced very near, then retired a little, and came on again several times, until our ranks became much thinned, and in our turn we retired, moving more to the left, our company being ordered to protect the left of our line, as the enemy were now moving round and menancing our flank in that quarter. Our Rifle Boys brought them down like wild ducks. At this moment a shot passed through the side of a brother officer in the same company with me. He exclaimed, " Oh ! Simmons, I am wounded." A horse being near, we luckily got him away ; he is likely to recover. In passing a road the fire was excessively hot from their cannons, their shells bursting continually above our heads in every direction. I was coming over with the rear section of the company when suddenly 300 or more French Dragoons dashed in among us, knocked down my sergeant, and cut down three or four men. A fellow brandished his sword in the air, and was going to bring it down upon my head. I dropped mine, seeing it was useless to make resistance. He saw I was an officer, and did not cut me. I looked round me to see if I had the least chance of escaping, and pulled my boat cloak off, which was buckled round me, when fortune favoured me : some of the 43rd and our own men gave them a volley. I took advantage of their confusion, rushed through them, and got through the breach in a wall our men were firing from, pleased enough at my good fortune. We were soon engaged in every direction, retiring very slowly, until about five o'clock most of the Brigade had passed the bridge. The French now

endeavoured to cut off the remainder ; every place 1810
was lined with them.   They now got possession of a
hill near the bridge in great numbers.   We were
ordered to advance up the hill and drive them from
the place.   A party of the 43rd, with Major M'Leod
at their head and several of their officers, as well as
our men and officers, ran up the hill, exposed to a
desperate fire, as the enemy had a strong wall to fire
over.   They did us much mischief before we got at
them.   It was a grand sight.   Our brave boys would
face anything.   They shouted.   The French became
panic-struck.   At this moment I had nearly come to
the wall.   A musket ball hit me in the middle of my
left thigh, and passed through a little upwards ; being
so near the man that favoured me with the shot, it
luckily went directly through, and took a small piece
of my cloth trousers with it, at the same time I
was also slightly hit in the leg.   I staggered on
a little, but fell ; the blood spouted out on both sides.
I put my hand into my pocket for my tourniquet,
but fainted.   Captain Napier of the 43rd, being near,
twitched his handkerchief round my thigh.   A sergeant
of the 43rd, with three of their men, carried me off.
By the time I got to the bridge I came to myself ;
there was a desperate fire at it.   A sergeant and
three of my company, came to my assistance
and relieved the other men.   They dragged me
up the hill, which was nearly a mile, up a very
rocky and steep place.   The blood kept pouring
'from my wounds.   I fainted several times.   The
Colonel of the German Hussars gave me some
wine and put me on a horse, an Hussar also with me.
I sent my men back.   In this way I was conveyed

1810 about a league, and put into a church, where I met
with numbers of men and officers in the same plight.
I was anxious to see my wound, and on examining it
I thought directly I should soon want a billet in
another world, but fortune has since favoured me.
The large artery in my thigh is not injured.   After
being dressed I was put upon a car drawn by bullocks,
and got into Pinhel about 10 o'clock at night, having
had nothing to eat all day except some wine ;   it
rained frequently, which made me uncomfortable.

In this way we travelled over rugged rocks and
mountains until the 31st of July, about 100 English
miles at the least ; we encamped on the river-side
near a small village.   The next morning we sailed
down the river Mondego about seven leagues to
Coimbra.   Moved to Figueira next day, a seaport, and
embarked on board the *Nestor* transport for Lisbon,
at which place I arrived on the 7th of August.
I have, after some trouble, got into an empty house ;
there is a mattress and sheets, things I have seldom
of late been used to.   My Colonel sent my servant
after me.   He is a trusty and good fellow.   I have
him here.   As I have the house to myself, I have no
one to disturb me.   The people are not worthy of
notice.   I met with great barbarity all the way.
They would let you die in the streets before they
would assist you.   Lisbon seems like every other
place.   If any of them come near to pity, it is only to
rob you, if possible.   I have several times on the
road been robbed of the bread I was going to make a
poultice of, and not had an opportunity of buying more.
My thigh is much better ; this day I have got a
crutch made.   I think of exhibiting in my room in a

day or two, and then I must hop out. I cannot bear 1810
to be penned up in this way. I hope, if I go on as well
as I am doing now, in six weeks I shall be able to join
my regiment and have another fight with the rascals.
We must have a general engagement soon. I hope
my dear Maud will not be so unlucky as I; he is
at present in very good health. The day after I
was hit I sent him an inventory of my little property
should anything happen to me. I expect a letter
daily from him. As I always take care to provide
against accidents, I have money sufficient for my
needs. When I found there was little chance of
recovering, I bought a silver snuff-box. I leave you
to guess who I meant it for. I also was going to
purchase a necklace for Ann, but I did not at that
time meet with one to please me. I directed Maud
to do it out of my money, but as things have taken
such a wonderful change for the better, I hope I shall
another day present my little affairs personally. I
look forward with pleasure to that time. I must
think of Betsy too. Yes, my dear parents, I think
of you all, and muse my fancy about you
daily. John I hope is at school, Charles, also Betsy.
Do not disappoint me, for God's sake. Maud I have
made something of. He writes better language. He
is afraid of doing otherwise. If he writes wrong, I
lecture him severely. I make every inquiry after
him. I am proud to say he is highly esteemed by his
brother officers. I have no doubt he will be a
dashing, brave fellow when tried. I beg you will not
talk to people of my being wounded or anything
else about me; it is truly ridiculous to satisfy every
idle person's curiosity. I will give you an old

1810 proverb ; put it into practice: " Shun the talkative and curious man, for what he hears he will relate again." God bless you all. Yours ever,   G. S.

Our Brigade had 18,000 French opposed to them ; our strength 3,000 ; they fought until 5 o'clock in the evening. The French sent a flag of truce. Both agreed to bury the dead. Our Brigade is near our army now. Lord Wellington is drawing the enemy on. We had two officers killed ; two have since died of their wounds ; six more are wounded. The papers will most likely enter more into particulars than I can. The French in the afternoon stormed the bridge five times ; their loss was very considerable. A French colonel came on in front of his men. Our Boys let him come upon the bridge and then shot him ; few of his men returned. The French certainly behaved very bravely. They are fine fellows. The officer that came upon the bridge to beg a truce observed to our officer that he was, as well as were all the French officers, much astonished at the determined bravery of the British soldiers ; it surpassed everything.

My brother will soon have a lieutenancy. He is a lucky fellow indeed. I regret much I did not receive my wound in a general action. I now live in hopes of a speedy recovery and to be well in time enough for one. I am confident of victory whenever Lord Wellington can bring them to a general engagement. Our troops are in good health and seasoned soldiers.

I had an account of our loss. In our company, I am sorry to say, thirty-nine were killed and wounded and

missing, also another officer and myself severely 1810
wounded. We sustained a greater loss than any
other company.

I hope my dear mother will not distress herself
about me. At best this life is very short, and should
I fall, I shall die nobly in the cause of my country,
and if I may use the words of a great man, " The
most precious tears are those with which Heaven
bedews the unburied head of a soldier."

In all probability by the time your answer will
arrive I shall have recovered sufficiently from my
wounds to enable me to join my regiment. Should it
be otherwise, I have left orders at the post office to
stop my letters till countermanded.

Direct Lieut. S., 95th or Rifle Regiment,
Brig. - General Craufurd's Light Division, Lord
Wellington's Army, Portugal.

CHAPTER V

Journal—15th August–30th September 1810

Removes to Pedroso for sea-bathing, accompanied by Lieutenant Harry Smith—The English merchant's wife's account of the French officers billeted on her in 1808—French opinions of the British before Vimeiro and after—A wounded French officer's description of British Rifle Men in action.

LETTER No. VIII

To his Parents, from Pedroso, Lisbon, dated 30th September 1810

Complains of inactive life due to wound, and reproves his father for styling the 95th Rifles *"a dangerous regiment"*—Description of the French plot in Lisbon—Much about brother Maud—Results of Colonel Sibthorp's well-meant endeavours to stop him joining the 95th—Dislike of the French to the *"green fellows"*—Severe comments on brothers John and Joseph.

Journal—1st October–31st December

Determines to leave Pedroso and rejoin his regiment—Joins a draft of convalescents marching from Lisbon to the front—The Rifle Men under Simmons ordered to do rear-guard to prevent desertion — Retreat of the British army on

Torres Vedras — Rejoins the Rifles at Arruda — Construction of the Lines—Rifles engaged at Sobral—On piquet with Lieutenant Hopwood—Captures two French soldiers —Lieutenants Strode and Simmons bury an old woman in the vault of a Portuguese grandee—Hatred of the Portuguese for the French—Description of the Lines of Torres Vedras — Arrival of English bell-tents — Retreat of the French under Marshal Massena — Advance of the Light Division in pursuit—General Craufurd is about to attack a supposed French rear-guard, but is stopped by Lord Wellington, who knows that the whole of Marshal Junot's Corps is in front of him—The Rifles engaged on the Rio Mayor—General Craufurd, with three Rifle Men, reconnoitre the French outposts, but disturbs a hornet's nest.   Simmons's wound begins to trouble him, owing to wet and exposure— He removes the *abatis* on the bridge across the Rio Mayor, assisted by three Rifle Men—Invalided back to Lisbon with fever and dysentery—Difficulties in obtaining a billet— Gets into quarters at last.

LETTER No. IX

To his Parents, from Lisbon, dated 16th December 1810

Describes life in the Lines of Torres Vedras—Visits his brother Maud at Bucellas — The advance from the Lines in November—Wanton havoc wrought by the French and miserable condition of Portuguese—Murders committed by French soldiers—Some candid opinions of the French nation —Pursuit of the French—Account of troubles due to his wound and during his return to Lisbon—Regrets as to his brother John's career, etc.—The French at "their wits' end" at having the worst of it whenever they meet Lord Wellington.

Journal—15th August–30th September

An Englishwoman married to a Portuguese shop-keeper informed my servant that the British sick and   1810 Aug. 15th

1810 wounded were to be put to death on that night, and that the people were to attempt to take the different forts and declare in favour of the French. He lost no time in making me acquainted with this news, which I laughed at as a nonsensical story. Later on, two officers who were billeted opposite me entered my apartment and told me that the soldiers were under arms, that the British ships of war were shifting their moorings with their broadsides towards the town, and that a number of Marines had been put on shore to co-operate with the soldiery. A number of Frenchmen had clandestinely entered Lisbon, and had succeeded in hatching a plot, which was luckily found out before it came to maturity. Several of the principal families were connected with them in it. By this incident I became acquainted with two officers, who visited me frequently, and made my days pass away more agreeably than before. The ringleaders in the plot were taken up, and terror and confusion were produced amongst the rest of them. So this business blew over and was soon forgotten.

Sept. 17th   I removed to Pedroso for the convenience of sea-bathing, my thigh being much better, which enabled me, with crutches, to move about. (The house belonged to a Frenchman named Chapellon.) Lieutenant Harry Smith [1] was also with me. I found great benefit from the sea-bathing. I became acquainted with a merchant's wife, who frequently sent me milk and butter. She was an Englishwoman, her husband being also of the same country. They were in Lisbon when the French under Marshal Junot entered

[1] Afterwards General Sir Harry Smith, G.C.B., the victor of Aliwal.—ED.

it, and having the whole of their property there, they 1810
determined to stay and abide the consequences.
She told me that she expected every moment to see
her husband dragged away to prison. A colonel and
a captain came to their house with a billet. They
were glad to lodge them and their servants and feed
the whole of them, which was done in such good style,
that the two officers interested themselves on behalf
of the English family and prevented any harm falling
upon them. In a little time they became very good
friends, and the French captain would call the lady
to the window and say, "Look at my fine company
of soldiers ; have you got anything like them in
England?" Her pride being hurt, she answered,
"Yes, indeed we have plenty." "Well, madam, I
hope one day or other to meet them in the field. I
have fought in many battles, but never against the
English, and really I have no good opinion of them
as a military nation." "You may learn, sir, to think
differently ere long," she observed to him. Time
passed away and the French had completely reduced
the Portuguese to obedience, when one day, suddenly,
during High Mass, the French were informed that the
English had landed on the coast. All the authorities
were assembled at the church and the people were keeping holiday, so that the inhabitants were highly pleased
to see the confusion produced amongst the French when
the English were named. The troops were assembled
and ordered to march to attack the invaders. The
captain informed the lady, "I am going to fight
against the English, and I will give you, my dear
madam, a good account of them when I return." She
very good-humouredly said, "Take care you do not

1810 burn your fingers." The captain's regiment marched and joined the French army previous to the battle of Vimeiro, where his company was annihilated and himself badly wounded. The lady was one day seated at her window and perceived a crowd of persons coming towards her ; curiosity made her anxious to know the cause. They soon approached near enough to show her that they were the wounded men upon bullock cars in great numbers. They passed along to the hospital, with the exception of one car, which stopped at her door. On it she perceived the poor French captain ; he was directly put into the chamber that he had occupied before, and every possible attention shown him. " My dear lady," he observed as soon as he saw her, " your countrymen have made me pay handsomely for my boasting. The fine fellows that daily paraded before your windows for so many weeks are now lifeless and inanimate clay, and will trouble you no more. Would to God it had been my fate also ! " He was now frightfully distressed with past recollections ; she left him to give him time to moderate his anguish. When he became calmer she returned, and he followed up his story. " I met the English. Oh, that morning was one of the most happy of my life ! My men to a man had the same feeling. I was sent out to skirmish against some of those in green—grasshoppers I call them ; you call them Rifle Men. They were behind every bush and stone, and soon made sad havoc amongst my men, killing all the officers of my company, and wounding myself without being able to do them any injury. This drove me nearly to distraction. In a little time the British line advanced. I was knocked down,

bayoneted, and should have been put to death upon 1810
the spot if an English officer had not saved me. I
find by my own feelings that I am not long for this
world. Our army has been defeated by your countrymen in a succession of battles, and you will have them
with you soon in Lisbon."

This officer sank in a few days, although every
possible care and attention were paid him by the
English family, who owed their preservation on a
former occasion to the good offices of this officer and
the French colonel.

LETTER No. VIII

PEDROSO, NEAR LISBON,
30th September 1810.

MY DEAR PARENTS—A friend made me a present
of this sheet of English paper, which I dedicate to you.
I have long been in expectation of a letter from you,
and luckily received yours, dated the 30th of August,
the other day. I am happy I had it in my power to
remove your anxiety, though I am sorry to say my
leg does not feel so strong as I could wish. I have
left Lisbon and removed into this small village by the
seaside for the purpose of bathing. I have already
found some benefit, and hope soon to be able to rejoin
my regiment. I assure you my feelings are much hurt
at being so long idle, and at a time when we daily expect a great battle is to be on the eve of taking place.

You make me blush at the idea or observation in
the letter, "*a dangerous regiment.*" My dear father,
" the more danger the more honour." Never let such

1810 weak thoughts enter your head. When I turned soldier it was not for the purpose of admiring myself like a peacock in gaudy plumage ; no, it was to meet the enemies of my country and go wherever my duty called me, and merit the name of a soldier, which I now say is the greatest pleasure I ever enjoyed. Thank God, I have succeeded far above my expectations in everything ; I mean I have established my name as a man worthy to rank with the veterans of my regiment, and am esteemed and respected by every brother officer. This, my dear parents, is a pleasure which makes me proud of myself, and increases when I think my friends must also allow I have done my duty and not mistaken my profession.

A most dastardly and nefarious plot was found out on the 13th of the month. The 15th was the day appointed for the conspirators to have assembled in the evening, or rather at midnight, to have rushed out and surprised the guards at their different posts, murdered them of course, and also assassinated all the wounded and sick English officers ; a fine reward for fighting for such a villainous set of cowardly rascals !

One-half of Lisbon was implicated ; two hundred of the first people in the town have been arrested and put into a fort. On the evening of the 15th inst. strong patrols of Dragoons were moving through the streets all night.

The Marines were ready to land at a moment's notice, but the affair was checked in time. Marshal Beresford took a leading character in the conspiracy, and gave timely notice, so every one was on his guard.

I could scarcely be convinced that any set of men would think of acting so infamously and illiberally.

Assassination is not now so common as it used to be 1810 in this country, but still the diabolical practice is not yet done away with.

One morning on looking out of my window in Lisbon, and asking what a man was laid in the street for, I was told that he had been stabbed in the night and must lie there until a sufficient quantity of money was collected to bury him.

I am quite delighted with my rural country situation. I have bought a nice little horse, and I now ride about the country, and live well and cheaper than in Lisbon. When I first landed I was carried on a mattress to an hotel. I soon found my pocket could not long stand out against such exorbitant charges. I spent a guinea a day. I had not half the comforts I should have had in an English house. I therefore was compelled to suffer myself to be lugged on a board along the streets for two English miles with a mob, who, finding out I was a wounded officer, followed from motives of curiosity.

I had a letter the other day from my Captain, who informs me there is every possibility of a battle soon taking place; he also informed me he fell down by accident and injured his leg so materially as to be obliged to leave and go to the rear. He was very anxious to be with me, and yesterday I was going to take a passage for Figueira, but was prevented by an order issued to prevent any officer not able to join his regiment from going to Coimbra, as, in event of a battle, room would be wanted for the wounded, so I daily expect the arrival of Captain O'Hare in Lisbon.

I had a letter from my brother, who mentioned

1810 they had been marching very rapidly to concentrate with the other Divisions of the army, and expected soon to give an account of the enemy. He is in very high spirits. I have no doubt but he will behave himself bravely and merit the appellation of a *British soldier*. I often receive an amusing epistle from Maud, and as I generally send mine with advice, he took the liberty to give me a few hints in that way as follows :—"I hope you will not think of returning so soon as you state, as you must be well aware should you subject yourself to harassing marches you would soon be again laid up." (I must beg leave to differ with him, knowing well my constitution is as strong as ever.) He then says, "Go to England, and if you find yourself better in two months, return here." I am well aware of his affection for me. I will just give you an instance of his generosity. His Colonel a few days back sent for him and informed him it was his intention directly to recommend him for a lieutenancy (my brother being, through good luck, at the top of the list of ensigns). It will be an additional increase of pay nine dollars monthly as well as the rank. The young rogue, thinking he might as well endeavour to kill two birds with one stone, told the Colonel I had a particular wish to be with him ; he said he would recommend me also and enumerate my services to the Commander-in-Chief. I was rather vexed at Maud asking favours for me without consulting me first. However, I know the reason that actuated him was from the most generous and brotherly feeling, which feeling I hope will always continue through life. He is a noble and generous youth in his sentiments. I am proud to have such a

brother ; how you must feel to have such a son. My 1810
dear parents, you have met with great misfortunes in
life, but you have children who love you, and in a
great measure counteract the ill-effects of adversity.
If I live you shall always command my last shilling.
I live for my family, and hope to see them all happy ;
it will ever be my greatest pleasure to assist them. I
believe I informed you that Colonel Sibthorp was so
highly averse to my leaving his regiment that he used
every scheme in his power to dissuade me, and being
so confident of success, stopped my recommendation
into the Line. The consequence was, instead of having
twenty second-lieutenants under me, they were gazetted
above me. If I had stayed in England Colonel
Sibthorp would have tried to have had it redressed.
Under this unfortunate interference I am now
receiving ensign's pay with the name of lieutenant
only. I hope in a few months to have my lieutenancy
through the regular routine of promotion.

I must say I should part from my regiment with
great regret. I live very comfortably, and if I escape,
in time, through the regular course of things, I must
get promotion very fast, much quicker than in any
other regiment. We have numbers of young men
who have got companies in five years. If I had
thought my lameness had been likely to continue so
long in the first instance, I should have left the country
for a short time, but now that there is a great probability of soon being able to move with my regiment
and once more enter the lists of fame, my duty commands me to remain. I must not think for a moment
of coming to England. I shall ride on horseback when
I am tired. I am not yet afraid of meeting the

1810 French, I assure you. I hope to see numbers more
bite the ground. Some deserters that came from the
enemy stated that the French did not like those *green
fellows* at all ; we made sad havoc amongst them,
particularly their officers. Numbers of our men are
most capital shots. It would astonish you to see
how coolly they go on and take the same aim as at a
bird. I feel great pleasure to be with such fighting
fellows and hardy soldiers. The men are so seasoned,
that rain or any other kind of weather makes no
impression. The intense heat now and then makes
the men cross into shady places. We have been in
want of tents for months together, sleeping on the
ground without any other covering than the canopy of
heaven. I never slept better than in such places.
This is the regiment to make the soldiers. I wish my
dear brother had had the same opportunity. The
French are very cautious when we are near them,
and go where they will, we always keep up with
them.

The officer that was taken on the 24th of July
was wounded ; he was very ill-used by the French,
nearly stripped and put in a common prison. He
contrived to make his escape, and is again with the
regiment. I was lucky in getting away from the
field of battle as I did.

My love to my dear Ann. Tell her not to dream
about my being again hit, for fear of her conjectures
being realised. I hardly know how I could comply
with her wish to have my picture, I am so ugly a
fellow, and particularly now my face is nearly black
from heat and exposure to every kind of weather.

I am much stouter even now than when in England, and never enjoyed better health ; if my wound 1810 did not ache now and then I should be quite saucy.

If Joseph behaves well and makes himself worthy of my assistance, I can in twelve months promise him an ensigncy, but I must have proofs of his improvement, as I should subject myself to great censure to recommend an ignorant boy ; let him know these are my sentiments. If he likes anything better I should be sorry to persuade him to enter the army.

I am glad you have procured a bull-dog for me. Take care of him, and I shall be happy to have him out here on the very first opportunity.—I remain, sincerely yours,

GEO. SIMMONS, Lt., 95th Regmt.

Send Charles and Betsy to school. God bless them. I desire any subject I may write to you upon may be kept secret, as it would be very unpleasant to have any of my affairs made public. As in all probability by the time you receive another letter I shall be with my regiment, direct Lieut. G. S., 95th or Rifle Regiment, Brig.-Gen. R. Craufurd's Division, Army, Portugal.

Journal—1st October–31st December 1810

Remained here (Pedroso) very comfortably, and 1810 bathed every day in the sea, which did me much good. Oct. Captain Mitchell, who was wounded through the elbow, came to live near us, and Lieutenant C. Eeles, who had landed with two companies of the 3rd Battalion, being unwell, remained with us. Being very tired of this inactive life, although my wound was not healed, I

1810 was determined to return to my regiment. Lieutenant Smith, who had a ball in his leg, and was also lame, was just as anxious as myself. Dr. Hossack, with some entreaty, allowed us to go, but the Commandant (Colonel Tucker, 29th Regiment) ordered us to take over money to subsist a number of men, and march with a detachment, which was a sad annoyance, having sufficient to do to take care of ourselves.

Oct. 7th   The detachment was formed at Belem under the command of Major Murphy of the 88th Regiment; he had men belonging to every regiment in the country, amongst whom several who had much rather remained at Belem than have paraded their bodies in a field to be shot at. We marched off about seven o'clock in the morning. The men of the Light Division who had been wounded with us and were well again, formed the rear-guard, and I travelled with it; but in spite of all my precautions several men skulked away unobserved, slipping into houses and other places. When we halted and called the rolls, 100 out of 800 that had marthed off were missing, which sadly annoyed Major Murphy. He asked me how many of mine were gone. "Not one," was my answer, "and depend upon it none will leave now." "Well, then, sir, take the rear-guard to-morrow and make any straggler a prisoner, and I will bring him to a Drumhead Court-Martial"; which order he made known to the detachment. The rain had fallen heavily all day. We got under shelter into miserable houses that had been left by their inhabitants at Lumiar.

8th   Marched under continued rain to Cabeza de Monchique, meeting numbers of poor people, making their

way to Lisbon in the most wretched plight, telling us 1810
the British army were in full retreat before the
French.   At the end of this day's march, another
one hundred *heroes* had disappeared, which made our
Commandant raving mad.   Smith called upon me to
assist him in a medical capacity.   I had a bucket of
spring water thrown upon him, which did him good ;
he had several fits, but this put an end to them, and
he was better after he had rested a night.

Still raining tremendously.   Arrived at Sobral. Oct.
The 1st Division entered the town, retiring before the 9th
French.   I soon found that the Light Division was
marching to Arruda, so I moved off with my detachment, and arrived in that place about eight o'clock,
wet through.   The Quartermasters of regiments
came in soon after, and then the town was divided ;
the troops followed.   I took possession of a good
house for Captain O'Hare's officers, and had a good
fire against their arrival.   They were glad to see me
again, and we passed some hours in a description of
the march of the enemy and the different fights and
skirmishes they had had since I left the army, which
was highly interesting to me.

This place, distant from Lisbon six leagues, is 10th
studded with rich merchants' country houses ; many of
them well built and adorned with the most splendid
furniture.   The people had left there from the dread
of falling into the hands of the French.   The British
army having retired before Massena to the iden-
tical spot where our gallant Commander meant to
oppose the enemy's further advance, our days were
now spent in making the position as strong as possible with *abatis*, scarping the ground and throwing

1810 up field-fortifications.   Long before we retired,
our General foresaw that in all probability, whenever the vast forces that the French could bring
against him were put in motion, we must have to
do so.   These very lines that we now occupy had
been planned out long before, and numbers of
Portuguese and British Engineers had been employed
for a considerable time building forts from the Tagus
to the sea.   So much for the wisdom of our gallant
Commander, Wellington.

Oct.   A body of the enemy's infantry moved against
12th the 1st Division near Sobral, but were repulsed in
good style, leaving a number of dead.   Lieutenant C.
Eeles, who had quitted the detachment and joined his
company when I passed through, was shot through the
body and put upon the road to Lisbon ; also Captain
Percival, who commanded the company, shot through
the wrist.   The 3rd Battalion company behaved *like
Rifle Men* and were complimented.

Our gun-boats went up the Tagus and fired upon
the working parties of the enemy at Villa Franca,
which annoyed them considerably.   Sir B. Spencer's
Division was placed in Zibreira, a little to the rear.
Lord Wellington's headquarters were at Pero
Negro, and Marshal Massena's at Alenquer.

13th   The company detached with the 3rd Caçadores
under the command of Colonel Elder to the heights
above Arruda, for the purpose of assisting in throwing up field-works, retired to a *quinta* at night, and
were hospitably treated by the Colonel.

21st   The whole British and Portuguese troops had been
daily employed in strengthening the position from the
Tagus to our extreme left at Torres Vedras, cutting

down trees and forming *abatis* wherever the ground 1810
was not bold and precipitous.   The enemy had also
been employed in throwing up some field-works.

This day joined Captain Mitchell's company Oct.
above Villa Mata, the country in our front being 22nd
covered with farmhouses and gentlemen's cottages,
which were generally well stored with provisions and
wine.   A number of French soldiers were observed
entering them and collecting the different articles,
which they carried to their encampment and distributed amongst their comrades.   We found the
enemy were suffering very much from want of food.

On piquet.   Two French soldiers entered a house 23rd
in our front.   Hopwood and myself with three men
crawled from our post into an avenue of trees, which
covered us from the immediate view of the French
vedette posted on a little eminence to apprise his
friends of any danger.   We succeeded in entering the
house unobserved, and surprised the two Frenchmen,
who were filling some canteens with wine, but sprang
to their arms.   One of them snapped his firelock,
but it did not go off.   They were instantly taken
from them.   A moment after, one soldier offered
me some brandy he had in a calabash slung across his
shoulders. ' I gave both a large goblet of wine, sent
a soldier to get all the canteens he could muster from
the piquet and return, we keeping a good look-out.
We filled sixty, then destroyed the hogshead, took
our prisoners to the piquet, and sent an escort with
them to the General.

Assisted, in conjunction with Lieutenant Strode, in 25th
depositing the remains of a poor old woman in a most
splendid vault in the church at Arruda.   I found her

1810 dead near the altar, where she had gone to offer up her prayers as a last effort, not being strong enough to fly with the inhabitants from the French, and had finished her mortal career. I looked round and saw a beautiful marble slab covered with armorial blazonry ; it caught my eye, and I said to my friend, "The old woman little thought what good offices an English soldier would perform when she entered the church." "What are they?" says he. "Why, she shall be put under that stone, and you must assist." We found a large crowbar, and soon finished the business to my satisfaction.[1]

Oct.   Deserters now very frequently came in and 31st informed us that the enemy were losing a number of men from disease, and that there was a great scarcity of provisions ; that Colonel Trant had assembled the Portuguese Militia in large force and had entered Coimbra, and had taken a number of sick and wounded officers and men and stopped the communications with Spain, cutting off the supply of provisions.

Massena begins to feel that entering a country with an army disposed to commit every description of brutal atrocity upon the unarmed inhabitants, and driving them like wild beasts to their fastnesses (which, from the nature of this country, abounds with such ground), has already kindled the spirit of revenge in their hearts. This has obliged the French to keep together, and they literally only have in possession the ground that their army for the moment occupies, and has also caused severe losses, for any straggler or sick man, unless he has an escort, is sure to be stabbed with the stiletto.

[1] Sir John Kincaid, in his *Adventures in the Rifle Brigade*, published in 1830, mentions having had a hand in this affair.—ED.

English bell-tents arrived for the Light Division, 1810
to replace the poor and small Portuguese ones, which Nov.
proved a great luxury.   2nd

The Duke of Brunswick Oel's corps joined the 13th
Light Division.   The enemy detached General Loison
for the purpose of obtaining possession of the bridge
of boats over the Tagus at Villa Velha, but the bridge
was destroyed on their approach.

As soon as the fog cleared away we found the 15th
enemy's piquets were gone and the position had been
vacated.   About three o'clock in the afternoon the
Light Division advanced upon the road to Alenquer
and bivouacked near it for the night.   I examined
several encampments that the enemy had occupied and
found them in a most filthy state, and in several huts
I found dead men who had fallen victims to the
inclement weather.   The enemy's fires appeared five
miles off.   Colonel Winch took command of the 2nd
Light Brigade, formerly commanded by Colonel
Barclay, 52nd Regiment.

The Light Division advanced at daylight and 16th
followed the enemy to Villa Nova.   They had attempted to destroy the bridge here, but we advanced
too rapidly for them.   Moved forward to Izambuja,
a town on the right bank of the Tagus, and remained
for the night.   We took a number of stragglers this
day who had been suffering sadly from starvation and
disease.   The road was found strewn with rags and
pieces of Frenchmen's appointments and caps, and
occasionally a dead horse, mule, or jackass to enliven
the scene.

The Light Division marched two leagues to 17th
Cataxa ; cavalry in front.   The enemy showed three

1810 battalions of infantry and six squadrons of cavalry as a decoy, the remaining part of Junot's corps being concealed from our view. General Craufurd fancied that he saw the whole of the rear-guard and had made his dispositions to attack them, when Lord Wellington arrived on the ground and stopped the attack, observing, " Are you aware, General, that the whole of Junot's corps is close to the advanced body you now see, amounting to, at least, 23,000 men, a large portion of which is cavalry?" The attack was, of course, abandoned. General Slade's Brigade of cavalry advanced and took up the line of piquets. The Light Division entered Cataxa for the night. I was on inlying piquet. The cavalry sent in 105 prisoners.

Nov. 18th   At daybreak we moved on, accompanied by Captain Ross's [1] Horse Artillery, which now is to remain attached to the Light Division. We advanced across a plain in considerable force, the enemy retiring before us and crossing a causeway and bridge over the Rio Mayor, the whole country in the neighbourhood of the river being a boggy impassable swamp. Our cavalry had a piquet close to the bridge, the advanced vedettes from which were dismounted, and occasionally exchanging long-shots across the causeway with the enemy. These men were highly pleased to see me arrive with some Rifle Men and take the post of honour from them, as the company I belonged to was sent on piquet, with orders to remain at the bridge. The French sent a few men forward to commence a fire upon us. I crawled on the bridge with three men, and lay down by a dead mule, where we had a good rest and took deliberate aim. The Frenchmen

[1] Afterwards General Sir Hew Ross, G.C.B.

soon became wary of showing themselves, which 1810
convinced me we had hit some of them. The
company, having had a hard day's work, were relieved
at night by a company of the 52nd, but we were
ordered to remain near at hand during the night as
a reserve to it.

The weather was very rainy, but, fortunately for us,
this part of the country was covered with olive-trees.
This wood is very hard and so greasy that it is as
inflammable as coal, so that, in spite of rain, we
managed to have good fires.   General Craufurd, over
his wine, took it into his head that the enemy was
moving off and he was anxious to be the first to find
it out. He came to the piquet and took three
soldiers and walked cautiously along the causeway
until the French sentry challenged and fired. The
General ordered his men to fire and retire. This
circumstance created so much alarm in the enemy's
camp, who imagined that the British army was
passing the bridge and falling upon them, that they
became panic-struck and commenced a tremendous
fire in every direction for some time. The balls came
rattling among the trees, and General Craufurd was
sadly annoyed at being deceived in his conjectures and
having caused such an uproar, with a great chance of
foolishly throwing away his life.

As soon as the day cleared sufficiently to see what Nov.
the enemy were about, we found that during the night 19th
they had been very busy cutting down olive-trees and
forming *abatis* on the position. This they had every
appearance of occupying for some time ; it was a most
commanding one, the left upon the Tagus, the
swampy Rio Mayor all along its front, with a *tête de*

1810 *pont* at the end of the bridge over the river. The country was very bold and hilly, with the large town of Santarem about a league in the rear of their position, which Marshal Massena had made his headquarters.

General Hill's Corps, about 12,000 British and Portuguese, crossed the Tagus at Vallada.

General Spencer's Division came to Valle this morning, and, with our Division, remained under arms all day. Lord Wellington reconnoitred the enemy's position, but no attack took place. Bivouacked in a wood near Valle. A deserter informed us that Junot's and Regnier's Corps were in position in front of Santarem.

I had left Lisbon to join my regiment before the wound in my thigh was quite healed, and from the continued hardship I had suffered, and being exposed night and day to very inclement weather, my health became very much impaired, but I was in hopes of being able to shake off disease.

Nov. 20th
Passed a most miserable night ; rain fell in torrents. The Light Division moved with some Dragoons towards the left of the enemy's position. They filled the wooded slope with numbers of Light troops. Some of them skirmished with our advanced parties. We returned at midday and were put into cantonments, the 52nd and 1st Caçadores and the Brunswick Oels into Valle, the 43rd into a large *quinta* above the village mentioned. The 95th Rifles were put into straggling farmhouses on the banks of the river, where we saw opposite to us, upon the wooded heights, numbers of Frenchmen on duty, observing our movements.

21st
I felt much refreshed from dry clothes and some-

thing to eat, but my thigh was getting worse and my 1810
body sadly out of order.
Nov.
Symptoms of dysentery.
23rd
On outlying piquet. A most dreadful night, which 25th
made me so ill that I could scarcely crawl.

General Craufurd came this morning and ordered 26th
the *abatis* to be advanced some yards upon the
bridge in case we should have occasion to blow up the
principal arch, which would then be clear. I got over
the parapet on the enemy's side and went forward to
the place the General had ordered the *abatis* to be
moved to. Three of my men began to pull it to
pieces and bring the wood. I expected the French
would fire at me from the *tête de pont*, and I was
suffering so much from disease that I was really careless
what happened, but I was allowed to finish my job
without interruption.

Worse and worse, and on the 2nd of December 30th
obliged to go from my regiment. I was put into a
boat at Vallada, and arrived at Lisbon about midnight.
By the greatest good luck, La Tour's Hotel was open,
and I got a bed there ; excessively ill.

Removed to a billet with much difficulty ; people Dec.
very uncivil.
3rd
Got another billet upon equally uncivil folks 4th
with bad accommodation. Ordered to be removed
by the Commandant, Colonel Peacock, as the family
had sufficient interest with him to put me out. I
found the people behaved ill to me for fear of bringing
a fever into their family, which induced them to try
every means to get quit of me. I was now in a very
forlorn state, my servant being obliged to go hunting
after a billet, which at last was procured upon an

1810 empty house. I was put into a large and gloomy apartment.

Dec. 6th   Made another attempt to get a billet of a comfortable description with the same ill success, which induced me to send a clear statement of the number of bad billets I had been sent to, and to request the Town Major to let me have a proper one. I had now the good luck to get into a comfortable house kept by an old gentleman and his two maiden sisters—the kindest people possible. They nursed me and paid me every necessary attention. I was exceedingly debilitated by a continued fever and dysentery. I remained very ill for some days, but gradually recovered.

Each army was occupied in strengthening their position and endeavouring (in case of an attack) to make them as strong as possible.

Lord Wellington took up his headquarters at Cataxa with General Spencer's Division. Nothing of moment occurred to terminate the year.

LETTER No. IX

LISBON, 16th December 1810.

DEAR PARENTS—I left Lisbon on the 7th of October. I was unfortunate at starting ; the rainy season had just commenced. I had a detachment of men from different regiments to bring up with me. Nothing but continued rain, bad quarters, my clothes never dry until I joined my regiment at a village called Arruda. I was extremely happy when I got to them,

I assure you. The last five miles I was obliged to 1810 walk, as my horse was quite knocked up. On the 12th, the French had brought up a great force. We had expected a battle, but the wary Massena took care not to bring on a general action. We had some very smart skirmishing. Our regiment lost two officers badly wounded. We are now in our Lines; our position remarkably strong; cannon mounted upon every strong hill. Every day we were in hopes the enemy would attack us, but were disappointed. I found my leg occasionally a torment to me, but took little notice of it.

I heard my brother's regiment was at Bucellas, a town famed for its wine, and about six miles off. I rode over to see him. He was delighted to see me, little expecting, from accounts he had received, to shake me by the hand again. I dined with him, spent the day; he would give me a bottle of cherry brandy. I was much pleased with his appearance. He has grown a very handsome and soldier-like fellow. He is very much respected and very happy, which is an additional gratification to me, and makes me very proud of him. Since that period he has several times visited me at the outposts.

On the 15th of November we got information of the French having retired. Our army immediately marched after them. The first night we passed through several French camps and found a number of dead bodies. We halted near a large village, and lay down for the night in the fields. In the morning we marched through a place, Alenquer, which was entirely sacked by the enemy, the windows and doors torn down and burnt, as well as most of the

1810 furniture in each house, beautiful china, pier-glasses and chandeliers all dashed to pieces, and every kind of devastation that is possible for savages to be guilty of. They had left numbers of miserable objects behind them in the houses, that were so ill as not to be able to march; these were of course put to death by the Portuguese when we happened to miss finding them out. On the 16th we followed the French as quickly as possible, took some prisoners, and spoiled their cooking. Found several peasants the French had murdered and left upon the road, also saw several French killed by the Portuguese. It was a dreadful sight to see so many fine towns without a creature in them. The poor unfortunate inhabitants only a few weeks back were living happily and comfortably, now destitute of everything and afraid of coming near their own property for fear of losing their lives. It is a dreadful consideration. Oh, happy England! may such scenes as these ever be unknown to my countrymen! The French are certainly the greatest curse the Almighty ever sent into the world. Universal conquest and ruin of everything sacred and binding between man and man is their sole aim. I hope their career will be checked sooner or later; they have long reigned almost uncontrolled.

On the 17th and 18th we continued marching after the enemy, taking occasionally a few stragglers and sick. On the 20th the enemy halted and began to throw up breast-works and *abatis* along a high ridge in front of Santarem; a very fine commanding position in front of the mountains; towards the river Tagus there was a plain covered with vineyards, and the opposite way and to our left, a perfect morass, impassable. We expected to attack them even in their strong 1810 position. The company I belong to were ordered on piquet, which was at a bridge over a river in front of the French. As soon as the enemy saw us coming they commenced firing upon us. We soon took and established our piquet ground, fired a few shots at the French, who went off to a more respectable distance and disturbed us no more. We luckily had no one wounded. A corporal going on the bridge with me shot a Frenchman who had just discharged his piece at him. That day our sentries were upon the bridge within two hundred yards of each other.

The excessive wet and bad weather has had great influence upon my constitution since I was wounded. I feel myself, I am sorry to say, quite a different man. This last march we have been exposed very much to the weather. We have had nearly a continuance of rain, and sleeping on the ground, the water making a gutter on both sides of one's body, was not pleasant to me. There was a time when I would not have cared a fig for it, but my leg, after lying thus, became very painful, and I felt as though I had to drag a ten-stone weight about with me. In the morning, possibly obliged to march for miles through grape gardens, fighting with the enemy, I limping along, and often finding difficulty to keep up with my men. Only a little while back I could run miles, always the first to go through or over anything ; judge how my feelings must be hurt at so serious a difference. I continued with my regiment as long as possible, until my mind became so much hurt and my body so much debilitated that I could hardly drag myself along. In this state I went on piquet ; rain all night. I was

1810 stationed at the bridge of Valle with a section of the company. I lay down occasionally by the fire. I was so ill I could not smoke a pipe, the greatest luxury a man can have in bad weather. The next morning I was relieved and went to bed, not a feather bed, but some straw in the corner of an old stable, with a knapsack for a pillow. I was recommended to start directly for Lisbon by my friend, the surgeon. I argued against it and said, as I had got a good comfortable bed, I should soon come round. Here, for the first time in my life, I was attacked with dysentery and in indescribable torture.

On the 3rd of December I found if I put off many days longer I should not be able to leave the regiment. I was conveyed on a mule to Vallada, on the right bank of the Tagus, took a boat, and arrived at Lisbon about twelve o'clock at night, got a bed by the merest chance and good luck, and the following morning procured a billet—a bad one, people uncivil. The next day got one on a very good house—people very friendly and kind. I am as happy as my unfortunate situation will admit of. I have kept my bed ever since my arrival here. My leg and thigh are frequently very painful. The dysentery has subsided in some measure, and upon the whole I feel much better to-day or I could not have given you this long epistle. I have had a medical examination. The medical men have ordered me to continue here six weeks. If I am not better in that time I shall procure leave to come to England. I hope that will not be the case. As God knows, I have little business to be at home at this period. I have got some curiosities taken from the French. I have a 1810 beautiful piece of silk for a pelisse for Ann, five or six yards, colour crimson. I mean to deposit my curiosities on board of some ship. Joseph, I hope, is going on properly. I have said enough about it already. If he does right and minds his education, I will—provided he wishes to come into the army—do everything I can to serve him, but he must make himself deserving of my intercession. If he chooses anything else, I should be sorry to dissuade him from it. He must not, as a soldier, expect to live in luxury and ease. He must often live hard and fight hard and expose his body to all kinds of weather and climate. I hope poor Charlie gets better. Do not quack with him. Get good advice, and he must recover. Let him take plenty of exercise at all times. I hope you will take care he is well educated. Send him to some good Latin school. Let me know how Betsy comes on ; I should suppose she is a tall girl. I shall take care of something for her if I come to old England again.

I am nearly worn to a skeleton. I was laughing at myself when shaving in the glass this morning at my hollow eyes and squalid visage. Now would be the time for Ann to have a likeness. I thought it would be worth staring at. This coming backward and forward to Lisbon makes a sad hole in my little savings, which does not please me at all. For the last eight days I could take nothing but Madeira with any degree of pleasure (three shillings a bottle here).

My best respects to Aunt. Maud, my brother, desires me when I write to remember him to her and my uncle. Any letter I receive from you I let Maud have the particulars directly. My love to you all. My dear mother I hope enjoys good health. I have often called out for her to nurse me. I am sorry to say I have often wanted so kind a friend. God bless and preserve her many years.—Yours truly and affectionately,

G. SIMMONS, Lt., 95th Regt.

I hope a little time will bring me round again. It would be a serious thing to be obliged to come home now after enduring all the hardships of so long a campaign without being present at a general action. I have one great consolation, if I am incapable of following the profession of a soldier, I can always get a living as a surgeon. I have not been idle even in this country, frequently attending hospitals, as I always endeavour to gain knowledge whenever I can find it, as it may one day or other be of use to me. I shall always be allowed to retire on half-pay, which would assist me very materially, but I am in hopes this will not be the case. I still fancy there is enough of me left to make a soldier. The French were never before put so much to their wits' end as at present; whenever they come on they always have the worst of it. Under Lord Wellington's command every one is confident of success. The Portuguese, led on by English officers, fight like tigers. They have behaved astonishingly well. I have witnessed several regiments of them come on with the greatest enthusiasm.

CAMPAIGN OF 1811

At the commencement of 1811, Soult was master of the whole of Andaluçia, with the exception of Cadiz, which place was blockaded by Victor. Soult, however, having been ordered in March to co-operate with Massena, thus leaving Victor unsupported, the Allies in Cadiz decided on a maritime expedition so as to raise the blockade of that place. General Graham embarked with some 4000 troops, and, landing at Algeçiras, joined La Peña and his Spanish force and marched on Cadiz. The battle of Barrosa was fought a few miles south of the Isla, the French under Victor being defeated and Graham marching into Cadiz.

At the same time, Soult was engaged in invading Portugal on the south of the Tagus, while Massena, unaware of the former's successes over the Spaniards, was retiring from before the Lines of Torres Vedras on the north of the Tagus.

Wellington at once followed in pursuit of Massena, and severe combats took place at Pombal, Redinha, Cazal Nova, Foz de Aronce, and Sabugal. Massena withdrew to Ciudad Rodrigo, and eventually, for want of provisions, to Salamanca.

Wellington now invested Almeida, on the Portuguese frontier, but Massena, having received strong reinforcements, advanced to raise the blockade, and encountered Wellington at Fuentes de Oñoro, but having been worsted, he retired across the Agueda.

Shortly after this, owing to a series of unfortunate mistakes, the French garrison of Almeida succeeded in cutting its way through the blockading troops and escaped.

Marshal Beresford had meanwhile been despatched to hold Soult in check south of the Tagus, and after a fight at Campo Mayor he laid siege to Badajoz, but learning that Soult was advancing from Seville to attack him, he raised the siege and

1811 took up a position at Albuera, where after one of the most sanguinary battles of the war, he defeated the French and they withdrew. Badajoz was thereupon besieged for the second time ; but Marmont having joined Soult and advanced with overwhelming numbers, the siege had to be again abandoned, the French entering Badajoz.

It was now September, and the war entered upon a new phase. Napoleon largely reinforced his armies in Spain, King Joseph commanding one about Madrid, Soult a second in the south, Marmont a third on the Tagus, whilst a fourth was styled the army of the north, under Dersenne.

This combination was too strong for Wellington to contend against, but he quickly noted that the fortresses of Ciudad Rodrigo and Badajoz were somewhat isolated, and decided to operate against them. Having also received strong reinforcements, he aimed at blockading Ciudad Rodrigo. Massena, however, at once advanced to its relief with a strong force, and Wellington, uncertain what was in front of him, took up a position on the Agueda. The combats of El Bodon and Aldea da Ponte now took place, after which, in November, Wellington withdrew once again behind the Coa and distributed his troops over a considerable area for subsistence.

CHAPTER VI

LETTER No. X

To his Parents, from Lisbon, dated 11th January 1811

Slow recovery from wound—Is joined by Colonel Beckwith, also wounded—Prospects of the coming campaign—Colonel Sibthorp's kindness — Admirable condition of British troops, and confidence in Lord Wellington in spite of "those fellows who are so ready to abuse him."

Journal—20th January–25th March 1811

Desertion of German troops—Recovers from wound and leaves for the front with Colonel Beckwith — German Hussars capture French cavalry advanced posts — The French retire through Santarem—The Light Division pursues—Shocking condition of Santarem and its inhabitants, due to French excesses—The Horse Artillery and Royal Dragoons take up the pursuit—Rear-guard actions—French Horse Grenadiers charged by 1st German Hussars—Advanced guard fight at Pombal — French driven off — Arrival of five British Divisions—Combat of Redinha—Dispositions of the French—The French flanks attacked by the Rifles —Defeat of the French—Narrow escape of Simmons and Lieutenant Kincaid—Action of Cazal Nova—Major John Stewart (in command of wing) killed, also Lieutenant Strode mortally wounded—Miserable state of the town—Brutality of French soldiers—The French retire during the night—

9

French stragglers saved from being massacred by the inhabitants by the British troops—Combat at Foz de Aronce—Marshal Ney's mistake—Lord Wellington takes advantage of it and orders Colonel Beckwith to "fall in" and attack at once—The Light Division attack—Kincaid again has a narrow shave—Stout resistance by the French ; hundreds driven into the river and drowned—Capture of their camp—The Rifle Men eat the Frenchmen's dinners—French hamstring all their baggage animals—Skirmish at Ponte de Murcella—Complimentary order by Lord Wellington on the conduct of the Light Division during the ten days' fighting, 8th March to 18th—Vigorous pursuit by cavalry and Horse Artillery.

Letter No. XI

To his Parents, from Mello, dated 26th March 1811

Brother John in trouble—Reported as having been taken prisoner by the French, who captured the merchant ship he was serving on—Recounts visit to brother Maud across the Tagus—Describes the pursuit of Massena and horrible brutalities committed by the French troops on the Portuguese inhabitants—Detailed description of the fighting—News of the battle of Barrosa and heavy losses of the Rifles (two companies 2nd Battalion, and four companies of 3rd Battalion engaged).

Letter No. X

Lisbon, *16th January* 1811.

My dear Parents—I embrace this opportunity of writing you by a friend of mine who is compelled to come to England for the recovery of his health, being rendered incapable of further service for some time, having two severe wounds.

I find the rest and comforts I have been able to 1811
procure here have brought me round much sooner
than I had any idea of. Shelter from the inclemency
of the weather and a warm bed have done wonders.
I am now as anxious as ever to return to my
regiment and share in its glorious achievements. I
am sorry to observe my leg is very little better. I
shall limp for life. Every change of weather affects
me most materially. I hope time will in some
measure eradicate these symptoms, though I am too
well acquainted with the injury my thigh has sustained
ever to expect recovery.

The Colonel of my regiment has been obliged to
come to Lisbon for the benefit of his health. He has
nearly recovered. I have at all times experienced
the greatest friendship from him. I dine often with
him. He had a great wish for me to live with him,
thinking he might soon recover, but not being able to
procure a billet for us both immediately, he would
not inconvenience me by taking me from a good one.
In the meantime he recovered. I have always been
fortunate in gaining the esteem of my superior officers,
and I am confident my Colonel will as soon as possible
do something for me. I have at this time an idea of
soon procuring a higher place.

I meant to purchase numbers of articles while in
Lisbon. I must curtail my inclinations, having been
at great expense since I arrived here. Everything
has altered much in price since I was in this place
before. However, I cannot rest longer without giving
my dear Ann some token of my affection for her.
These baubles will occasionally serve to remind her
that her brother George, though far away, still loves

1811 and adores her. I wonder much at not hearing from you. I hope you do not conceive I am careless of your affairs. I think you know me better than to suspect it. I have not had a letter since September last. The French are bringing up all the men they can muster, and concentrating them in different Divisions near us. The weather has been so intolerably wet and bad that it would be impossible for the two hostile armies to commence the work of death and destruction at this time. We are in hopes the sun will begin to shine upon us and dry the earth sufficiently to enable us soon to commence. Our men are in the highest spirits imaginable, and the Portuguese also are determined to fight to the last. We shall soon have noble work. The French are a set of impudent rascals. I certainly expected to find them stand much better than in the two or three instances where I have been, with others of my regiment, opposed to them. They are certainly brave men, but do not like close quarters. When charged by Britons they run off.

When anything particular transpires I will write you. I have at present several articles, but cannot find any conveyance for them. I shall leave them at Lisbon. My brother Maud has the history of everything belonging to me. He sent me a letter the other day requesting I would accept forty or fifty dollars, as I must be in want of money. I thanked him, but desired him to take care of it until he arrived in England, where it would be of use. He laughed at my delicacy. He is an impudent fellow, I assure you. I also told him it astonished me exceedingly to find he could keep any money ; I wondered it did not become a burden to him. He wanted one day to wager with me on that 1811 head, but on showing him twenty-five guineas besides dollars, he passed it off and abused me for covetousness. I expected a letter from him, and would have enclosed it, but he is too idle to write, as I generally contrive to give him all my news. I received a very kind letter from Colonel Sibthorp this morning. By some accident it has been detained in England ever since I was at Lisbon before. He says he fully expected me home, and had fitted up a quarter for me in his house. He was extremely happy when he heard through the Adjutant of the Lincoln, with whom I correspond, that my health was again re-established ; and in some measure to palliate the disappointment he experienced in not seeing me, he sent me £25 for my present use. He concludes his letter with again observing that if I should be obliged to come home from wounds or illness or any other cause, his house will always be open to me. I assure you this letter gives me great pleasure. I know well it is in Colonel Sibthorp's power to befriend me in my profession.

I send Ann a gold chain ; it is, I am informed, a curiosity in England and is the purest gold that can be formed, also a gold cross set with topaz, a pair of earrings ; the same I could not procure smaller, or should have liked them better. I send my mother a ring set also in topaz, and a silver snuff-box. I hope the whole will arrive safe. I send them at a venture, and durst not risk more money. I have often laughed at the cause of my buying the box at Coimbra. It was when I had experienced a severe march after being wounded, and was feverish and continually talking of

1811 my dear mother and annoying every one near me. I would not be satisfied until my servant had procured some boxes from a jeweller. The one I send was my choice. I wrote a long letter settling my little affairs, stuffed it into the box, and then felt very happy. The next day my wound was more favourable. You know the rest. I think I see my mother opening the box and recounting this little tale. When the officer lands he will give the parcel to the clerk at some mail coach office (by my orders). Pay the booking. I think there is no chance of its miscarrying. You may on receipt of this, occasionally send to the post office to inquire for a small parcel directed as usual, Osborne Street, Kingston-upon-Hull. The whole cost me £7 or £8. I have more curiosities, but durst not risk them all at once.

I hope two months will nearly enable us to decide the fate of Portugal. It is my continued prayer for a general action. That day will be tremendous. I have no fear as to the result. The troops are seasoned, weather-beaten veterans, commanded by the best General in the British service. I wish some of those fellows who are so ready to abuse him were for a night posted within 200 yards of the enemy; they would not talk so nonsensically. It is easy for them to do so fighting battles over a good fireside at home with a pot of old October before them.

My love to you all, particularly my uncle and aunt. I remain the same, still and for ever, your affectionate son,   G. SIMMONS, Lt., 95th Regmt.

I hope Joseph attends to my injunctions. It will in the end be himself that must reap the benefit.

"Education is fortune sufficient to a man who will 1811 make good use of it."

Journal—20th January–25th March 1811

Considerable reinforcements have joined the Lisbon. French army, several of the Brunswickers have deserted to the enemy, and some were detected in the act of going over. Three of them were shot and the corps sent to the rear. Deserters, both officers and men, very frequently came over from the French army.

I found myself quite restored to health, and went Jan. to the Italian opera, San Carlos. Also went on board 20th the *Tonnant*, 80 guns, to see the brother of Lieutenant Stokes, a friend of mine, who was exceedingly kind, as well as the whole of the officers, and showed me the greatest hospitality.

The remains of the Marquis Romana were brought 27th on shore at Belem. Minute guns were fired. The body was taken to the Church of San Justine, where it was interred with much pomp and ceremony, the British and Portuguese soldiers being all under arms, and police guards also.

The shock of an earthquake at 11 o'clock P.M., Feb. which alarmed the inhabitants. 3rd

Having enjoyed myself for some time now in Lisbon, and being quite restored to health, I became anxious of again associating with my brother soldiers.

Took my departure, in company with my worthy 4th friend, Colonel Beckwith. He had been some time in Lisbon with intermittent fever, but was now restored to health. Halted at the house of Major M'Neal, a

1811 friend of the Colonel's, at Alhandra, where we were very hospitably treated. It being a rainy morning, and the Major pressing us to stay another day, we did so.

Feb. 6th   Rode to Valle and joined Captain Beckwith's company, which was in the same house and stables I left it in five weeks before, although it had changed its captain.

8th   Colonel Drummond took command of the 2nd Brigade of the Light Division *vice* Winch deceased.

9th   Cornet Streunitz, of the German Hussars, surprised an advanced post of the enemy near Rio Mayor, consisting of an officer and thirty men. Cavalry desertion from the enemy very frequent, and constant reports brought in that they cannot remain much longer in their present position, as the soldiery are suffering sad privations.

22nd   Cornet Streunitz took another party of the enemy, one officer and fifteen men, who had been placed in ambush to endeavour to surprise our cavalry piquets. I got leave to visit my brother Maud, who was in General Hill's Division across the Tagus. I passed it in a large boat of a rough structure filled with men and horses, and very bunglingly navigated ; however, I was landed safely. I mounted my horse and rode to Almeyrim, where his regiment was stationed (2nd Battalion 34th). I found him well, and we fought over our battles together, over some bad wine.

30th   Returned to my corps, as the reports of the enemy's moving off gain ground daily.

March 4th   Two deserters came over ; they report that the enemy are burning everything that they cannot remove, such as gun-carriages, carts, etc.

The cavalry have advanced a little way on our left, 1811
and the Divisions in rear are closing up to us. March

The *juiz de fore* of Santarem sent a peasant to 5th
give information that the enemy had retired through 6th
the place at two o'clock this morning and were in full
retreat. The Light Division followed the enemy at
daybreak and entered Santarem, where we remained
about an hour. How different this town now
appeared; when I last was in it all was gaiety and
happiness, and the shops abounding with every luxury,
and a smile upon every one's face; but now the
houses are torn and dilapidated, and the few miserable inhabitants, moving skeletons; the streets strewn
with every description of household furniture, half-
burnt and destroyed, and many streets quite impassable with filth and rubbish, with an occasional man,
mule, or donkey rotting and corrupting and filling the
air with pestilential vapours.

My heart ached as I passed through it. We
marched to Pernes. The enemy had blown up the
bridge over the river Pernes, which was repaired
by Captain Todd, Royal Staff Corps. The poor
inhabitants had been persuaded to remain by Marshal
Junot, under fair promises, but they ill performed these
assertions. The houses were nearly all unroofed, and
the people in a starving condition. Two young ladies
had been brutally violated in a house that I entered,
and were unable to rise from a mattress of straw. On
the line of march, comparing notes with other officers,
I found that they all had some mournful story to
relate of the savage French Vandals which had come
under their immediate observation.

Followed the enemy's rear-guard to Torres 7th

1811 Novas, and halted near La Marrosa. The Horse Artillery and Royal Dragoons came up with the French rear-guard and harassed it. We passed several of the enemy's killed and wounded men upon the road as we advanced. The unfortunate inhabitants that have remained in their villages have the appearance of people who have been kicked out of their graves and reanimated, and the sight of them rouses the fiercest passions within us, and will make us, when we come up with the enemy, take ample vengeance upon them for their unheard-of and disgusting cruelties to this unfortunate nation. O happy England! surrounded by an element over which thy sons in their wooden walls triumphantly sway, and on thy happy shores the arms of that tyrant who has deluged Europe in blood can have no influence. May it ever be so is my earnest prayer!

March   Light Division marched at daybreak, and came up
8th with sixty sick Frenchmen upon donkeys in a wretched plight from disease and fever. We followed the rear-guard to Venda dos Carvalhos. The enemy moved off when we came in sight. The cavalry and Horse Artillery pressed them so hard that the enemy blew up four tumbrils and destroyed a quantity of gun tackling.

9th   Advanced early this morning, and after marching five hours, came up with the enemy's rear-guard at the junction of the road from Leyria and Lisbon to Coimbra. A large body of cavalry showed itself, and infantry in force was halted in rear. An advanced squadron of the 11th French Horse Grenadiers were charged by the 1st German Hussars in pretty style, and twelve of them taken. The French had taken two Hussars two days before, and it was believed had

coolly sabred them. The Germans were so incensed 1811
at the report that they were going to put some of
these men to death, but were luckily prevented and
persuaded to desist. One of the enemy was a very
handsome man and an Italian. He had a narrow
escape, as he was upon his knees and the sword
uplifted to slaughter him when Colonel Gilmore
begged him off. About forty straggling soldiers fell
into our hands on this day's advance, and the road was
often covered with dead Frenchmen, gun-carriages,
waggons, and pieces of different military equipment.

Returned half a league and bivouacked in a pine March
wood. Sir William Erskine took command of the 10th
Light Division. The enemy appeared in great force
for the purpose of checking our advance, in order that
their heavy guns, baggage, etc., might gain some
advantage by moving rapidly away. Towards evening
our forces were considerably augmented by the arrival
of General Pack's Brigade and a Brigade of the 1st
Division. In short, our army was moving up as
quick as the nature of circumstances would admit
of it.

FIGHT OF POMBAL

The enemy moved off before day, and our cavalry 11th
and Horse Artillery set out in pursuit of it. They
were obliged to halt a little way from Pombal, and
the Light Division were sent forward to dislodge
the enemy's Light Infantry and Voltigeurs from the
enclosures. The castle, an old ruin situated upon
an eminence, was very spiritedly attacked by the 95th
Rifles and the 3rd Caçadores. Although the enemy

1811 disputed the ground obstinately, which, from the nature of it, was very defensible, yet they were driven sharply through Pombal. Some officers' baggage was captured.

The enemy remained on strong ground at a little distance from us. The 1st, 3rd, 4th, 5th, and 6th Divisions arrived near us in the course of the evening. The town of Pombal is frightfully dilapidated, and the inhabitants as miserable as I have before represented them in other places.

COMBAT OF REDINHA

March 12th   The enemy took up a position to receive our attack in front of Redinha, his right resting on the river Soure, protected in front by heights covered with wood, and his left beyond Redinha upon the river. The front part of his line was much intersected with deep ravines. In the centre was a beautiful plain filled with infantry, formed in good order but a motley-looking set of fellows in greatcoats and large caps, a body of cavalry supporting, and other bodies moving according to circumstances. The wooded heights were attacked by a wing of the 1st Battalion (Rifles), commanded by Major Stewart, who carried them in gallant style. The other wing attacked the left, the Light Division acting in unison with these attacks, our columns moving rapidly into the plain, forming line and moving on, and also the cavalry. It was a sunshiny morning, and the red coats and pipe-clayed belts and glittering of men's arms in the sun looked beautiful. I felt a pleasure which none but a soldier so placed can feel. After a severe struggle we drove the enemy from all his strongholds and down a

steep hill to the bridge.   We pushed the fugitives so 1811
hard that the bridge was completely blocked up, numbers
fell over its battlements, and others were bayoneted ;
in fact, we entered pell-mell with them.   The town
was set on fire in many parts by the enemy previous to
our entering it, so that numbers of them, to avoid being
bayoneted, rushed into the burning houses in their
flight.   Lieutenant Kincaid [1] passed with me through
a gap in a hedge.   We jumped from it at the same
moment that a Portuguese Grenadier, who was following, received a cannon shot through his body and
came tumbling after us.   Very likely during the day
a person might have a thousand much more narrow
escapes of being made acquainted with the grand
secret, but seeing the mangled body of a brave fellow
so shockingly mutilated in an instant, stamps such
impressions upon one's mind in a manner that time
can never efface.   A man named Muckston laid
hold of a French officer in the river and brought
him out.   He took his medal, and in the evening
brought it to me.   I took it, but should have felt
happy to have returned it to the Frenchman.

The enemy cannonaded our columns crossing the
bridge and occasionally gave the skirmishers some
discharges of grape.   Notwithstanding, it did not
deter us from following them and driving them some
distance, when we were recalled and formed up.   The
British army bivouacked for the night.   Lieutenants
Chapman and Robert Beckwith wounded.

The Light Division advanced at daylight and found March
13th

[1] Afterwards Sir John Kincaid, author of the spirited sketches,
Adventures in the Rifle Brigade, and *Random Shots by a Rifleman*.
—Ed.

1811 the enemy strongly posted in front of Condexa.   The
3rd Division took a detour by a mountain road and
turned the enemy's left, which obliged *Johnny* to move
off ; we followed through the town close to them ; the
houses being generally unroofed and others that had
been quarters for French officers, were deliberately
set on fire.

In one instance I ordered some soldiers to remove
several chairs and some straw under a staircase which
was then on fire.   By this timely removal, the house
was saved, and most likely many others.

ACTION OF CAZAL NOVA

March   As soon as the fog cleared away, we found the
14th enemy very strongly posted, the ground for miles
in their rear being one continued series of good
positions.   The heights and village of Cazal Nova
were spiritedly attacked by Major Stewart with the
left wing 95th Rifles, and the other wing soon
followed.   Then, soon after, the whole Light Division
was engaged skirmishing, which continued from hill to
hill, and a combined movement (on the enemy's flank)
by the 3rd Division assisted us very materially in making the enemy quit the many strongholds which, owing
to the nature of the ground, gave him repeatedly the
advantage over us.   About three in the afternoon a
regiment formed up and hid itself.   Our advanced
skirmishers, going over the slope of a hill, came within
a few yards of this regiment, when the men fired a volley
into our faces.   It was quite ridiculous ; the balls went
whizzing over our heads, and they scampered off.
Our Horse Artillery generally gave the enemy a few

rounds of shrapnel to amuse them before we gave 1811
over our day's work. These battalions of the enemy,
by our rapid movements, were forced upon the main
body at Miranda do Corvo, on the Deuca, and had
sustained considerable loss. From the hard fighting of
this day many brave fellows had fallen. Major Stewart,
a fine gallant little fellow who commanded the attack
so spiritedly, was wounded. Lieutenant Strode, in
the company with myself, was also wounded.[1] I was
placed on piquet at the entrance of the town of Loũsa,
and a little after dark patrolled into it. Houses in
every direction were on fire, and a few wretched inhabitants standing about in the streets with despair and
horror marked in their faces. Kincaid and I went into
a house where an old man was seated ; he had been
lame in both legs for many years. A French soldier,
on leaving the house, had given him two deep sabre
wounds on the head and another on the arm. This
place was a true picture of everything that was
wretched.

I was sent on this morning with a party of the March
piquet. Found near the roadside, quantities of 15th
ammunition that had been buried by the French, also
a French officer and numbers of men dead ; a deserter
from the Brunswickers I took prisoner. The enemy
had retired in the night so as to have a little start of
us, as the battalions engaged yesterday had been too
severely handled. At every step this morning we found
sick and dead Frenchmen, gun-carriages, waggons, bag-

[1] Major Stewart, as many others have done, asked me if he
was mortally wounded. I told him he was. He thanked me,
and died the day following. Lieutenant Strode died of his
wound some little time after at Coimbra.—G. S.

1811 gage ; horses, mules, and donkeys abandoned by their masters, not being able to carry their loads farther, some from frightful sore backs, others from lameness and starvation. We passed through Miranda do Corvo in pursuit of the enemy. The town was almost filled with sick, wounded, and dying men, abandoned to their fate, and dead. The rascally French had even plundered this place and committed every sort of wanton atrocity upon the inhabitants, and then left many of their helpless countrymen for the infuriated inhabitants to wreak their vengeance upon. Luckily for these poor wretches, we followed the French so rapidly that they fell into our hands, and were put in charge of British soldiers, or they would have been butchered indiscriminately.

COMBAT OF FOZ DE ARONCE

After marching a league from the latter town, we found the enemy's rear-guard had taken up a position at Foz de Aronce, with their back to the river Ceira, and the bridge behind them blown up. The remainder of their army was in position on the other side, having passed by fording, but in consequence of heavy rains, the river became so swollen that it was in a few hours impassable. Our gallant chief observed with his penetrating eye the egregious mistake that the officer, Marshal Ney, who commanded the French rear-guard, had made. We were all hungry and tired. I was frying some beef and anxiously watching the savoury morsel, when an order was given by Lord Wellington himself to Colonel Beckwith : " Fall in your battalion and attack the enemy ; drive in their skirmishers, and I will turn their flank with the 3rd 1811 and 1st Divisions." The whole Light Division were smartly engaged. The enemy opposed to the company (Captain Beckwith's) I was with, were behind a low wall. The approach was through a pine wood, and the branches were rattling about our ears from the enemy's bullets. Lieutenant Kincaid got shot through his cap, which grazed the top of his head. He fell as if a sledge hammer had hit him. However, he came to himself and soon rallied again. Lieutenant M'Cullock was shot through the shoulder. The attack commenced about five in the afternoon and lasted till after dark, the rain falling abundantly during part of the time. The French fought very hard, and, some finding resistance to be in vain, threw themselves upon our generosity, but the greater part rushed into the river, which was tumbling along in its course most furiously, and there soon found a watery grave. The enemy so little dreamt of being disturbed this night that their cooking utensils were left upon their fires for strangers to enjoy their contents. Such are the chances of war! I was quite exhausted and tired, and was with about fifteen of the company in the same state, when we made a great prize. One of the men found a dozen pots upon a fire, the embers of which were low and caused the place to escape notice. Here we adjourned, and soon made the fire burn brightly. We found the different messes most savoury ones, and complimented the French for their knowledge of making savoury dishes, and many jokes were passed upon them. The men looked about and found several knapsacks ; they emptied them at the fireside to see their contents and added to their own kits, shoes and shirts

10

1811 of better quality than their own. In every packet I observed twenty biscuits nicely rolled up or deposited in a bag ; they were to last each man so many days, and he must, unless he got anything else, be his own commissary. We had been very ill-off for some days for bread, so that some of these proved a great luxury.

March At two o'clock this morning the enemy had the
16th arches of the bridge more effectually blown up. The weather began to clear at daylight. We saw numbers of the enemy dead in the river, and lying about near the bushes as the water had left them. It was judged about 700 or 800 had been drowned, and the 39th Regiment lost their Eagles in the water. A great quantity of baggage must have been destroyed or thrown into the water, as there were a great many mules and donkeys close to the river-side, hamstrung in the hind leg. These poor animals looked so wretched that one could not help feeling for them, and disgusted us with the barbarous cruelty of the French. To have killed and put them out of their misery at once would have been far better. We remained in bivouac.

17th The Light Division forded the river, a little more than knee-deep now, which the day before yesterday had caused so many Frenchmen to wind up all worldly accounts. Bivouacked for the night in a pine wood after a short march, as, owing to our rapid advance, it became difficult to get up a sufficient supply of rations for the army from Lisbon. Some deserters say the enemy has buried many pieces of cannon. Gun-carriages, ammunition-waggons, and every material of war is abandoned by the enemy, which makes us regret that provisions should be the cause of delay in

not pursuing more effectually the great advantages we 1811
have already gained. A deserter informed us that
after dark the other night the enemy sent several
battalions down to the river to assist, if possible, the
rear-guard in passing the river, but that they got into
confusion and fired upon each other.

Advanced early this morning to the river Alva, March
found the bridge blown up, and the enemy in 18th
position on very strong ground at Ponte de Murcella
with some guns in position commanding the approach
to the river. We formed opposite the enemy and
had a fine view of a large body of them. Some nine-
pounders were soon got up, and commenced pounding
their columns. I never saw *Johnny* go off in such
confusion. The cavalry followed for some distance.
The Light Division went into bivouac in the pine
woods for the night.

An extract from the General Orders of the Day
shows the high estimation in which our gallant
Commander holds the three British regiments of the
Light Division for their services in the field for the
last ten days.

Adjt.-General's Office, Loušā,
16th March 1811.

"The Commander of the Forces returns his thanks
to the general and staff officers, officers, and troops
for their excellent conduct in the operations of the
last ten days against the enemy, and he requests
the commanding officers of the 43rd, 52nd, and
first battalion 95th (Rifles) to name a sergeant of
each regiment to be recommended for promotion to
an ensigncy as a testimony of the particular approba-

1811 tion the Commander of the Forces entertains for the conduct of these regiments.

"E. PAKENHAM, *Deputy Adjt.-General.*"

March A wooden bridge having been thrown across the
19th river during last night, we passed over this morning and advanced through Sobreira. A league farther we bivouacked in a wood of pines. The cavalry followed the enemy's rear-guard, and in crossing a plain took 800 prisoners. One was a Portuguese and aide-de-camp to Loison. He had a Spanish girl in a Hussar uniform as his companion. This fellow, on his arrival in Lisbon, will be put to death as a traitor to his country if he has not better luck than he deserves.

20th Light Division moved through Galizes and went into bivouac in a fir grove near Vendas Novas. The French rear-guard was vigorously pursued by the cavalry and Horse Artillery, who took numbers of prisoners and stragglers. We found numbers of tumbrils, carts, waggons, and other articles abandoned by the French. Occasionally we found Portuguese peasants that had been most wantonly shot by the enemy.

21st The Light Division marched on to the fir groves above Maceira and bivouacked. Two hundred more of the enemy taken by the cavalry.

22nd Went into houses at Moimenta da Serva in consequence of the weather being very bad. Several of the poor people gave us a melancholy account of the cruelties they had suffered from the French; and in every village on the line of their march they had murdered many of the inhabitants in a most savage manner. A priest in the above village dead, and his body mutilated.

Marched in front of Sampayo and bivouacked in a 1811
wood.   March
Lodged in the town of Mello.   23rd
                                                                                                       24th
Bivouacked in a wood. Supposed to be waiting 25th
for supplies.

LETTER No. XI

MELLO (NEAR CELORICO), PORTUGAL,
26th March 1811.

MY DEAR PARENTS—I received the melancholy
account of poor John with sorrow.[1] It is a great
misfortune, and under the present circumstances it is
utterly impossible to give him the least support. I
hope by this time you have received more authentic
information as to his situation. It is entirely out of
my power to gain any knowledge of him or be of the
slightest use, distant as I am from England. Your
plan will be to make inquiry through the Transport
Board, but it is so entirely out of my way, I cannot advise
you how to act with certainty. In a mercantile place
like Hull you will find numbers very well acquainted
with the business. If it would be possible to remit
him money occasionally, it would be the best way of
serving him. It would be cruel of me to say anything
further regarding my displeasure when I heard of him
binding himself in so low a capacity ; it is done, and
the result has proved truly unfortunate. We cannot
foresee evils, but we should endeavour to prevent

[1] Brother John had entered the Mercantile Marine, and on
his first voyage his ship was captured by a French privateer, and
he himself killed in the engagement. At the time of writing this
letter it was believed that he was alive and a prisoner of war.—
ED.

them. If he had been a soldier, or a sailor in a King's ship, he would, though a prisoner, have had some little liberty, but in his situation he will not be noticed, but mix with men of all descriptions. I endeavour to look upon his unfortunate situation in the best manner possible. I flatter myself an exchange of prisoners may take place before long. I hope his constitution is good. He may possibly make his escape, though when once safe in France, it is unlikely. I sometimes fancy he may get away after recovering from the wounds he received, being near the coast. If he is enterprising, I think he may have several chances ; but, poor fellow, his youth may make him careless. I wish I had the chance of attacking the escort that guards him on the road. I think you would then soon have a favourable account of him. Give me all the information you can about him in your next.

I joined my regiment at Valle on the 22nd of February, the place I left them at, my health quite restored and my thigh much better. I heard of Maud's regiment being on the other side of the Tagus in good quarters ; it induced me to go. He was delighted to see me. He regretted much the account of poor John. I dined with him, and stayed until late the day following. Before I left his quarters he gave me an excellent dinner and plenty of good wine. I was much pleased with his manner of living, having a good stock of useful and necessary things, a canteen with knives, forks, plates, etc.—in short, every-thing useful, with a donkey to carry them. He is very steady, and has saved money. I paid him some very high compliments on his conduct. He is taller than I, and I assure you a very handsome, stout 1811 fellow. I told him about the little trinkets I had sent Ann from Lisbon, which, by the bye, I hope have arrived safe ; acquaint me regarding them in your next. He means to make Ann some presents when he returns. The officers of his regiment behaved very politely, and invited me to spend some days, but that was impossible. My brother came a little way with me, and with regret we parted. We continued at Valle within pistol-shot of the enemy's sentries until 6th March. At daybreak we found the enemy had left this strong position and withdrawn his piquets. Our Division directly followed. The French went off in the night, consisting of the rear-guard of 12,000 men. They had been for some days taking sick and baggage to the rear and heavy cannon also. We passed through the fine town of Santarem, which was dreadfully sacked. I was in the town when full of people and wealth ; this sight hurt my feelings much. A few half-starved miserable wretches came to cheer us, nearly dead with hunger. I looked for the house I was once billeted upon, but, alas ! only the bare walls remained. The unfortunate owner was a fine liberal old man, and treated me very kindly. I made some inquiries, but could hear nothing. We halted for the night in a village.

At daybreak we followed the French, and passed through several towns on fire. We did not come up with them. This night was on outlying piquet. A little cottage by the roadside struck my fancy. I took up my abode in order to have my pound of meat cooked and to be sheltered, being rainy. The woman of the house welcomed me in and offered me her chair. She had four children lying near her literally starving.

The French had robbed her of everything worth
taking. Some of the soldiers cut her with their
swords for endeavouring to stop them from taking
away her daughter, and one villain had the meanness
to return to the house and tell her, "Your children are
starving ; if you will give two dollars for this loaf, you
shall have it." She went where the last of her money
was secreted ; he watched her, and took the money,
abused her, and walked off. The poor creature and
her children appeared so wretched ; she was continually
praying the English would revenge her wrongs. I
did what I could to console her, and gave them
some of my little stock of provisions, which, circum-
stanced as we are, we must, from real necessity, be
very careful of, as the towns are all left by the
inhabitants.

It is beyond everything horrid the way these
European savages have treated the unfortunate
Portuguese. Almost every man they get hold of
they murder. The women they use too brutally for
me to describe. They even cut the throats of infants.
The towns are mostly on fire—in short, they are guilty
of every species of cruelty. I have seen such sights
as have made me shudder with horror, and which I
really could not have believed unless an eye-witness of
them. It is needless for me to enter into particulars,
as I could fill a volume with their barbarities. We
continued marching, daily taking French sick and
stragglers. If they fell by any chance into the hands of
the Portuguese, they either dashed their brains out or
stabbed them without ceremony. From the Portuguese they certainly deserve no quarter, for they give
none.

On the 9th, one company of us had some little 1811 skirmishing. The Hussars and the 16th Light Dragoons, amounting to two troops, charged double the number of French; killed and wounded fifteen and took ten horses.

On the 11th we followed the enemy; two companies of ours drove them from the woods; the enemy halted at Pombal, and occupied the heights and castle. After some sharp fighting the enemy were driven from their position, on the 3rd Caçadores (pronounced *Cassadores*) coming up. One officer wounded and several men.

On the 12th we passed through several towns on fire; about eleven o'clock A.M. we came up with the French, and found them posted upon some heights in great force, both cavalry and infantry. On their right and left were woods filled with sharp-shooters. Our columns moved up and our regiment, the 43rd, 52nd, and Portuguese Light Infantry, amounting to 5000, extended to the distance of three miles. The order was given, and we filled the woods. The French threw numbers of shot and shells, which only killed a few men. The woods were of fir-trees and upon the sides of steep hills; as soon as we gained the top, the French gave us a volley. It was of no consequence; our Boys would not be stopped. The French, finding they could not stop us, retired in the greatest confusion through the town of Redinha, which was on fire. We kept at their heels, and the town was filled with our men in a moment. We plied the enemy so hard that numbers threw away their arms, and upwards of fifty fell over the bridge and were drowned. A party of my men were blazing away at the rascals; one espied

1811 an officer endeavouring to get through the water ; he jumped in and brought him out by the neck. He gave the soldier thirty-six doubloons and a medal dedicated to the Legion of Honour. The soldier gave me the medal. I should have returned it to the officer, but having something of a more serious nature to mind, I afterwards had not an opportunity. Halted for the night in a wood.

No fighting of consequence on the 13th.

On the 14th we drove in the enemy's piquets at daylight. Our whole Division was engaged. Lieutenant Strode of the same company was badly wounded in the thigh, and Major Stewart mortally wounded. We continued fighting until three o'clock P.M. Strode when he fell called to me to take his rifle, exclaiming, " This, Simmons, may be of service." I had no time to stand on ceremony, but moved on. The French were driven back on all sides, and very glad to give over fighting.

A very good town near where we halted was on fire, and numbers of the inhabitants murdered.

At daybreak on the 15th found the enemy were gone. We immediately followed, and came up with them at half-past four o'clock P.M. occupying a very strong position and in great force. We began to build huts about a mile from them and cook our breakfast, dinner, and supper all at once ; soldiers eat when they can. However, we were disappointed, an order coming from Lord Wellington for an immediate attack. Every man to his post, and in ten minutes exposed to a heavy fire of shot, shells, and musketry. In passing the plain to get at the enemy in the wood, I was for the moment startled ; a musket ball struck my rifle

(Strode's), and shattered the butt to pieces, which 1811 luckily saved my right thigh. I laughed and pushed on.

We here had some very hard fighting, having twelve French battalions opposed to us. Our men and the Portuguese went in skirmishing order up to their line. The French fired volleys. Their officers behaved very gallantly. Just at dark the enemy were beaten back in all directions, and as caution is necessary, we gave up the pursuit. This fight took place near, and in, the village of Foz de Aronce. Above 500 of the enemy were driven into the river and drowned, numbers killed and wounded, nearly 300 mules and asses killed for fear of falling into our hands. We quartered ourselves in the French camp; they left us good fires. I roasted some pork which the French left, and had plenty of biscuit, took a glass of grog and a pipe, and talked over the business of the day with my brother-officers. Very happy to find I had a whole skin, which was more than I expected; rolled myself in my cloak, lay by the fire, and slept as well as I could wish.

In the whole of these affairs we have had one major killed, a very fine gallant soldier, and six lieutenants wounded; I cannot say how many men. The *Gazette* will give a more circumstantial account. The 43rd and 52nd have also suffered severely. Some light companies of other regiments were with us. The Portuguese deserve every praise; they fight like lions. We have paid off the French for old scores, and also taught them what they must expect to meet with if ever they dare to invade our happy country. As for my gallant countrymen, I

1811 cannot say too much for them; proud I am indeed
to be worthy the name of a Briton. I have confidence and pleasure in feeling I have done my duty
under all the privations I have laboured under, and
at a time when hardly recovered from a very bad
illness. I have great reason to thank the Almighty
for His merciful goodness to me, and for my preservation hitherto. I hope it is for a good purpose. I
must own it would grieve me to leave you under your
present circumstances. I yet flatter myself some day
or other I shall have it in my power to show some
mark of my affection to the best of parents; if
not : God's will be done. My last words will be
prayers for the welfare of those dearer to me than
life.

I have seen a letter from Cadiz. I find the rascally Spaniards have deceived General Graham, but
the English *alone* gave the French a terrible beating.
Our regiment had one lieutenant-colonel wounded,
one captain killed, and four lieutenants wounded. Our
regiment gets terribly cut up. We think nothing of
it. Every man glories in doing his duty, and those
that survive must be promoted.

The French said they would drive us into the sea,
but Lord Wellington, the finest General in the British
service, has, from his penetration, starved and nearly
driven them back out of Portugal. We are at Celorico,
only six leagues from the frontiers of Spain, and in a
few days I shall once more see Almeida. I hope not
to be so unlucky as before. If we can bring the
French to a general action, you will have a fine
account of the result. I hope it will be the case in
a few days. Our men have got quantities of money

and plunder from the French.   In the whole business 1811
we have taken 1500 prisoners.   I cannot ascertain
how many were drowned in the two rivers, but the
last business was a glorious one for us.   The river
appeared covered with bodies of fine handsome
fellows.   We march in the morning, but the enemy
seem to wish to be off and have no more to do with
us.—I am, your affectionate son,

Geo. Simmons, Lt., 95th Regmt.

Joseph, I hope, is at school; Charles and Betsy
also.   My love to my dear Ann.   She must endeavour
to spell better.   Always let me see some of her writing.
Joseph may as well likewise give me a specimen.

When I am richer I shall send some things of
more value to Ann.   The snuff-box, I hope, will
please my dear mother.   Be particular in stating when
you write, which must be on receipt of this, whether
the trinkets have safely arrived.   I have no doubts upon
the subject, as the officer I entrusted them to is a
particular friend.   You must excuse omissions in this
letter, as I had only a little time to give you this
account, and that after a hard day's march, when I
ought to have been sleeping instead of writing.

CHAPTER VII

Journal—26th March–25th May 1811

French dislodged from Freixeda and their baking operations
stopped—Death of Lieutenant James Stewart (Brigade-
Major)—Dreadful murder of a Spanish woman by the
French—Action of Sabugal—Desperate fighting—Lieutenant Arbuthnot killed—Advance resumed—The Spanish
frontier crossed—The Light Division takes up the old line
of outposts on the Agueda—Reconnaissances of Almeida,
held by the French—Defence of the bridge of Marialba—
The French driven off—Lord Wellington rejoins the army
— The Royal Dragoons and 14th Light Dragoons hold
the advanced posts—The French occupy Gallegos—The
Light Division falls back—Marshal Massena concentrates a
strong force in front of Fuentes de Oñoro—The British army
forms up behind the town—Combats at Fuentes de Oñoro—
Battle of Fuentes de Oñoro—The Chasseurs Britanniques
repulse a charge of French cavalry—Successful charge by
British cavalry under General Stewart — The French
occupy the village, but on debouching are charged by the
74th and 88th Regiments and driven back—Bivouac on
the battlefield—French and English outposts in touch—
General Brenier evacuates Almeida, blowing up his magazines and destroying his guns—Marshal Beresford invests
Badajoz—News of the battle of Albuera (the *only* general
action in the Peninsular War in which some of the Rifles
were not present).

Letter No. XII

To his Parents from Espeja, dated 18th May 1811

Graphic account of the action near Sabugal—A running fight
for two miles—The 43rd Light Infantry and Portuguese
Caçadores support the Rifles—The skirmishers suddenly
come upon the French posted in strength, and have to fall
back—Colonel Beckwith's coolness in action—Picton's
Division arrives—Gallantry of the French officers—The
French retire—Skirmishing about Almeida—The fighting
prior to the battle of Fuentes de Oñoro—The inhabitants of
the town ordered to clear out—Battle of Fuentes de Oñoro
—Losses of the Rifles—Exceptional amount of fighting
which fell to them—Anxiety as to the welfare of his family
—Scarcity of food and clothing—A *brown* " Green jacket "
—Wants a good " spy-glass."

Journal—26th March–25th May 1811

Marched to Celorico. The enemy evacuated it 1811
yesterday, and had an officer and thirty men taken March
by our cavalry.   26th

The Division remained in bivouac.   27th

The Light Division (with the exception of the 28th
right wing 95th) crossed the Mondego and occupied
the villages of Baraca and Minhoeal. That wing
made a forced march to Alverca da Beira, where the
cavalry had their outposts. A party of Rifles (100),
under the command of Captain Beckwith, was sent to
dislodge a body of the enemy from a mill in the front
of Freixeda, at which mill, *Johnny* was busily employed grinding flour, and another body of the enemy
was baking it in the town. The enemy were driven

1811 from the mill, and twenty prisoners captured, but we had to regret the loss of a gallant fellow in Brigade-Major Stewart, who was killed on incautiously entering the town, some French soldiers firing at him quite close, from a window. I was requested to examine his wound by Colonel Beckwith, and report how he came by his death, as his head was deeply cut in the forehead and it was feared by some that when wounded he had been deliberately murdered. I gave my opinion that from a musket ball having entered his left breast, and passed through his heart as he rode forward, he had instantly fallen upon his head. The place he was riding over being granite rocks, and he being a heavy man, the fall had scarred his head as it then appeared. My supposition satisfied every one.

March 29th   Before day we deposited poor Stewart in his last worldly tenement, wrapped in his cloak, near the village, and then moved forward towards Guarda after the enemy, the 3rd and 6th Divisions co-operating. We expected to have had warm work, but on perceiving us move to attack in the direction of Sabugal, *Johnny* moved off in the greatest possible hurry, followed up by cavalry and Horse Artillery, who took near 200 prisoners.

The 3rd Division occupied Guarda, and saved the church, as well as many houses, from being burnt. The doors of the church were on fire.

In a village in the front of Guarda, named Carapeta, I saw a woman laid in the street near her own door, murdered. The ruffians had placed upon her bosom a huge piece of granite taken from the market cross, so heavy that it took me and six men to remove it. The blood was running from her ears and mouth. Her dress

upwards was most respectable, but her lower habili- ₁₈₁₁
ments had been dragged off her. A peasant informed
me that she was the wife of the *juiz de fore* of the
village (that is the Mayor). The Division occupied
all the villages at the foot of the high hill that Guarda
stands upon. I was quartered in Carapeta. I visited
Guarda, which stands very high and upon a ridge
named the Sierra de Carapeta, connected with the
Estrella mountains, and is the most elevated town
in Portugal, and also very ancient, with a castle,
and encircled by a dilapidated Moorish wall. The
cathedral is very ancient and the church superbly
finished. The organ must, from its large size, have
produced a great musical effect. The church had been
converted into a stable and the organ sadly cut and
hacked about in the most wanton manner (by *Catholics*).

Marched to Pega, where we halted an hour. April
Very rainy. Moved forward to Quintas de San Bar- 1st
tolomé, near the Coa and opposite Sabugal, where
the enemy was in great force. A most dreadful
night and very close. On piquet, with orders never to
quit the post, in case the enemy attacked me during
the night, and to be very vigilant indeed.

Went into quarters at a village.   2nd

ACTION OF SABUGAL

Colonel Beckwith's Brigade crossed the river Coa ; 3rd
the sides steep ; the 95th led. It was deep and came
up to my arm-pits. The officer commanding the
French piquet ordered his men to fire a few shots
and retire. On getting footing, we moved up in
skirmishing order and followed in the track of the

1811 piquet. We were met by a regiment, and kept skirmishing until the rest of the Brigade came up, when
we pushed the enemy through some fine groves of
large chestnut-trees upon the main body (Regnier's
Corps or 2nd). Two guns opened on us and fired
several discharges of round and grape. The guns
were repeatedly charged, but the enemy were so
strong that we were obliged to retire a little. Three
columns of the enemy moved forward with drums
beating and the officers dancing like madmen with
their hats frequently hoisted upon their swords. Our
men kept up a terrible fire. They went back a little,
and we followed. This was done several times, when
we were reinforced by the other Brigades, and the guns
were taken. But from the enemy's numbers being
very much superior, the combat was kept up very
warmly until General Picton's (3rd) Division came
up and pushed out its Light companies on their
flank, the 5th Regiment forming a line in support.
The 5th Division, under General Dunlop, soon
crossed at this bridge and passed through Sabugal.
The enemy gave way and went off in confusion ;
the rain now fell in torrents and materially assisted
their retreat. Our cavalry was unluckily too distant
to take advantage of the loose manner in which they
moved off. The Light Division was put into the
town for the night, as a compliment for its conduct on
this day, and the remainder of the army in bivouac.
Lieutenant Arbuthnot was killed, Lieutenant Haggup
wounded, Colonel Beckwith wounded and his horse
shot. Lieutenant Kincaid and I, with our baggage, were
provided with a dilapidated habitation. We had very
little to eat, but were sheltered from the pelting rain.

In one corner of the place several miserable human 1811 beings were huddled together, nearly starved to death. I gave a poor little child some of my bread, but then all the wretched creatures began to beg from me. I could not assist them, not having enough to satisfy the cravings of a hungry stomach, and being aware of another rapid march awaiting me, and more exertions and dangers to encounter before we could put the French over the frontiers of Portugal; and as Sancho says, "It is the belly that keeps up the heart, not the heart the belly."

The Light Division marched to Quadrazaes and April Val d'Espinho, formed a junction with the 3rd 4th Division, and passed through Alfayates, where the latter halted. We moved forward to the frontier village of Forcalhos.

Marched to Albergueria. Once more upon Spanish 5th ground, and now able to get something more comfortable to eat and a good mattress to sleep upon.

The enemy retired across the Agueda, leaving a 6th garrison of 1000 men in Almeida under General Brenier.

The 2nd Battalion 52nd joined from England 7th on the march from Ponte de Murcella, and were put into Colonel Drummond's Brigade. Remained in quarters.

Marched into Fuentes de Oñoro. 8th

The Light Division took up the old line of out- 9th post upon the Agueda, occupying the villages of Gallegos, Espeja, and Fuentes de Oñoro, and forming the line of advanced posts to the Duas Casas, the fortress of Almeida being now blockaded by the British and Portuguese.

**1811
April
10th** Captain Cameron, Lieutenants Cox, Coxen, and myself went with 150 Rifle Men to San Pedro, near Almeida.

11th Before day, marched close to the town with a company of the 2nd Battalion 52nd, under Captain Snodgrass, who supported us. Several cannon shot were fired from the town at us. We succeeded in making the garrison take within its walls several bullocks and sheep that were feeding under the range of their guns. When it became dusk we returned to San Pedro.

12th Marched to near Almeida and attacked the party that were guarding the cattle. The cattle were taken into the town. The enemy fired some heavy guns repeatedly at us. Sergeant M'Donald was killed. Continued watching near the town amongst the rocks, but the cattle were kept within the gates. Returned at dusk for the night to San Pedro.

13th Returned to Almeida, fired at the cattle, made the enemy take them within the walls. This was a very unpleasant service, attended with more risk than profit. If we had been able to obtain a sirloin of beef occasionally it would have been well enough.

14th Went as usual to Almeida.

15th Returned to Fuentes de Oñoro and joined my company, as the detachment belonged to several companies. Two complete companies marched to Malpartida to perform this daily service.

16th Marched to Molino dos Flores and found the Light Division upon the heights, expecting to move forward to intercept a convoy on the road from Salamanca to Ciudad Rodrigo, but did not effect our purpose and returned to quarters. Some of our cavalry got between 300 French infantry and the 1811 town; the enemy took shelter in an old ruin; the party was asked to surrender, but refused. The officer should have immediately sent for some infantry, but he waited too long before he decided upon it, and a body of French came from Ciudad Rodrigo to release them. Heavy firing of cannon and small arms at Almeida. Lord Wellington left us to visit the Corps in Alentejo.

Two battalions of French infantry and a squadron April of cavalry came by Carpio to the heights above 22nd Marialba, on the Azava, where they halted, and sent a party forward to attack the 52nd piquet, stationed at the bridge. The pass was disputed with spirit, and soon after another company, with some of the 95th Rifles, came to their assistance, and the enemy were compelled to retire. The enemy moved away in the direction of Ciudad Rodrigo.

Some piquets that the enemy had outside Almeida were driven in, which caused the firing mentioned.

The 6th Division is stationed before Almeida 24th under General Campbell; it is now most rigorously blockaded. Sir Stapleton Cotton has arrived from England, and is appointed to command the whole line of outposts. Sir B. Spencer commands the army in the absence of Lord Wellington.

Colonel Beckwith's Brigade occupied the villages 26th of Sexmiro, Barquilla, and Villar del Puerco, which are near each other and to the left of Gallegos.

Marched early in the morning to Almeida, and 27th then went to the rear of Gallegos, where our Brigade was assembled.

1811   Colonel Drummond's Brigade was now assembled in front of this place. The piquets exchanged a few shots with the enemy. We were informed by deserters that Marshal Massena had arrived at Ciudad Rodrigo, and that the French army was concentrating its force in the neighbourhood for the purpose of relieving Almeida.

April   Lord Wellington returned to the army. The
28th   Royal Dragoons and 14th came to the advanced posts and entered Sexmiro, Barquilla, and Villar del Puerco. A sortie was made by the garrison of Almeida, but effected nothing of consequence; a sergeant and three soldiers were made prisoners.

30th   Marched to Sexmiro, as a strong piquet of French infantry was placed at the ford over the Agueda not far from it.

Six squadrons of cavalry and a column of French infantry made their appearance about noon on the heights of Carpio and Marialba, and withdrew after remaining some hours.

The 3rd Battalion 1st Foot marched to Almeida to support the Light Division. The outpost at Sexmiro was confided to the cavalry.

May   Marched to Almeida. Marched to Espeja and
1st   joined the Brigade. The enemy in force; cavalry, infantry, and guns moved forward a little after daybreak upon Gallegos and Espeja. Colonel Drummond's Brigade joined ours. The Light Division retired before the enemy about three miles and formed column of regiments in a very extensive wood. The British cavalry were drawn up in a plain to our front. It was occupied by them for the night. Bivouacked.

Yesterday the French army had concentrated in 1811
our vicinity ready to advance, and having a large May
force of cavalry (far more numerous than ours), we 2nd
retired, without firing a shot, through the village of
Fuentes de Oñoro, and found the British and Portuguese troops in position, with the Duas Casas River in
our front, the right of the army resting upon a
Portuguese village—Nava de Avel. Don Julian with
his guerrillas, horse and foot, and some light guns,
were also there for the purpose of acting upon the
enemy's flank. Our centre was behind Fuentes de
Oñoro, and parallel with it (our position being much
higher), our left being upon Fort Concepçion and Aldea
de Obispo, which was four miles in front of Almeida.
We overlooked the villages and adjacent country,
where we observed the enemy moving into position
and advancing towards us along the same tracks we
had a few hours before been passing over. It was
obvious that Marshal Massena had concentrated
this large army either to attempt to carry off the
garrison of Almeida, or to throw succour into it.
Lord Wellington was determined to prevent him,
and placed his army as I have described. About
mid-day the enemy's light troops, supported by
columns of infantry, entered the village, and were
met by Light companies of the 3rd Division, and those
of Generals Nightingale's and Howard's Brigades and
the King's German Legion, supported by the 83rd
Regiment (2nd Battalion). The village being built
of granite, and the walls intersecting it in every
direction of the same material, the contest became
amusing and lively, and was supported on both sides
with great bravery. A very heavy column now

1811 entered and was carrying all before it, when the 24th, 71st, and 79th Regiments were thrown into the village, and checked its advance. At daybreak the firing ceased on both sides. The Light companies and the 83rd were withdrawn, leaving the 71st and 79th supported by the 24th.

May   The Light Division was kept in reserve the greater
3rd part of the day directly behind Fuentes de Oñoro, and a line of the 3rd Division was formed ready to enter into the spirit of any attack made in this quarter, which, being the key to our position, in all probability would be assailed with the most vigour. The Light Division towards evening moved to the left, as the enemy appeared in great force in that part of our line. A brisk cannonade was kept up by the French during the whole of the day, although they had gained no advantage, but lost a great number of men in Fuentes de Oñoro.

4th   The enemy's General made a reconnaissance of our position. Smart fighting in Fuentes de Oñoro.

Major-General Craufurd assumed the command of the Light Division, having joined from England. Towards evening the Light Division moved in the rear of the centre to support it in case of an attack, being the key to our position.

Battle of Fuentes de Oñoro

5th   This morning we observed the enemy had concentrated a large force of all arms in the vicinity of Fuentes de Oñoro. The Light Division was moved to the right and also some distance to its front, and entered a large wood, throwing out skirmishers to our front, as it was expected from the enemy's 1811 manœuvres that a large force was concentrating there under cover, for the purpose of making a sudden attack upon the right of our line. Their skirmishers kept up a fire, but did not attempt to drive us out until a large body of their cavalry had debouched some distance to our right and when clear of the wood, wheeled to their right, so as to intercept our retrograde movement. The enemy's skirmishers then followed us up, keeping up a smart fire until we left the wood and formed column at quarter-distance ready to form square at any moment if charged by cavalry, and in this way we marched to that part of the position where the Guards were formed in line. A body of cavalry hovered about us, but from our formidable appearance and the steady manner with which the movement was conducted, the enemy did not charge us. A company of Guards wheeled back, their battalion being in line ; we passed through and then halted in column and became a support to that part of our line. The 7th Division was on the right of our line. A heavy column of French cavalry moved upon Nava de Avel as well as infantry, and Don Julian, with his guerrillas, horse and foot, retired before them. The French columns were passing from the wood towards the right in large bodies, which made it obvious what were the intentions of the enemy. Our illustrious Chief, having the eye of an eagle, in an instant penetrated through the designs of Massena and ordered the 7th Division to refuse its right, which was effected so well that the enemy gained no advantage. The Chasseurs Britanniques, a regiment in our service in the 7th Division, principally composed of renegade

1811 Frenchmen, was charged by a body of the enemy's cavalry in line, and repulsed them in good style. "When Greek meets Greek then comes the tug of war." We were highly amused at this rencontre. Some squadrons of ours, headed by General Stewart, attacked a large body of French cavalry and hacked their way through it, bringing off a colonel of Dragoons and several men, besides leaving a number *hors de combat.* The enemy passed the Duas Casas at Paya Velha ford, and occupied the place where part of the 7th Division had retired from, in consequence of the right of the army being thrown back. Five companies of Rifle Men occupied some rugged ground through which the Turon pursued its course, on the right of the 1st Division, and between it and the 7th. The enemy attempted to penetrate this valley, but were kept in check by our men and some Light companies of the 1st Division. The left of the 7th Division rested upon the Turon, and its right towards the Coa, covering the road to Almeida. The 5th Division was stationed at Fort Concepçion and Aldea de Obispo. General Park's Portuguese Brigade and 2nd Regiment blockaded Almeida. A company of the Guards, who did not get out of the wood at the time we retired (from mistake, I suppose), were sharply attacked, and Colonel Hill, who commanded, was taken prisoner as well as several men, and some killed. The enemy's guns kept up a very heavy cannonade upon our line. Our heavy artillery was drawn up in front of the 1st Division, and kept up a well-directed fire upon the enemy's guns and silenced several. As our men were lying down in column just behind the line of the 1st Division, ready to be slipped at anything that might be thought necessary, 1811 a body of French cavalry menaced a charge upon our guns and came up in the boldest manner, receiving repeated discharges of grape-shot, that literally made lanes through them. Finding it of no use, the cavalry moved off. The enemy, not being able to make any impression upon our right, attacked the village of Fuentes de Oñoro with great vigour, continually bringing up more men to the assistance of those engaged. The 24th, 71st, and 79th defended the upper parts of the village with great resolution, and repeatedly repulsed the different attacks. The enemy ultimately arrived at the head of the village by the principal road, and were beginning to make a formation upon the plain opposite our line, when the head of their column was repulsed in grand style by the 74th and 88th Regiments. They were led by Colonel Pakenham, D.A.G., a most able soldier.[1] The place was covered with dead, and a number of officers who had led the head of this imposing column were killed. No further operations of importance occurred during the day. The Light troops on both sides kept up a continual tiralade from behind the village walls, and many gallant little affairs took place by individuals that were known only to those who were principals on that occasion. Night put a stop to further havoc, and the British soldiers rested upon the field of battle, with that proud feeling which a man only can have under such circumstances —of having fulfilled his duty to his country by

[1] Afterwards Major-General Sir Edward Pakenham, who was killed in the disastrous attack on the lines of New Orleans, 1815.—Ed.

1811 repulsing a much larger force of cavalry and infantry at all points, and that under one of the enemy's most able generals, Marshal Massena, Prince of Essling, the "spoiled child of Fortune" (for so Massena was designated by the French Emperor). The Light Division relieved the piquets. I was on piquet in the lower part of the village, near a little stream of water which passed through part of the town. The enemy had a captain's piquet on the opposite side of the little rill, and a heavy column of infantry was formed behind a small church, either waiting for orders or fearing an attack. We gave some badly-wounded Frenchmen to the piquet, and the officer allowed some of ours to be given up. A French officer said to me, "This place is appropriately named the Fountain of Honour ; God knows how many of our friends on both sides have drunk deep of its waters, and with to-morrow's dawn most likely many more will do so." My only reply to this was, "The fortune of war will decide that, and we are ready to try its chances when our illustrious chief gives the order to advance." The remainder of the night was occupied in knocking down many an honest man's garden wall and making a strong breastwork to fire over as soon as the day dawned. Only a few random shots were fired during the night. Before day every man stood to his arms and carefully watched its dawning.

May 6th   The enemy we found, when visible, to be not inclined to fight us ; they had been busily occupied in getting their wounded and heavy guns away to the rear, as well as all incumbrances, in order to be able, if pressed, to make a clean start and be off. Relieved from piquet.

Remained as yesterday. Went on piquet in the village in the evening.

Relieved as before by the 2nd Brigade, Light Division. The weather very warm, and great numbers of dead, all stripped naked, were spread in every direction and swollen in a disgusting manner from putrefaction and exhaling most offensive smells. Such is the general result of a hard-fought battle when the dead are not buried.

On piquet.

At daybreak found the enemy had moved off and only left a small cavalry piquet here and there along the line of posts they had before so strongly occupied as a rear-guard. Our columns were soon moving forward and the French withdrawing to join a very strong body of cavalry, which kept ours in check and prevented us from taking many prisoners. The Light Division went into quarters again at Gallegos and Espeja. This night the garrison of Almeida under General Brenier, after mining the works and fixing the loaded cannon muzzle to muzzle and having the trains laid to fire them, left the town and passed over the very bodies of the blockaders in a close column. The pickets followed and fired upon them, the French now and then firing a few shots, but making the best of their way to Barba del Puerco, where they arrived at daylight, and were attacked by some of the 4th and 36th Regiments in winding through the intricate passes over the Agueda. In the eagerness of pursuit the 36th Light company passed the bridge and went too far, and a body of French from San Felices moved to assist their comrades and beat back the Light company with loss. Colonel Cochrane, who

1811 commanded the regiment on that occasion, was very much annoyed at some remarks afterwards made. Brenier's mines exploded most effectually, and the guns also were split in pieces; in fact, altogether it was a most masterly movement. Colonel Bevan was too late at Barba del Puerco with his regiment, owing to Sir W. Erskine, by accident, not sending him an order in time. Poor Bevan was censured by Lord Wellington, which circumstance preyed so much upon his mind, knowing that he had done his duty, that he blew his brains out. The order alluded to was sent from the headquarters by Lord Wellington's direction, and Sir William Erskine forgot to forward it, and literally after the business was over found the document in his pocket. What trifles some men's fate hangs upon!

May 12th A Brigade of French Dragoons moved forward to the heights of Carpio this morning. Our cavalry piquets retired towards Espeja, followed by a squadron. The 1st Brigade, Light Division, moved in front of the town, and skirmishers (Rifle Men) fired upon the French. They retreated, and our cavalry reoccupied their post at Carpio, beyond the Azava.

16th Lord Wellington left the headquarters at Valermosa and went to visit Marshal Beresford, who had commenced the siege of Badajoz.

Accounts of a sanguinary battle having been fought there on May 16th arrived. Marshal Beresford had marched from before Badajoz to Albuera, where he encountered, with the British, Portuguese, and two Divisions of Spaniards, under Blake and Castaños, the French army, commanded by Marshal Soult, and eventually, after sustaining repeated attacks, drove it

back. On the night of the 17th the French moved 1811
off, and Badajoz was again invested on the 19th.
My brother Maud, Lieutenant, 34th Regiment, commanded a company, his captain being killed early in
the action.

Letter No. XII

Espeja, Spain, 18th May 1811.

My dear Parents—This very wet morning, being
disengaged, I feel great pleasure through the medium
of this sheet to impart my adventures since I last
wrote from Celorico on 26th March, which I am well
aware will be gladly received by my dear mother
when she finds her son has always had the good-
fortune to be engaged in every affair with his
regiment against the enemy. After halting one day
at Celorico, we marched towards the Coa, first
driving the French from the strong position at
Guarda. In a skirmish at Freixeda we lost a
valuable officer, shot from a window. Our men were
so enraged at the circumstance as to be with difficulty
prevented killing some rascals we took. The Light
Division moved near Sabugal on the 2nd of April—
a very bad day. I was with half our company on
piquet, our sentries within pistol shot of the enemy,
and being a very rainy and stormy night, it was necessary to be much upon the alert for fear of surprise.
By the bye, the enemy have been so severely handled
in five or six attempts to surprise piquets of the
Light Division in the night as to make them very
cautious how they attempt such manœuvres. I smoked
my pipe to keep me warm, and had an immense

1811 wood fire, round which our lads sat joking and passing the night with the greatest cheerfulness.

Early the next morning the piquets were called in, and Lieutenant-Colonel Beckwith's Brigade ordered to cross the river and attack the enemy. The river was rapid and at the ford took me to the waist. I fully expected the enemy would have greeted our approach with grape-shot and shells, but they suffered us to pass unmolested. As soon as the Rifle Men crossed, they extended and moved up the steep hills, covered with mountain heath and brushwood. On approaching the summit of the first chain of heights, the enemy commenced skirmishing. By this time the 43rd Light Infantry and Caçadores had joined us. The enemy were driven from one chain of hills to another for two miles, when suddenly, on gaining the top of a third chain of hills, our whole line in skirmishing order came in contact with seven columns of French.

The company I was leading on pounced upon a column, and, owing to the situation of the ground, came literally within twenty yards of it before we could see it. Guess my astonishment! The most hideous yelling assailed my ears (the same in every direction of our line), the French drumming, shaking their bayonets, and calling out "Long life to the Emperor Napoleon." Luckily the ground was thinly patched with stout trees, which afforded our men good shelter in retiring. Nothing could intimidate our brave fellows, retiring and keeping up a hot and destructive fire upon the enemy's close column so as to annoy them very materially. I now began to think we were always to have ill-luck on the banks of this infernal river, but fortune, under many circumstances, favours the brave.

Colonel Beckwith rode along the line in the most cool 1811
and gallant style, cautioning the men to be steady,
knowing well that if we maintained our ground for one
hour or so we should have two or three Divisions of
our army to our support, and that if we did not keep
our ground the whole Brigade would be drowned or
bayoneted.   As our Division had so recently driven
about 500 French into a river and drowned them, the
same way of retorting to the joke would have been
delightful to the enemy.   We retired very steadily
about fifty yards into a deep valley, the French firing
from a great number of cannon, throwing grape and
shells, which splintered the trees and naturally killed
several men.   Finding the enemy did not advance
farther, the Colonel formed part of the 43rd Regiment,
our little line of skirmishers moving up at the same
time and making a desperate attack upon a gun that
was keeping up a very destructive fire.   Every one near
the gun was bayoneted or shot.   We were driven back,
attacked again, but were again obliged to retire, when
luckily the other part of our Division moved up, and
the gun was ours.   Colonel Beckwith on the second
attack, had his horse's side pierced by a grape-shot ; a
bullet hit him slightly on the eyebrow ; as he wiped
the blood away he called out, " My brave lads, I am
no worse ; follow me."   General Picton's Division
advancing now upon our left, the enemy moved off in
the greatest confusion.   This battle was the most
trying and glorious I ever beheld.   They must (from
their numbers alone) have annihilated us, but fearing
some trap was laid, *Johnny* durst not move on.   Our
loss this day was severe.   The carnage on the enemy's
side was dreadful ; the most handsome men I ever

12

1811 saw were biting the dust. The enemy on every occasion oppose us with their picked and best troops ; their officers are certainly prodigal of life, often exposing themselves ridiculously. One French officer came capering on, to show off to his regiment what a fine fellow he was, and actually made a cut from his horse at one of our men, who shot him. Occurrences of this nature frequently happen. One lieutenant of ours had his head dashed to pieces by a cannon shot—a very brave young soldier.

The enemy now retired by one forced march over the Agueda, leaving a garrison in Almeida, which was directly invested, our Division establishing their piquets on the same ground they occupied last year. A party of men was sent (I was one of the number) to attempt the destruction of the enemy's bullocks that were sent out to graze under the walls of Almeida. The enemy threw a number of shot and shells at us. The bullocks were so near the garrison as to render it impossible to kill the animals without losing a number of them, and the object gained not being worth the risk, the party were ordered to join the regiment. Our piquets and the enemy's were frequently skirmishing, the result always terminating in our favour.

On the 2nd of May the enemy again advanced. We had previously been informed by the peasantry that Massena had been collecting all the force he could muster, and meant to relieve Almeida and fight a general action.

Massena moved over the Agueda with 35,000 infantry, 5500 cavalry, and also a very respectable train of field artillery. We retired leisurely and

halted in a wood. Some part of the enemy occupied 1811
our quarters in Espeja.

On the 3rd the enemy's whole force advanced.
Our Division retired without any loss to our position
just above Fuentes de Oñoro, and to my agreeable
surprise our army, amounting, in this quarter, to
31,000 British and Portuguese, were ready formed, and
making every necessary preparation to receive the
enemy. As this unfortunate village was situated about
the centre of our line and in a hollow, it would be one
place of attack. Under those circumstances, the inhabitants were told that if they attempted to stop they
would be killed by the shots and shells thrown into it
unavoidably by both parties. The poor unfortunate
people were obliged to run off directly. In this place
I had lived for some months at different times, the
people very kind. I looked with sorrow at the poor
inhabitants, heaving a sigh, expressing at the same
time delight and confidence that the happy shores of
Britain would never be cursed with these detestable
monsters while her gallant sons are ready to lay down
their lives with eagerness in defence of the most happy
land in the universe. May England ever fight her
battles in a foreign land! O happy, happy country!
you are ignorant of the miseries and wretchedness that
one-half of Europe is continually exposed to, and may
you ever enjoy the same happiness! My poor old
patron (landlord), happening to single me out as he
passed through our martial band, came and caught
hold of me, the tears running down his aged cheeks.
" Oh, sir, I hope God will guard and protect you. If
you beat these monsters, I do not care though my house
and everything I have left is destroyed." He then

observed with what delight every eye seemed to sparkle at the advance of the enemy, and with agitation, observed their numbers, expressing at the same time wonder at the light way in which every one viewed them.   The enemy drew up their whole force opposite ours in a line about a mile and a half distant from us, and as the ground was high on both sides, with a little rivulet between us, they saw us and we saw them.   It was the grandest sight I ever beheld.   The enemy sent men behind the stone walls, and were making their approaches towards the valley.   About four o'clock in the evening a very heavy cannonade commenced on both sides, and severe fighting continued till dark.

4th. Early this morning we expected an attack, but nothing of consequence was done.   At daylight on the 5th of May the enemy were moving on in all directions. Our Division moved to the right of our line and into a wood in front ; skirmished ; ordered to retire.   The enemy making a rapid movement round the right of the wood, some Light companies of different regiments and a company of ours were sadly mauled by the cavalry. The French have a very great superiority of cavalry. Our Dragoons amounting to only 1500, they could not possibly check so vast a superiority of cavalry in every place.   Every one exulted with soon bringing the enemy to a general action.   Massena made a slight attack on our right, a vigorous one at the village in front of our centre, and a slight one on our left, in all which they suffered most severely.   The enemy threw numbers of shot and shells, which were returned in grand style by our artillery.   Suddenly, when every man's hopes were raised to the highest pitch, the Prince of Essling, seeing the centre could not be attacked, and also being beaten back on the left, ordered his army to retire. For want of cavalry we were not able to follow after them. I never regretted anything so much. The result of the business was about 5000 officers and men of the enemy killed, wounded, and prisoners; and about 600 of ours (including Portuguese) killed, wounded, and prisoners. This day, Massena made a very fine speech to his men, saying he would drive us beyond the Coa and relieve Almeida.

By some means or other our Division was sent to different parts of the line, where it was expected we should be most wanted, and by a mere accident, for the first time we were not hotly engaged. One of our officers was killed and another badly wounded, and a few men wounded. If the enemy could have been brought to a general action we should have lived peaceably this summer, instead of which we shall be in perpetual hot water. I am astonished to see the ridiculous nonsense put in the English papers by the friends of young men who are as ignorant as themselves. I beg you will not by any means publish my letters to any one, as it would only be attended with unpleasant consequences.

Since our advance from Santarem on 6th March, seven of our officers have laid down their lives, and a great number have been wounded. I soon expect to have my lieutenancy. If I live, I shall get a company sooner in this regiment than any other. My dear brother wrote me wishing to get into our regiment; he is very comfortable in his present one, and not half so liable to be exposed to hardships. I have advised him to continue in his regiment. In six months we see as much service as half the army can boast of in ten years. It is just the life for me while I have health. I am happy to inform you my thigh begins to fill out and gets stronger daily, so much so, that I begin to take one hour's exercise at football very frequently. I am very anxious to know if you hear anything of John, whose fate often costs me many an uneasy hour. Make every inquiry after him, and if possible send him money. Joseph by this time ought to be very clever. I expect to see him write as well as I do. I hope you are very strict in making him attend to his education, as it is fortune, along with good conduct. I hope Charles is at a good grammar school. He is old enough to commence Latin. It is from the purest motives I take such interest in my family. If I see them advance and flourish in the world I shall be the happiest of mortals ; if otherwise I shall be the most miserable.

My dear father, recollect these words, and should casual circumstances estrange me from you, and my pen cease to dictate the love I bear my family, your children will live to reward your kindness. My sister Ann's letter gave me great pleasure. I hope she continues to amuse herself in endeavouring to acquire knowledge. I am proud of her, and hope she will be an ornament to her family. My dear little Betty ! I shall send her some little things, but the uncertainty and inconvenience of sending articles prevents me. If I find the last article safe, it will induce me to do the same again. I often amuse myself with the thoughts of your comfortable fireside, when exposed, wet and hungry, to the inclemency 1811 of the weather, though the pride and pleasure in doing my duty for my country overcomes every other consideration. I hope my dear mother is well, and I hope to see her another day in company with Maud, who is now a lieutenant. My best respects to my uncle and Aunt Maud. I feel myself in duty bound to thank her for her kindness to my mother. I bought a shawl, and am sorry I have not had an opportunity of sending it to my aunt.

Lord Wellington is adored by his army ; wherever he is, confidence of success is the result. The French own it that, next to Buonaparte, he is the first Captain in Europe. I wish his lordship had Buonaparte to contend with instead of Massena ; we should sooner settle the business. I have received no letters since I last wrote from Celorico. I wrote a long letter to Colonel Sibthorp the other day.

My brother is a bloody-minded young rogue, and is thirsting to be engaged with the French. By this time I daresay the army under Marshal Beresford has been engaged. My brother's regiment is in Alentejo. I am proud to say I am confident he will do his duty most gallantly. We expect to organise the Spaniards, and if the system is successful, to attack the French in Spain. The Spaniards are handsome-looking fellows, but proud and haughty. The Portuguese have on all occasions behaved bravely. The Spaniards have behaved remarkably well to the prisoners taken by the French, and at the risk of their lives bring them back to us, which is a very good trait in their character. Every article of food is enormously dear : bread 1s. a pound, butter

1811 4s. a pound, wine bad and dearer than in England. Clothes are expensive and bad. My jacket is brown instead of green. Never was seen such a motley group of fellows. I luckily got some French shirts and other articles, or I should be nearly naked. If you ever meet with a good spy-glass, buy it, as I should be glad to give any price for a good one. I suppose you have the dog " Rifle " ; if a good one, still preserve him. My respects to my friend Whitaker. I hope his son volunteered. If he has done so into this or my brother's regiment, we shall be very happy to serve him. I hope to see a great number of volunteers come out soon, cavalry and infantry, as we shall soon want a fresh supply. I hope many will fancy a green jacket, as our ranks are very thin, having lost a number of brave soldiers. I remain, with best wishes, your affectionate son,

GEO. SIMMONS,
Lieut., 95th or Rifle Regiment.

CHAPTER VIII

Journal—26th May–21st August

The Light Division falls back and recrosses the Coa—Simmons
visits the graves of those who fell in the combat of the
previous year—Finds the remains of his friend, Lieutenant
M'Diarmid of the 43rd Light Infantry, and buries them—
Marches and counter-marches—Is ordered to take a convoy
of sick to Lisbon, but takes "French leave" and marches
to rejoin the Rifles—Four companies, 3rd Battalion, under
Colonel Barnard join the Light Division.

LETTER No. XIII

To his Parents, from Mortiago, dated
26th August 1811

Condoles with his father — Colonel Beckwith invalided to
England—Is promoted to 1st Lieutenant—Arranges for his
brother Joseph to be sent out to the Peninsula as a "Volunteer" to the 34th Regiment—Moralises on the uncertainty
of human life and the depressing influence of continuous
losses of good men on active service—The proper spirit
with which to go into action.

Journal—29th August–30th September 1811

Is sent out on a reconnaissance by General Craufurd—Marshal
Marmont advances in force—The Light Division falls back

across the Agueda—The Light Division chaplain oversleeps
himself and falls into the hands of the French—Narrow
escape of General Craufurd from capture by French
Dragoons—Marshal Marmont, having effected his object,
falls back into Spain.

LETTER No. XIV

*To Lieutenant Maud Simmons, 34th Regiment, 2nd
Division, Portugal, from Aldea Velha, Portugal,
dated 1st October 1811*

Describes General Marmont's concentration and advance to
protect the convoy destined to revictual Ciudad Rodrigo—
The position at El Bodon—General Picton attacked—Lord
Wellington withdraws on Aldea da Ponte—The Rifles on
rear-guard—The French advanced guard press them, but
are driven back—The French cavalry capture some Portuguese guns, but the latter are recaptured by the 5th Fusiliers
with the bayonet — The British army draws up on the
heights of Alfayates, but Marmont refuses action and falls
back—The Light Division "out of a scrape" for the first
time without losses—Regrets at this.

Journal—1st October–20th December 1811

Gets the ague, the result of repeated drenchings—Don Julian
Sanchez, the guerrilla chief, captures General Renaud, the
Governor of Ciudad Rodrigo—The Light Division ordered
out to endeavour to intercept the new Governor reaching
that fortress—Simmons's stable on fire—Nearly loses his
horses—Again attacked by ague—Lord Wellington inspects
the three British regiments of the Light Division (43rd,
52nd, and 95th Rifles) near Fuenteguinaldo—The Light
Division goes into cantonments for the winter.

LETTER No. XV

To his Parents, from Atalaya, Spain, dated
8th December 1811

Anxious inquiries about brother Joseph, and further instructions
as to his voyage out, his uniform and equipment—How to
make an officer's cocked hat—Severe lecture to his father.

Journal—26th May–21st August 1811

The Light Division marched to Nava de Avel 1811
and Aldea da Ponte, fully expecting to proceed to May
Alentejo. Countermanded and took up again the 26th
line of outposts from the 5th Division in front of 27th
Espeja and Gallegos.

Having correct information that the enemy's June
cavalry had been collecting in large force for some 5th
days upon the Agueda, made us much upon the
alert to know where the attack would be made, and
before day we marched out of Espeja (Beckwith's
Brigade) and bivouacked in a wood in rear of that
place. Returned about noon.

The Light Division retired, the outposts being 6th
put back with a body of cavalry. We passed through
Aldea da Ponte and bivouacked in the wood near
Alfayates. We heard that Marshal Marmont commanded the French, and that Massena had been
recalled to Paris to explain to Napoleon why he
had been repulsed and beaten at Fuentes de Oñoro;
so the deserters inform us.

The Light Division marched and crossed the Coa 7th
at the same ford (to the right of Sabugal) we did

1811 when on the 3rd of April we passed in the face of a
French Division. I had very different feelings
now, coolly and deliberately entering a river
after marching some distance with a burning sun
over one's head, the perspiration running in streams
from every pore. Although I was well used to
such movements it was not pleasant, but on the
former occasion I took the water as kindly as a water
dog, for the French skirmishers were firing in our
faces. We bivouacked in a wood of chestnut-trees,
where several of our brave fellows had been buried,
and whose bones had been dug up by wolves and
were strewn above their graves. A gallant young
fellow, Lieutenant and Adjutant M'Diarmid, 43rd
Light Infantry, who was wounded with myself at
Almeida, and who joined again when I did, had
fallen in fight here. I went to see if his grave had
escaped the general disturbance. I found his skull
lying at some distance ; I was convinced that it must be
so, as the hair was still in patches on it. There was no
mistaking it ; his hair, when alive, was auburn and
very curly. His bones were partly eaten and thrown
about in the same way. This appearance of a friend
whom I had esteemed and had so often associated
with, and so recently too, produced many gloomy
reflections. I collected the straggling relics and replaced them and covered them over as the last tribute
I could pay him.

June   Marched to Maimoa, the day excessively hot.
8th Bivouacked there to cook. Moved to Penamacor in
the evening. This town is situated upon a most commanding eminence, from which you have a bird's-eye
view of the country round.

Marched to San Miguel d'Acha. Bivouacked 1811
and halted. June

By some mistake of the Staff, commenced the 9th 10th
march under a vertical sun at midday ; the heat was
so great that several men fell out of the ranks, not
being able to keep up with the column.

Passed the 1st Division at Louza, and halted near 11th
Escalos de Cima in a wood.

On our march, passed Castello Branco, and halted 12th
for some time near Sarnadas, which is close to the
valley of the Tagus. In the afternoon moved to the
pass at Villa Velha. Over the Tagus, a bridge of
boats was moored.

Passed over and marched to Niza. Bivouacked 13th
in a wood. I felt myself very unwell. Got a bed in
the town.

Marched to Alpalhão, and on 15th to Portalegre, 14th
and remained in these good quarters until the 19th,
when we marched to Arronches.

Rode to San Olaya to see my brother Maud. He 21st
had gone to the rear ill the day before. I felt sadly
disappointed.

Marched to an encampment upon the Caya, about 23rd
three miles in the rear of Campo Mayor, and took
up our ground in position with the army. Lord
Wellington was compelled to leave Badajoz and
recross the Guadiana, owing to Marshals Marmont
and Soult having formed a junction and concentrated
their forces in its neighbourhood.

Visited my *patrona* in Campo Mayor ; she was 24th
very glad to see me. Returned to the camp in the
evening.

Rode to Elvas and visited Fort de Lippe.

1811
July
3rd   Lord Wellington took the cavalry and crossed the Guadiana to reconnoitre the enemy ; he found they were gone.

20th   General Craufurd frequently has the Division out for exercise. Nothing else worthy of notice has occurred. The Light Division broke up from this tiresome sort of monotonous life led here. Marched a league and a half and bivouacked.

22nd   Marched to Portalegre.

23rd   Castello de Vide. Occupied several *quintas* round the town. A splendid garden was attached to the one I was billeted upon. I feasted upon a variety of good fruits as well as quantities of mulberries.

29th   Marched to near Niza and bivouacked upon the same ground as before.

30th   Passed the Tagus at Villa Velha over a pontoon bridge lately placed there. Bivouacked in an olive grove.

31st   Marched about two miles and bivouacked.

Aug. 1st   Marched to Castello Branco.

2nd   Marched to Louza and Escalos de Cima.

3rd   Marched to Bemposta. Bivouacked.

4th   Marched to Maimoa. Bivouacked on the same ground as on a former occasion.

6th   Moved to the heights on which the village stands.

7th   At daybreak the Division marched towards the northern frontier. I was sent back with forty-five sick men, and had a number of mules for the sick to ride upon to facilitate their conveyance to a hospital station. Marched to Pedrogão. Halted during the heat of the day, and in the evening moved forward.

8th   To San Miguel d'Acha. Bivouacked and marched to Escalos de Cima. Halted in the place during

the heat of the day.   In the evening moved forward 1811
to Castello Branco and gave up my charge.

Halted.   I had my baggage with me and the Aug.
horse I rode ; two horses to take care of, and no 9th
servant.   By accident I met with a half-starved
Portuguese boy in the street, whom I engaged for a
servant.   I found the Commandant wanted to send
me " on command " with a detachment of sick men to
Lisbon.   I requested he would allow me to proceed
and join my regiment, observing that as in all probability it would soon be actively employed, I should
feel sadly disappointed to be absent from it.   My
anxiety, he said, was highly praiseworthy, but he felt
it necessary for the good of the service to send me in
another direction.   I found it useless to argue the
question further, but I determined to start back, let
the consequence be what it would.

At one in the morning took " French leave " and 10th
marched to Escalos de Cima.

Marched to San Miguel d'Acha in the cool of the 11th
evening.   Moved on to Pedrogão.   Bivouacked near
a rivulet ; made tea.   My Portuguese boy very unwell.   I cut grass for my horses and tied them close
to where we lay down for the night.

Started up with the dawn, saddled my horse and 12th
loaded my baggage, and proceeded to Maimoa in the
evening.

Proceeded to San Estevão.   Bivouacked and 13th
marched to Sabugal.

Marched to Alfayates.   Bivouacked during the 14th
heat of the day.   In the evening to Aldea da Ponte.

Marched to Fuenteguinaldo.·   15th

Marched to Mortiago and joined the Battalion. 16th

1811 Colonel Beckwith complimented me for returning, and although the Commandant had made a formal complaint of me to headquarters, I had nothing said to me upon the subject. I found the Light Division thus distributed : 52nd and Horse Artillery in Saugo, 43rd and right wing of Rifles at Martiago, one troop of Royals and left wing of Rifles and 1st Caçadores at Lariquella, and the 3rd Caçadores at Villarejo.

Aug. 21st Colonel Barnard joined the Division with four companies of the 3rd Battalion Rifles ; these men had been with the army stationed in Cadiz. They were placed in Colonel Beckwith's Brigade. Marched to Villarejo, and the 3rd Caçadores to Las Agallas.

LETTER No. XIII

MARTIAGO, SPAIN, 26*th August* 1811.

MY DEAR FATHER—I received your letter dated 19th of May, which affected me most sensibly.

Your misfortunes affect me most seriously. Would to God it was in my power to prevent them. At present it is not.

After the battle of Fuentes de Oñoro we enjoyed ourselves in the advance near Ciudad Rodrigo, the Spaniards being convinced we had given the French a good drubbing. We had dances with the villagers every night. I do not ever remember spending a more happy time.

On the 28th of July we again made a rapid march and retraced the ground back to the north. We are now farther advanced into Spain than ever before. I expect some fighting soon. *Johnny* will not suffer us to remain long quiet, if he can disturb us. A number of our officers are ill ; one died the other day. I never was better in my life. My Colonel has gone to England sick. Previous to his departure I dined with him. He presented me with a letter, couched in the most flattering way, stating my services, which was addressed to Lord Wellington. I presented the letter the next day. I am in consequence promoted to a 1st Lieutenancy. The Colonel has at all times shown me great favour. I regret his departure. I hope in two or three years to get a company through the influence of my friends.

Maud has his Colonel's leave for Joseph to come here as a Volunteer. In two or three months after he joins, between us we can procure him a commission. I transmit you a bill amounting to £23 : 9s., which will nearly equip Joseph. You may procure the amount at any banking house in England. Directly on the receipt of this write me, for I am anxious to know, as I have two more in case this one is lost or miscarries. The articles to equip him will not cost much money.

I hope, if I live through these turbulent times, to be able greatly to assist you in a few years. Let me be where I will in the world, the welfare of my family will ever be uppermost in my thoughts and my first consideration. I have made many friends since I embraced a military life. In my situation I am content and happy, and meeting the enemy never costs me a second thought. It of course makes one gloomy to see so many fine fellows fall round one, but one day or other we must all go.

1811 The difference is very immaterial in the long-run whether a bullet or the hand of time does your business. This is my way of moralising when I go into a fight (which has been very often), and if for the good of old England, I do not care how soon we have another. I go with the determination of doing all the injury in my power to the enemies of the human race, of which the French certainly merit the appellation. I am sorry I cannot be of service to my dear sister. It afflicts me much. Tell her to bear up against present misfortunes, and recollect she has brothers who will be able to send her money occasionally. After we have done for Joseph, I shall not forget her. Give me an account of Charles and Betsy. Keep them at school. I want to know if Charles is better. In another year I think I can take him off your hands entirely. Poor John! make inquiry about him, and let me know if you can gain intelligence of him.

My dear mother—you do not say much about her. I want to know if her constitution is as good as when I was at home. I flatter myself she will yet see us all round her. Our promotion in the army will put it in our power to assist you very materially in a few years. Maud has been lucky indeed. He is senior lieutenant to me, and if we continue on service, he, as well as myself, must get forward. My respects to my uncle and aunt.—Believe me yours,

GEO. SIMMONS, Lt., 95th Regmt.

Direct, 1st Batt., 95th or Rifle Regiment, Light Division, British Army, Portugal. Write directly and let me know when I may expect Joseph.

He must have a fustian haversack, a tin pot, and a 1811
large pocket-knife. You will be able to judge by the
soldier's haversack ; his may be a little smaller.

Journal—29th August–September 1811

Marched to Atalaya. In the evening I was Aug.
ordered by General Craufurd to go forward through 29th
a wooded country and by a circuitous route to get
upon the road leading to Salamanca, and then, discre-
tionally, to move on for the purpose of finding out
when the convoy was likely to leave Salamanca for
Ciudad Rodrigo. I had a corporal and three men
of the German Hussars with me. I reconnoitred
Tenebron and cautiously entered the place, left it, and
bivouacked for the night within the woods.

Moved forward to Boca Cara and also to Santi- 30th
espiritus, and gained information from a party of Don
Julian's guerrillas that the convoy had left Salamanca,
but was compelled to return owing to several guerrilla
parties having formed up and made an attack upon it.
I returned to my quarters at Atalaya.

Major-General Drummond died at Fuenteguinaldo, Sept.
and Major-General Vandeleur was appointed to com- 7th
mand the 2nd Light Brigade.

Moved to Horquera and bivouacked. 8th

Rode over to Las Agallas and dined with Colonel 11th
Elder.

Moved to Villarejo. 16th

The Division moved and assembled upon the 23rd
heights near Horquera. The enemy's Dragoons
entered Atalaya in force. Our cavalry piquets retired
from it, and crossed the stream behind it.

1811
Sept.
24th

Marshal Marmont was now moving forward with 6000 cavalry and four Divisions of infantry, and bringing a convoy of provisions for the use of the garrison of Ciudad Rodrigo.

25th

The French passed through Tenebron and Santi-espiritus yesterday. The Light Division formed at Las Agallas, marched to Cespedosa, and bivouacked for the night. General Picton's Division partially but sharply engaged about noon near El Bodon. Major Arentschildt's Brigade of nine-pounders (Portuguese) did much execution at this place. The enemy made a dash at these guns, and were in possession of them, but were soon driven away by the 2nd Battalion 5th and the 77th Regiments and some Portuguese infantry, supported by three squadrons of British cavalry.

26th

Moved to Fuenteguinaldo, and found the British and Portuguese concentrated upon the heights in front of it, the right resting upon Perales, in the Gata mountains, and the left at Nava de Avel under General Graham. Some Spaniards were observing the Coa.

The Light Division retired by Robleda across the Agueda, and made a circuitous route to Fuenteguinaldo, as the enemy was nearly round us. A field-work was thrown up, upon some commanding ground about the centre of our position, which gave us an idea that Lord Wellington meant to receive the attack of the French army, and put us all in high spirits. General Cole's Division had some fighting on this day.

After dark our army retired, and the Light Division formed the rear-guard and left the ground about midnight, having kept up the fires in such a manner that the enemy imagined we were still in bivouac. The Light Division parson, Parker, went into a house to make himself comfortable for the 1811 night, and slept very pleasantly.   Some time after day-break he heard strange noises within doors, and soon after, a French Dragoon entered his room.   Giving his sword two or three menacing flourishes, he asked him for his money.   He was followed by others, who were apt scholars in imitating a good example; pillage and rapine they glory in.   The poor parson found him-self stripped of everything, and, almost naked, was driven over rugged ground for twenty miles without shoes, and then put into a prison amongst a group of others and left to cogitate upon his hard fortune and upon his own stupidity for sliding away to make a lodgment in a house unknown to any one in such critical times.

The Light Division passed through Casillas de Sept. Flores.   General Craufurd was pressed sharply by 27th some French cavalry, and came galloping in rather too hastily.   Some Rifle Men and 3rd Caçadores, being halted on both sides of the road, ran forward amongst the brushwood and fired a few rounds at the advance of the French (a few cavalry), who put to the right about and scampered off.   Some sharp fighting followed.   General Pakenham with the Fusilier Brigade drove the enemy from Aldea de Ponte.   Moved to near Alfayates and bivouacked.

Retired a league before daylight, and took up a 28th position upon the heights near Soita amongst some of the most extraordinary chestnut-trees for magnitude I ever beheld ; several were hollow.   Ten men might be accommodated and sheltered for a night in the hollow trunks of some of them.

Marshal Marmont, having effected the principal

1811 object the force he had collected was destined for (viz. to protect the convoy to Rodrigo), as he did not wish to hazard a battle, commenced his retreat into the interior of Spain.   His army, we were led to believe, amounted to 60,000 men and 130 pieces of cannon in the field-train.   Weather unfavourable. Remained in bivouac.

LETTER No. XIV

ALDEA VELHA, PORTUGAL,
1st October 1811.

MY DEAR BROTHER—According to our expectation, the enemy advanced with supplies for the garrison of Ciudad Rodrigo.   About the 21st of September the convoy left Salamanca.   We were informed the cars loaded with provisions amounted to 1100.   As General Marmont was determined to give battle, he had collected a very formidable force of 60,000 men, with a vast train of field artillery.   A very pretty escort.   You will wonder, as well as many others, how the devil he could collect such a force at one given point in so short a time, and particularly when we are taught to believe they have so few men in Spain, having lost so many in different affairs with the Spaniards, according to the accounts we received from different parts of Spain.

Our Dragoons were driven in, as the enemy advanced.   Our Division were ordered to occupy very strong ground in rear of a small stream, which runs at the bottom of a very deep ravine a little way in the rear of Atalaya.   The 3rd Caçadores were posted in the mountains to the

right, and at two or three passes in front of Las 1811
Agallas. Our regiment occupied several strong places,
being divided according to circumstances, and keeping
up a chain of posts communicating with the 3rd
Caçadores on our right, and 43rd Light Infantry on
our left.   The 52nd were also posted in the same way,
with Rifle Men of our 2nd and 3rd Battalions in
different fastnesses and mountain roads.   General
Picton's Division were upon the left bank of the
Agueda at El Bodon ; so you will perceive our
situation was rather critical, being so far advanced
and having the river Agueda in our rear ; but it is
very obvious that this was highly necessary in order to
put Marmont to as much inconvenience as possible
and make him bring up his whole force.   On the afternoon of the 24th, the enemy's cavalry drove our
Dragoon piquets over the different fords of the
stream in rear of Atalaya, and established their posts
opposite us.

About twelve o'clock at noon on the 25th the
enemy, in terrible force, attacked General Picton's
Division at El Bodon, which place being immediately
to our left rear, and also over the Agueda, we began
to think ourselves placed most curiously, though every
one felt the greatest security in Lord Wellington's out-
manœuvring *Johnny*, and bringing off the Division in
safety.   The cannonading was tolerably well kept up
on both sides, and repeated volleys of musketry.   The
enemy were continually driven back, and could not
effect their purpose, which was clearly to cut off the
Light Division.   In the evening, the Division were
ordered to assemble at Las Agallas just after dark, and
then circumambulating [*sic*] towards Fuenteguinaldo

1811 (Lord Wellington's headquarters), the Division halted
in a field near Cespedosa. Our baggage had gone
some little way farther and had nearly been taken by
the enemy's Dragoons. Some of the 11th saved it,
luckily for us. The enemy's patrols were upon the
same road and in our rear.

On the 26th at daylight we moved towards Fuenteguinaldo. The enemy might have cut in between us,
but did not like to risk such a manœuvre. We passed
the Agueda at a ford at Fuenteguinaldo in safety. We
found the army all collected ; several commanding
heights were strengthened and breast-works thrown up.
Every one expected a general engagement would ensue.
We took up our ground on the position, and there was
some partial skirmishing with cavalry when the enemy
established his advanced vedettes. At twelve o'clock at
night the other Divisions of the army were ordered to
retire immediately by the roads, principally towards
Aldea de Ponte, and at two o'clock the Light Division
were also ordered to form the rear-guard and move off.
We moved through Casillas de Flores ; in consequence
of innumerable impediments on the line of march,
we moved very slowly. *Johnny's* advanced guard
pushed in our cavalry, about a squadron, rather un-
mannerly, which caused us to halt and throw out a
few Rifle Men to stop his career. Two or three of
the most valorous were knocked off their horses, and
the remainder retired to a most respectable distance,
where they could amuse themselves by taking long
shots—an amusement they are fond of.

On our line of march we saw the enemy's cavalry
cutting wonderful capers upon the plain and their
infantry moving up in vast columns. General Picton's

and Cole's Divisions retired before the enemy's 1811
cavalry in squares in the most cool and steady manner.
About eleven o'clock A.M. on the 27th the enemy
commenced cannonading our cavalry, which was returned with equal spirit on our side.   The light
troops of General Picton's Division were also smartly
engaged at this time.   The enemy's cavalry in a vast
body charged and took five Portuguese guns, which
were instantly retaken in the most gallant manner by
the 5th Regiment of Foot, who attacked the cavalry
with the bayonet and fairly beat them off.   Colonel
Pakenham, with the Fusilier Brigade, marched up in
ordinary time to meet the enemy's cavalry, who durst
not face them.   The firing ceased about two o'clock.
The enemy's columns were moving up and concentrating opposite us.   Our army were drawn up in front of
Alfayates upon the commanding heights.   The Light
Division and Light Artillery, which, by the bye, I had
forgotten to mention before, were drawn upon the right,
fronting a wood, which was filled with the enemy's
Light troops and a Light Division and Artillery, which
had followed us all the way.   Near sunset the enemy
appeared to be advancing, wishing to try whether or
no he could induce us to retire.   Our first line formed
and also moved forward some paces, the Light Division
throwing out skirmishers towards the woods.   This
manœuvre induced the enemy to give up the project,
at least for the night.   Immediately after dark the
other Divisions of the army retired.   About two
o'clock A.M. we moved off also, and retired to Soita, a
village about a league and a half in front of Sabugal.
The army we saw formed upon the heights in the
rear of this place, and this was called the position that

1811 we were to fight upon—at least, we fully expected it from present appearances. *Johnny* being tired of cutting such a caper after us, and Portugal not being quite so congenial to his comforts, he made a retrograde movement towards Ciudad Rodrigo and Spain.   You see the Light Division has for the first time got out of a scrape without receiving any further injury than from excessively harassing marches. I hope it will never happen again. I have no wish to come off scot-free. When a man's mind is worked up to meet his enemy and fight, it is a great disappointment.

I have now told you all the news I know of. This morning, 1st October, we moved into cantonments. Right wing, 95th, in Aldea Velha. Alfayates is the present headquarters of the Division. I believe the other Divisions of the army are all in cantonments behind the Coa. One company of our 2nd Battalion arrived the other day from England, and a batch of subs. also for us. I received a letter, or rather three in one, from some fair dames in Kent ; one of them says she has entirely given me up— I shall never return. As I am in the humour, and to pass off a dull and rainy day, I am writing nonsense for their amusement ; not love, I assure you.

I have not yet received an answer to the letter I wrote home. I am very anxious about it, as upon it depends the future welfare of Joseph. If I do not receive an answer soon, I shall write again and send a second bill, as delays are dangerous. I think there will be no necessity for making any arrangements at Lisbon until we have a letter knowing when we may expect him. I hope he has not gone on a long voyage. I wrote you some days back 1811 since I received your last. I mentioned in the letter an agreeable surprise I met with in the hovel of an unfortunate refugee. I shall soon begin to feel the benefit of a 1st Lieutenant's pay, as well as the payment of a company, which I have already had for three months, and as yet met with no losses. I am excessively ill-off for clothes and cannot purchase anything. I hope soon to procure some cloth from Lisbon. I am at present a perfect guerrilla, have broken my sword, lost my sash, and am as ragged as a sweep, with just the clothes I have on my back. I have paid the fees of Commission, and have fifty dollars beforehand, so I am in a fair way to soon recover my balance.—I am, dear brother, your most sincere friend ever,

GEO. SIMMONS,
Lt., 95th or Rifle Regt.

P.S.—So uncertain are we what is to happen to-morrow, yesterday I wrote this letter fully expecting to rest for some time. To-day we have again entered Spain. Oct. 2nd, Fuenteguinaldo. In a day or two I think we shall make another advance to our old quarters. This morning we had accounts from near Salamanca; the people say that the guerrillas destroyed several deposits of stores to a vast extent, and killed numbers of stragglers from the French army. The French cavalry suffered exceedingly from our guns.

Journal—1st October–20th December 1811

Marched to Aldea Velha.   Oct. 1st
Light Division was cantoned in the adjacent villages. 2nd

1811 Fuenteguinaldo. Weather very rainy.
Oct.
8th Transferred to the left wing and moved to
Castillejos de Duas Casas and to Robleda on
15th.

17th Marched to Atalaya.

30th Marched to Fradamora and took the command
of Captain Balvaird's company. Having for some
time back been very often completely drenched with
rain night and day, for the first time in my life
I got the ague, which I found a very unpleasant
companion, particularly as this post was taken so as to
prevent supplies from being carried into the garrison
of Ciudad Rodrigo by the peasantry, which required
me to be very vigilant in the performance of this
duty. On 15th October Don Julian Sanchez, with
a number of his guerrillas, surprised the Governor of
Rodrigo (General Rénaud) and took him and five
officers, as well as 200 head of cattle belonging to
the garrison.

Nov. 1st Withdrawn to Atalaya and joined my company.

2nd Information had been received that a body of
French troops were escorting a new Governor to
Rodrigo. The Light Division moved towards the
fortress this morning, and the 3rd Division also
made a forward movement to support us to
Fuenteguinaldo. It soon was ascertained that the
Governor had entered it, as the enemy were in
bivouac two leagues in the rear. Their purpose
being effected, they returned to Salamanca.

Ordered to reoccupy Fradamora and keep a
good look-out. Succeeded in capturing a number
of peasantry that were going to the French garrison
with wine, onions, bread, and eggs for sale. I

purchased what I wanted, and then sent them under 1811
escort to our Commissary.

At daylight the place where my horses were put Nov.
up was on fire.   I had some difficulty in getting 7th
them out.   Luckily, having water at hand, with great
perseverance the fire was soon got under.   Next to
the stable was deposited a large quantity of flax,
which luckily remained uninjured.

The Spaniard to whom the premises belonged
was chattering so fast and in so frantic a manner that
I did not for some time understand him until he
jumped before the barn, then nearly all in a blaze,
and roared out, "Oh, my money!   I am a ruined man.
Oh, my money!   For the love of God, bring me my
money."   As these people were in the habit of hiding
their money to prevent the French from robbing
them, I instantly perceived his distress and ordered the
men to throw water upon the spot he pointed to,
and had the pleasure of getting his store of wealth
and giving it into his hands, which so delighted
him that he d——d the barn, and said that as
he had got his money, it was of no consequence.
The annoyance I felt and my exertions on this
occasion to get the fire under, brought on the ague
with redoubled violence.

Marched to Atalaya.   Had the ague daily, and kept 16th
my bed from its debilitating influence.   I took bark
in very large doses, combined with opium, and placed
a hot stone on my bosom and two at the soles of my
feet as soon as there was any appearance of the cold
fit.   From treating myself in this way I soon dislodged this insidious enemy from my body and
gradually recovered.

1811
Nov.
21st

The Light Division now occupy the villages of El Bodon, Martiago, Zamarra, and Atalaya, more effectually to blockade Ciudad Rodrigo.

A very brilliant affair took place on the 28th of last month, at which my brother Maud was present, in the surprise of part of General Gerard's Division of the French at Arroyo dos Molinos in Estremadura by General Hill with the 2nd Division of the British army.

24th   The 43rd and 3rd Caçadores moved to Martiago, both Battalions of the 52nd to Zamarra, Horse Artillery and 1st Caçadores to Las Agallas, and the Rifle Men held Pastores, La Ençina, and Villarejo.

Dec.
20th

The three British regiments in the Light Division were seen by Lord Wellington near Fuenteguinaldo, after which they returned to cantonments. Don Julian, with his guerrillas, are very active, and occasionally pick up Frenchmen. The garrison is now blockaded completely; Tenebron and Santiespiritus are now occupied by British Dragoons. Nothing further worthy of notice has taken place during this month, which finishes the operations of this eventful year. Looking forward anxiously to the time when we are to be ordered to commence the siege of Ciudad Rodrigo.

LETTER No. XV

ATALAYA, SPAIN, *8th December* 1811.

MY DEAR PARENTS—About the end of August, after receiving your letter, I wrote an answer. For these two months past I have daily expected to have had some account from you, and as I have received none, I cannot put off any longer. I must 1811 inform you that the account of Joseph being sent to sea made a very serious impression upon my mind, and in order to save him from *perdition and ruin*, I directly raised all the money I could, and enclosed in my letter in the latter end of August, a bill amounting to £23 : 9s. It is now above three months since, which circumstance makes me apprehensive the bill is lost; if so, still hoping the bill may not have been cashed, I send you the second. You must in that case, stop the payment of the first, but should you have the first in your possession, burn this, my second.

When I had your account of Joseph's unfortunate situation, I directly wrote to my brother to know if there was a vacancy for Joseph, as in my regiment there was not, having three volunteers with us.

My brother spoke to his Colonel, who immediately said he should be happy to have an opportunity of serving him, and desired Maud would order his brother to proceed and join the 34th, and on his arrival he would directly recommend him for an ensigncy.

If you could procure a passage for him from Hull to Lisbon, it would save a great deal of unnecessary expense; but if this cannot be done, he must go to Portsmouth, and on arrival, inquire for the office of the General who commands there. He will tell the gentleman in the office he is a volunteer going out to join the 2nd Battalion, 34th Regiment, and will thank him to give him an order for a ship. He will then be sent to the Agent of Transport's office, who will inform him what ship is going to sail.   He will then be provided with a passage, and have rations from the day he goes on board, with the use of a cabin. Only, if there are officers on board, he will be the last allowed to choose a bed-place, as he will on all occasions rank as junior.   I only make mention of this because some forward young fellows give themselves great airs and get themselves offended, which will never happen if a young man conducts himself as a gentleman and does not give way to chattering and nonsense.   I hope he will not be showing his agility on board the ship in climbing about the ship or using sea phrases, as such proceedings would make the officers have a bad opinion of him.   In short, he will not have any business to go from the quarter-deck on any occasion.   On his arrival in Lisbon he must inquire for the Town Major's office, where he will find the post office for British officers' and soldiers' letters.   There is now a letter there directed for Mr. Joseph Simmons, Volunteer, 2nd Battalion, 34th Regiment, to be left till called for by himself, so there can be no mistakes.   In the letter, he will find every necessary instruction.

A gentleman—luckily a great friend of my brother —is stationed at Lisbon, and likely to remain some time, his name Lieutenant Richardson, who has the command of the sick detached from the 34th Regiment.   Joseph will find this in the instructions. This officer will take him to his house, and keep him until a favourable opportunity offers to send him to the army.   By the bye, Lieutenant Richardson lives at Belem, so if Joseph lands from the ship at Belem stairs, he will be only three or four hundred

paces from the barracks, where he may make 1811
inquiry of any soldier he sees which is the 34th
barracks.   As soon as he meets with a man of the
regiment, he then must make him go and show
the house of Lieutenant Richardson.   Should he
be absent from home, wait until he returns.   On
his making himself known to him, he will be
kindly received.   I think I have stated the business
so clearly that it would be almost impossible for
Joseph to err.   You must procure Joseph a superfine
red jacket.   I was thinking of letting you get him a
regimental 34th coat, but I am afraid it would be too
expensive, although it would be in the end a great
saving, as cloth is extremely dear in Lisbon ; however,
do as you can.   The collar and cuffs, white Kerseymere, a white Kerseymere waistcoat, two pair of strong
grey trousers, made wide like sailors' trousers, three
pair of strong shoes (one pair short), strong leather
gaiters.   I have always found them the most pre-
ferable, as they keep your shoes from slipping off, and
also prevent sand and gravel getting into your stockings.   Three pairs of socks.   If you could purchase
a sword (not a sabre) similar to the officers' swords
you may have observed on parade, and can get it
cheap, buy it ; its being new is of no consequence.
An old sash also you might procure cheap ; it would
answer as well as any other.   However, these things
are now and then to be met with here.   He must
have a haversack made of dark fustian (not too large),
a clasp-knife, fork, and spoon ; also a tin mug,
which will serve him for wine, soup, and tea.   You
may also buy some pasteboard and make a cocked
hat, or at least have it cut out in order that he can

14

1811 put it into his baggage, with some oil-silk, some broad
black ribbon for a cockade, and some broad stuff for
a binding.   The tailor of the regiment will form it ;
a gold bullion for each end.   His baggage must be
as small as possible, as the convenience of carriage is
very scarce—three shirts will be enough.   He must
also have a black leather stock with a buckle, a
common rough greatcoat ; let it be big enough (any
colour, it is of no consequence).   Could you get
three or four dozen of buttons like the 34th ?   They
would be very useful afterwards.   He must bring
two or three tooth-brushes and three little towels, or
any other little thing that may have slipped my
memory which may strike you.   His brother is a
methodical young rogue, and will provide him with
many comforts and conveniences, as the regiment is
always in good quarters, which gives them every
opportunity of being comfortable.   If the money I
sent is lost, it will prove a most unfortunate circumstance.   In consequence of my fears on that head I
had the opportunity of sending a note to a person in
London by a friend going home, as I had a little
military account unsettled.   I empowered him to
receive the balance and transmit the amount to you.
The balance will be from £10 to £20.   I am not
exactly certain ; however, whatever it is you will
have it.   I directed him to send it, and gave my
friend your direction—Osborne Street.

I hope you will make no delay about Joseph, as
the Colonel often asks Maud about him.   I must
say, my dear father, you did very wrong to send
Joseph to sea.   I think, if you refer back to my
letters, you would find I had laid down a line of

conduct, that, if you had been guided by me, you at this moment would have had him well educated and fit for anything. However, the opportunity is lost, the best must be made of it, and should he be a good boy, he may still fetch up what is lost. I assure you the misfortunes of my family often cost me many a bitter pang, and if it was not for the hopes of being able some day or other to be of service to you and family, I would not care how soon I made my exit. I am only a poor soldier ; with my sword I must defend myself, and I am proud to say I have often drawn it in the defence of my country, and as yet, thank God, it is untarnished. I have no fears that, while I live, it will be ever so. I have as bright a prospect as most men in my profession—my brother the same. My brother was with General Hill's Division in this last fight in the Alentejo. He took a French captain and dismounted him ; he also took from him a handsome sword. We have been very actively employed all the winter so far. In the mountains near Ciudad Rodrigo it is as cold as in England. After being roasted all the summer, it nips one to pieces to be out in this weather. I have had the ague very severely, but I am now better. I pray for the warm weather, which we all do. Our officers and men have in general been sickly, but they are coming round wonderfully. We shall have warm work in the spring, I think. It is wonderful to see the gallantry displayed on all occasions by a British soldier.

My best respects to my uncle and aunt. I hope they are well. I feel much obliged to my aunt for her kindness to my family, and should I ever return to England, I hope to have the pleasure

1811 of thanking her in person.   Let me know if you hear
anything of poor John.   I am very anxious.   I hope
Charles is better.   For God's sake, mind he is not
ruined by a pack of d——d quacks ; let some regular
practitioner see him.   I must request you will take
care of his education as well as Betsy's.   I shall
charge my mother with neglect if this most
essential point is omitted.   My dear Ann, I hope,
is well and attentive to my mother.   I have a lot of
trinkets for her if I can find means of sending them.
Some days back I sent a Spaniard into Ciudad
Rodrigo to buy some buttons (curious silver ones).
I shall preserve them for Ann.

On the receipt of this note, write immediately and
let me know when I am to expect Joseph.

I remain, with my love to my dear mother and
family, your affectionate son,

GEO. SIMMONS,
Lt., 95th or Rifle Regiment.

CAMPAIGN OF 1812

The commencement of the year 1812 found the British army in the Peninsula much scattered by reason of the difficulties of provisioning it.

Soult, operating in Andaluçia, had towards the close of 1811 detached a force to besiege Tarifa, and at the end of January attempted to storm it, but was repulsed with heavy loss and retired on Cadiz.

Napoleon at this time was concentrating all his energies on his disastrous attempt to subjugate Russia, and in order to augment his forces in that country, had recalled some 60,000 of his best troops from Spain. It was at this juncture that Wellington, taking advantage of the disorganised state of the French forces in the Peninsula, which, in addition to being divided into three separate armies, were widely distributed in order to obtain supplies, decided on a winter campaign, and unexpectedly invested the strong fortress of Ciudad Rodrigo.

After a siege of only twelve days, pushed forward with extraordinary vigour, with the object of obtaining possession of the place before Marmont could assemble a sufficient force to render assistance to the besieged garrison, Ciudad Rodrigo was stormed. In this desperate undertaking Generals Craufurd and Mackinnon, fifty officers, and 650 men fell in the breaches. The French loss was only 300.

Marmont, having failed in his attempt to collect sufficient forces to raise the siege, on hearing of the fall of the place, retired on Salamanca.

Wellington now directed his attention on Badajoz, so as to impede the junction of Soult and Massena, and marching rapidly thither, laid siege to it. Soult, confident in the strength

1812 of the place, set to work to collect a force sufficient to attack the Allies, but before he could do this, Badajoz was stormed. The losses of the assailants in this terrible assault were very great; sixty officers and over 700 men were killed, and the total number of killed and wounded during the siege was 3500.

Having thus made himself master of Badajoz, Wellington contemplated driving Soult out of Andaluçia, but was met by so many difficulties, political as well as military, that he abandoned this scheme, and decided to operate against Marmont in Estremadura and Leon. Having surprised and captured the fortress of Almaraz, he advanced to the Tormes and laid siege to the forts covering the bridge of Salamanca. Marmont shortly appeared at the head of a strong force and endeavoured to succour the forts, but without success, and upon their being stormed by the British, he fell back to the line of the Douro near Tordesillas, Wellington following him as far as Rueda.

Massena, having received some reinforcements, crossed the Douro and sought to turn Wellington's right flank. Now ensued the remarkable manœuvring on both sides which, after the sharp combats of Castrejon and the Guareña, culminated in the battle of Salamanca. After this disaster to the French arms, Massena retired on Burgos, and King Joseph, who, too late, had come to aid Marmont, returned to Madrid. Clausel fell back through Valladolid, which town Wellington occupied, thus separating Marmont from King Joseph. The Allies now advanced on Madrid, which the King quitted in haste, and ordered Soult to abandon Andaluçia and to join him at Valencia.

The Allies occupied Madrid, and remained there for some months, but Clausel having reorganised his forces and reoccupied Valladolid, Wellington advanced against him.

Clausel fell back on Burgos, followed by the Allies. No less than five assaults were made on this fortress, but without success. Meanwhile the French received reinforcements, and eventually the siege of Burgos had to be raised, and Wellington was forced to retreat on Madrid, several sharp combats taking place on the way thither.

King Joseph, with Soult and Jourdan, now moved on Madrid, and the French force being thus overwhelmingly

strong, Wellington evacuated the capital and fell back 200 1812
miles to the line of the Tormes, followed by Soult and
Jourdan.   His position there being turned by Soult, he resumed
his retreat on Rodrigo, and after a sharp combat on the
Huebra, reached that place in November, and went into winter
quarters.

CHAPTER IX

Journal—4th January–30th July 1812

The Light Division advances on Ciudad Rodrigo and fords the
Agueda—Storming of Fort San Francisco—Commencement
of the siege of Ciudad Rodrigo—The convents of Santa
Cruz and San Francisco captured—Work in the advanced
saps—Storming of Ciudad Rodrigo—Simmons is told off for
one of the ladder parties—Rencontre with General Craufurd
—The Forlorn Hope and storming parties advance and carry
the breaches—The Rifles bivouac on the ramparts—Heavy
losses of the Grenadiers of the 45th and 94th Regiments—
Effects of the explosion of the magazine—Death of
Lieutenant Uniacke—General Craufurd dies of his wounds
—The Light Division marches back into Portugal—
Advances again on Badajoz—Ground broken before Fort
Picurina—Sortie of the French—Their cavalry enter the
British camp—Storming of Fort Picurina—Lieutenant Stokes
of the Rifles, the first man in—The British entrench themselves in the work under a heavy fire from the French—
Batteries in Badajoz—Duty in the trenches—Simmons
with forty good shots pick off the French artillerymen and
silence the guns—A French officer endeavours to return the
compliment, but is "put out of that" by a Rifle Man—
Accident to Simmons—Storming of Badajoz—Major O'Hare
of the Rifles in command of the storming party—Desperate
fighting at the breaches—The Light Division unable to
enter—Carnage in the ditch—The Light Division ordered
to withdraw—The 3rd Division escalade the castle—Lord
Wellington orders the Light Division to renew their attack—

The town occupied—Simmons enters the house of the French
Quartermaster-General and finds a sketch-map of the breaches
showing the expected British lines of advance—At day-
break visits the breaches—The *chevaux de frise* and
obstacles created by the French—Finds the body of Major
O'Hare—"*A Lieutenant-Colonel, or cold meat in a few hours*"
—Heavy losses of the Rifles and of the Light Division—
Brother Maud comes to see if he is alive—The soldiers
plunder the town—The Light Division marches towards
Salamanca—Fighting near Salamanca—The British enter
the town—Simmons' views of the priests and monks—
March towards the Douro—Gets a good quarter at
Nava del Rey—The armies on opposite banks of the
Douro—Lord Wellington reconnoitres the French, and
nearly falls into the hands of their cavalry—The British
army retires, closely followed by the French—The marches
previous to the battle—Skirmish on the Guareña—The
French endeavour to turn the British left, but are checked
by the 27th and 40th Regiments—An unlucky young
Rifle Man—Marmont steals a march on Wellington—The
British army fords the Tormes—Great thunderstorm—Battle
of Salamanca—Simmons catches a partridge during the
fight—Pursuit after Salamanca—Brilliant charge of the
German Heavy Cavalry under General Bock—The Hussar
officer and his brother—Visits the grave of General Férey
and finds the Spaniards have exhumed him—The Rifle Men
bury the body again.

Journal—4th January–30th July 1812

A general movement of the troops took place.
1st Division marched to Gallegos and Espeja; 4th
Division crossed the Agueda and occupied San Felices;
3rd Division occupied Martiago and Zamarra;
Light Division entered Pastores, La Encina, and
El Bodon. The latter place I marched to. A stormy,
cold, incessant rain during the day. The Agueda
much swollen. Forded it nearly up to the shoulders.

1812 The men obliged to put their pouches upon their knapsacks and lay hold of each other to prevent being forced down with the current. Some time exposed before there was any possibility of getting lodged. Officers, men, and all huddled together. Got our men better regulated and had three houses for the company.

Jan. 8th Several regiments had been ordered to prepare gabions and fascines, which we were aware could only be for the siege. The Light Division was ordered to move before day, and crossed the Agueda at a ford above the convent of La Caridad. Our march was conducted out of the range of shot from the town to the north side, and behind a hill in the vicinity of San Francisco. A redoubt was established here. We halted. Several French officers made their appearance, and politely took off their hats and spoke to us. They of course were very anxious to know what all this meant.

Colonel Colborne, with 360 men from the 43rd, 52nd, and 95th (Rifle Men) stormed the fort of San Francisco after dark. Three pieces of cannon, two captains, and forty-eight men were made prisoners, besides what fell by the bayonet in the assault.

9th Began immediately to break ground, and before morning dawned we had commenced our first parallel and completely covered ourselves. The enemy kept up a most tremendous fire all night. I became perfectly familiar with the difference of sound between the two missiles, shot and shell, long before day. Returned to our quarters, and the 1st Division relieved us in the trenches.

12th Marched back and resumed our work in the

trenches. The weather was keen and it froze sharply. 1812
Our poor fellows had to cross the river nearly up to
their shoulders, and remain in this wet state until they
returned to their quarters, some working and some
covering the working parties by firing upon the works
of this town ; others were ordered to get as close as
possible and dig holes sufficiently deep to cover themselves, and take deliberate aim at the enemy's
embrasures, which a good marksman would easily do
by observing the flashes of their cannon, although it
was dark.   Jan.

Returned to quarters at El Bodon.   13th

Twenty-two pieces of British cannon opened most 14th
musically upon the town. *Johnny* has hitherto had
it all his own way in administering to the comfort
of many, and most suddenly and unexpectedly sent
them, I trust, to another and better world. For
on this little spot all the fiercer passions of the
human heart are busy in the breasts of each
individual of both parties, investing and invested.
Moralising will not do now ; death or glory, a golden
chain or a wooden leg, " England expects every man
will do his duty." These are the only feelings that can
make the scene of death and destruction palatable to a
Christian : King, Church, and Country to fight for.

Marched and again entered the trenches. The 16th
enemy had got the range to such a nicety that their
shells were literally dropped into our works.

The convent of Santa Cruz was taken by surprise by
General Graham with the King's German Legion on
the night of the 13th ; thus on the night of the 14th the
convent of San Francisco and Santa Clara and suburbs
were all in our hands. I had charge of a party to

1812 carry earth in gabions, and plant them upon the advanced saps in places where the ground was an entire rock and could not be penetrated. The enemy fired grape, and consequently numbers fell to rise no more from the effects of it. I ran the gauntlet here several times, and brought gabions of earth, always leaving some of my poor fellows behind, when I returned for more, and glad enough I was when the Engineer said " We have now sufficient."

Jan.
17th   Returned to quarters in a whole skin.

STORMING OF CIUDAD RODRIGO

19th   Marched and passed the ford as before. Halted for one hour near the convent of La Caridad, then moved forward and halted behind the convent of San Francisco with the 3rd Division. We were now informed that two breaches in the wall had been effected, and that when the arrangements were made, we should storm the town. I must observe here that I was so anxious to be speedily employed that when Lieutenant Smith, Brigade-Major, came to a fire near which I was standing and said, " One of you must come and take charge of some ladders if required," at the impulse of the moment I took with me the men required, and followed him to the Engineers' camp, where the ladders were handed to me. I marched with them to General Craufurd, who was with the advance. He attacked me in a most ungracious manner. " Why did you bring these short ladders?" " Because I was ordered by the Engineer to do so, General." " Go back, sir, and get others; I am astonished at such stupidity." Of course I went back, but was sadly crestfallen. This is what I deserved for over-zeal. I returned with the 1812 ladders. A Portuguese captain and his company were waiting for something to do, so I said, "Here, my brave fellows, take these ladders," and handed them over with every necessary instruction for the good of the service. I then instantly returned to the company I belonged to, which was posted at the head of the column ready to proceed. The 3rd Division moved to attack the right breach, and the Light Division the left or small breach. The Forlorn Hope and storming parties moved on at about seven o'clock, and the head of the column followed close behind. A tremendous fire was opened upon us, and as our column was entering the ditch an expense magazine on the ramparts near the large breach blew up and ignited a number of live shells, which also exploded and paid no sort of difference to friend or foe. The night was brilliantly illuminated for some moments, and everything was made visible. Then as suddenly came utter darkness, except for the flashes from cannon and muskets, which threw a momentary glare around.

The breaches were made in the curtain, before which a traverse was fixed in the ditch to protect and strengthen it. In my hurry, after descending into the ditch, I mistook the traverse for the top of the breach, and as the ladders were laid against it, I ascended as well as many others, and soon found our mistake. We crossed it, and slid down directly opposite the breach, which was soon carried. The town was entered by armed men at every point, and in the dark there were many mistakes made by men shooting their friends instead of their enemies. The prisoners were collected and huddled together upon the ramparts

1812 like so many sheep, and there guarded until daylight. My battalion formed up upon the ramparts and made fires, as the night was a clear and frosty one. Some men brought me wine, ham, and eggs. I soon made a hearty meal, and washed it down with some good French Burgundy, putting my feet to the fire, and enjoyed as calm a sleep as I ever did in my life before, for three or four hours.

Jan. 20th At daylight I walked round the ramparts and found numbers slaughtered. The 94th and 45th suffered sadly, particularly their Grenadiers, who literally had fallen in line with each other upon the large breach. The explosion I mentioned had killed numbers more of the French ·than of the English ; they were mangled in a most shocking manner ; headless trunks, and others torn into masses of lacerated parts, which it was hard to fancy ever belonged to human beings. General M'Kinnon, who commanded a Brigade in the 3rd Division, was blown up and his body sadly mutilated, but being a very tall man, it was not difficult to make him out. A circumstance which probably saved me from being blown up with a friend of mine, Lieutenant Uniacke, was, when we got into the ditch together he observed, " This is the way." In the bustle I said, " Impossible. Here are the ladders. I shall go up them," fancying my Portuguese friend had placed them right, so that ultimately the ladders served me. Poor Uniacke got round the corner just in time enough to get scorched from head to foot in a frightful manner, and died a few hours after in great agony. General Craufurd, who commanded the Light Division, was mortally wounded, General Vandeleur, Colonel Colborne, and

Major Napier were badly wounded ; also Lieutenants 1812
Cox, Hamilton, and Bedell.

About nine o'clock in the morning we marched from
that part of the rampart where we had been resting
for so many hours, seated before good fires. We
passed out of the town and then halted. The French
prisoners followed, guarded. We had scarcely left
the gate when a tremendous explosion took place,
which blew up numbers of Frenchmen, and also some
Englishmen. Directly under the place we had so
recently left were deposited several barrels of gun-
powder, which had taken fire from some cause or
other. That face of the rampart was a pile of ruins
in one instant. I really thought this was a kind act
of the Almighty towards us.

We marched back to our cantonments and met part
of the 5th Division upon the road coming to Ciudad
Rodrigo to bury the dead and put the works in
order, as the men who have stormed a town are
seldom fit for anything but vice and irregularity for
some time afterwards, if left within its walls. The
soldiers were laden with all sorts of things, and
looked like a moving rag-fair. Some, liking their
bellies better, had their swords fixed, and stuck upon
them large junks of corned beef, ham, pork, etc.
I was glad to get back to my peaceable habitation. The
Governor, 78 officers, and 1700 prisoners were taken,
besides the killed and wounded. General Craufurd
was buried at the foot of the little breach with
military honours by the Light Division.

The French army under Marshal Marmont had
no idea we should be able to take Rodrigo from them
so quickly. The enemy moved forward to ascertain

1812 the fact, and finding the news too true, left us in quiet possession of it.

Jan. 31st   Marched to Fuenteguinaldo.

Feb. 26th   The works of Ciudad Rodrigo having been completely put in order, and a garrison of Spaniards having entered it, the army was ordered to proceed towards Estremadura. Marched to Alfayates in Portugal.

27th   Val Morisco.

28th   Passed through the town of Sortelho, situated most romantically amongst stupendous and rugged mountains and surrounded by an old Moorish wall. It is nearly at the foot of the Sierra da Estrella. Halted at Castelhera.

29th   Marched to Capena.

Mar. 1st   Marched to Alpedrinha.

2nd   Alcainz.

3rd   Castello Branco, and under very different feelings than when I left it before. If I had obeyed the orders of the Commandant, I should not have been at Rodrigo.

4th   Halted.

5th   Marched to Sarnadas.

6th   Marched to Niza, crossing the Tagus at the bridge of boats over it, and through the pass of Villa Velha.

7th   Castello de Vide and Esuesa.

8th   Visited the town of Marvão, surrounded by a wall in good preservation, and situated upon a high mountain. It has a few guns mounted upon the ramparts. It ought to be almost impregnable, if in good hands, when besieged.

14th   I had been very unwell, and had kept my bed for some days. Suddenly this morning, the order to march came ; my servant brought me the news. I instantly 1812 jumped out of bed and dressed myself. Dr. Burke, our surgeon, saw me mounting my horse. " What, sir, are you mad ? You cannot go in your present state with the Division. I have got a car to send you away with the sick." I thanked him, but observed, " I am determined to try." I was exceedingly ill, but during the march I was violently attacked with vomiting, and in a very debilitated state got into a billet with my captain at Portalegre upon a *padre* (clergyman), who gave me some chocolate and a comfortable bed, and I was somewhat better the following morning and went with the Division to March Arronches. 15th

Marched to Elvas and found myself getting better. 16th

Marched to the camp before Badajoz. The 3rd and 17th 4th Divisions were upon the ground. Some time after dark, broke ground before Fort Picurina and the town.

On piquet with the company near an old ruin 18th some little distance from the town, and from which we had a good view of the working parties' operations in the trenches.

Weather for some days back cold and rainy. 19th The enemy collected a body of horse and foot and made a sortie upon our works. They had a number of men to take away our tools and fill up the trenches. They drew back very soon. At the moment of the attack our different parties were relieving, and the weather being very dull, accompanied with a drizzling rain, the enemy got very close before they were observed. The enemy's cavalry dashed through our camp, and at the spot where the Engineers

15

1812 were engaged in carrying on the work for the siege, captured an officer, and a Dragoon tried to drag him away with him. Our people in the camp at the moment fancied they were the Portuguese cavalry, but soon were undeceived, and a number took up arms and ran forward to attack them. They made their way back as rapidly as they had moved forward. The officer, Colonel Seres, who commanded the sortie, died of his wounds in the town.

March   About twelve o'clock A.M. our first battery opened 25th and played handsomely upon Fort Picurina.

STORMING OF FORT PICURINA

26th   A storming party was ordered a little after dark, and part of our working party, under Lieutenant Stokes, was ordered to carry the ladders to mount the walls. He was, after placing the ladders, the first in the place. This fort was very strong, and the French officer had not the least idea we could take it. The enemy fought resolutely, but were soon made prisoners (those who remained alive when the officer sur-rendered). When it fell, we commenced breaking ground in front. I knew well, as soon as the enemy were aware of the place being in our possession, that they would commence a fire of grape, so that I made my men work hard to cover themselves. About midnight a most furious fire of shot, shell, and grape went over us, and did us no harm. Before daylight our trench was perfect. Curiosity led me to see the fort and obstacles the men who stormed it had to encounter. Upon the parapet were pointed palisades, and live shells all round, ready to be lighted and

thrown into the ditch. There were also numbers of 1812
other shells and powder for the purpose of injuring
the assailants, but the determined and spirited manner
in which the men stormed the work prevented the
enemy from doing the mischief they had premeditated.

Regularly upon working or covering parties in March
the trenches every twenty-four hours. Our batteries 30th
were soon formed, and our artillery began to play
upon the wall with great effect.

I was with a party of men behind the advanced April
sap, and had an opportunity of doing some mischief. 4th
Three or four heavy cannon that the enemy were
working were doing frightful execution amongst our
artillerymen in their advanced batteries. I selected
several good shots and fired into the embrasures.
In half an hour I found the guns did not go off so
frequently as before I commenced this practice, and
soon after, gabions were stuffed into each em-
brasure to prevent our rifle balls from entering.
They then withdrew them to fire, which was my
signal for firing steadily at the embrasures. The
gabions were replaced without firing the shot. I was
so delighted with the good practice I was making
against *Johnny* that I kept it up from daylight till
dark with forty as prime fellows as ever pulled trigger.
These guns were literally silenced. A French officer
(I suppose a marksman), who hid himself in some long
grass, first placed his cocked hat some little distance
from him for us to fire at. Several of his men handed
him loaded muskets in order that he might fire more
frequently. I was leaning half over the trench watching his movements. I observed his head, and being
exceedingly anxious that the man who was going to

1812 fire should see him, I directed him to lay his rifle over my left shoulder as a more elevated rest for him. He fired. Through my eagerness, I had entirely overlooked his pan, so that it was in close contact with my left ear ; and a pretty example it made of it and the side of my head, which was singed and the ear cut and burnt. The poor fellow was very sorry for the accident. We soon put the Frenchman out of that. He left his cocked hat, which remained until dark, so that we had either killed or wounded him. My friends in camp joked me a good deal the next morning, observing, " Pray, what's the matter with your ear ? How did the injury happen ? " and so on.

Weather for some days good.

STORMING OF BADAJOZ

April 6th The Engineers now proclaimed the breaches practicable. Arrangements were made to storm the town. My old captain, Major O'Hare, was to lead the storming party. I wanted to go with him, but those senior demanded it as their right. The two Brigades of the Light Division fell in and moved on a little after dark, preceded by the Forlorn Hope and storming parties to the glacis. The 4th Division also were to storm the breaches with us, the 3rd to escalade the castle, and the 5th Division to attack Fort Pardeleras and escalade the town on that side. Our storming party was soon hotly engaged. Our columns moved on under a most dreadful fire of grape that mowed down our men like grass. We tore down the palisading and got upon the glacis. The havoc now became dreadful. My captain

(Gray) was shot in the mouth. Eight or 1812 ten officers, and men innumerable, fell to rise no more. Ladders were resting against the counterscarp from within the ditch. Down these we hurried, and as fast as we got down rushed forward to the breaches, where a most frightful scene of carnage was going on. Fifty times they were stormed, and as often without effect, the French cannon sweeping the ditches with a most destructive fire. Lights were thrown amongst us from the town that burnt most brilliantly, and made us easier to be shot at. In this way we remained for a considerable time. I was in a sort of frenzy stamping one of these lights out when an officer laid hold of me, saying, "Leave it, or when the light goes out your feet will be blown to pieces, as there is a live shell connected with it." The ditch now, from the place where we entered to near the top of the breaches, was covered with dead and dying soldiers. If a man fell wounded, ten to one that he ever rose again, for the volleys of musketry and grape shot that were incessantly poured amongst us made our situation too horrid for description. I had seen some fighting, but nothing like this. We remained passively here to be slaughtered, as we could do the besieged little injury from the ditch. We were ordered to leave the ditch and move away from the works. The Light Division formed up on the plain at some distance from the town. Here we observed the 3rd Division assailing the castle and escalading its walls.

In consequence of the breaches being so furiously attacked, the French Governor, Phillipon, drew nearly the whole of the garrison to defend them, or the 3rd

Division must have suffered infinitely more, as the walls were very high and the place difficult to enter.

The castle being taken, the town was commanded. A heavy gun was dragged to the gate connected with the town and fired through it, which blew it open. The enemy now finding the castle in our possession, and also finding the British entering another part of the town by escalade, were obliged to oppose them with a greater part of their force. I was lying upon the grass by my comrades, having the most gloomy thoughts of the termination of this sad affair, when a staff officer rode up and said, "Lord Wellington orders the Light Division to return immediately and attack the breaches." We moved back to this bloody work as if nothing had happened. Never were braver men congregated together for such a purpose. We entered the ditches, and passed over the bodies of our brave fellows who had fallen and dashed forward to the breaches. Only a few random shots were now fired, and we entered without opposition. Firing was now going on in several parts of the town, and we were not long in chiming in with the rest of them. The prisoners were secured and the place was given up to be plundered and pillaged. I am sorry to say our soldiers were now become nearly as great adepts as any Continental soldiers in this work of destruction.

I went into a genteel house. The Spaniard told me the French Quartermaster-General had lived with him. He showed me the officer's room. I found a bottle of wine and two glasses upon the table. There was a piece of paper upon which he had made a rough sketch of the two breaches, and had represented the

way our columns would move to the attack. He also 1812
had marked where the ladders would be placed to avoid
some water in the ditch, and which latter was the only
place where their shot could not have effect. I suppose
the water had been turned into the ditch for this purpose. The Spaniard said that the two officers went out
in great alarm. I sat down and drank the bottle of
wine and got some eggs and bacon fried. When the
day dawned I went to see the breaches. I found a
breast-work of sand-bags upon them, constructed for
the enemy to fire over a strong *chevaux de frise*.
Placed in front and across the breaches here and there
were large beams studded with long spikes irregularly
thrown about to impede our advance. Behind these
breast-works the ground was cut and intersected with
deep trenches and covered with planks, to enable the
enemy to get to the breaches and ramparts. In the
bottom of these trenches were placed swords and
bayonets fixed upon pieces of wood to wound those
who fell upon them. Holes were made in the ramparts
big enough for a man to sit in, with a deep groove to
lay his musket in and fire. In short, the Governor
had done everything in his power to make the place
as defensible as possible, and displayed a great deal of
ability and judgment in his masterly arrangements.
The ramparts were lined with live shells and barrels
of powder, cart wheels, and lumps of wood and iron,
ready to be thrown into the ditch.

I saw my poor friend Major O'Hare lying dead
upon the breach. Two or three musket balls had
passed through his breast. A gallant fellow, Sergeant
Flemming, was also dead by his side, a man who had
always been with him. I called to remembrance poor

1812 O'Hare's last words just before he marched off to lead the advance.   He shook me by the hand saying, "*A Lieutenant-Colonel or cold meat in a few hours.*" I was now gazing upon his body lying stretched and naked amongst thousands more.   Our loss was very severe, but principally fell upon the young officers. Capt. Diggle, Lieuts. Hovenden, Cary, Stokes, Allix, Croudace, killed.   Lieut. Freer (wounded in the trenches upon the day of the sortie), Capts. Crampton, Balvaird, M'Diarmid, wounded.   Lieuts. Manners, Johnstone, MacDonnel, Macpherson, Stewart, Foster, Gardiner, Fitzmaurice, and Farmer wounded (two died a few days after).   The 43rd and 52nd Light Infantry lost about the same number as ourselves.   I am only astonished how any one escaped, but I was not touched in any part of me. I went away from the town to the camp as soon as possible.   The 2nd Division was stationed near Talavera Real, about three leagues from Badajoz, to watch the movements of Soult, who was collecting an army to attempt to raise the siege of Badajoz.   My two brothers were with that Division, and they were looking towards Badajoz from their encampment with great anxiety, as they distinctly heard the continued peals of cannon, and saw the sky over the town illuminated from time to time, which gave them a pretty good idea that rough work was going on there.   I had only just got into my tent and thrown myself down upon my blanket when my brother Maud entered. I sprang upon my legs and seized him by the hand. He was so affected that he was obliged to sit down. He burst into tears.   I observed, " Why, this is woman's work.   My brave fellow, you ought to laugh. I am sound and untouched." He observed, 1812 " I entered your encampment with an aching heart. I was some time before I durst ask for you. At last I summoned up resolution to do so, and asked a man, who told me you were killed, ' but that is his tent,' he added. I was so agitated that I rushed towards it scarcely knowing what I did, when you jumped up and shook hands with me." He lay down for some time to compose himself. In the afternoon I walked over to Talavera Real and met my brother Joseph. We spent a pleasant day together.

I returned to camp and found the soldiers in April possession of all sorts of things brought from the 8th town, and crowds of country people bartering with them for clothes and other articles. These two sieges had demoralised the men very much, and coercion was necessary on many occasions (with men that had never behaved ill before), and obliged to be resorted to. The men were made to throw away a quantity of things, and to prevent them secreting any of the articles, their packs were examined, and the plunder that had not been made away with was collected into heaps and burnt. A garrison of Spaniards were put into Badajoz and the place was put in order. Marched to Campo Mayor. 12th

Marched in front of Arronches. Bivouacked in a wood. 13th

Marched to Portalegre, 14th to Niza, 15th to Sarnadas, 16th to Castello Branco, 17th halted, 18th to Escalos de Cima and Louza, 19th halted.

Informed by the peasantry that the enemy was in 20th force at Sabugal and San Miguel d'Acha.

Marched to Penamacor, 22nd to Quintas de 21st

1812 San Bartolomé, 23rd to Alfayates. Bivouacked in front.

April 24th Marched and bivouacked near Castillejo on the Azava.

25th Halted in bivouac. My horse, which had been for some days ill, died—a sad loss to a poor soldier in such hard times.

May 6th Marched to Campillo.

27th Reviewed by Lord Wellington with the rest of the Division between Fuenteguinaldo and El Bodon. He told us we *looked well and in good fighting order.* Our men's clothing was covered with patches of all colours, and many of the officers' dresses were in little better plight.

June 6th Marched to El Bodon.

11th Marched in front of Ciudad Rodrigo and bivouacked in a wood.

12th Visited the town. The Light Division collected here, and with the rest of the army on the 13th made a forward movement near Alba de Yeltes. Bivouacked in a wood upon the river Yeltes, a small stream.

14th Marched and bivouacked near Sanchobueno.

15th Marched and bivouacked near Matilla.

16th Marched a few miles in the direction of Salamanca.

17th Marched and forded the Rio Tormes above the town, bivouacked in a wood for the night. General Hill remained with the 2nd Division on the Alentejo frontier, as a check upon Marshal Soult's army, which was in Andalucia. In May, General Hill, with his Division, took two forts near Almaraz, on the Tagus, by storm, viz. Fort Napoleon and Fort Ragusa, and some works of minor importance. My two brothers were in these affairs.

The enemy retired from Salamanca as the British 1812 army approached, merely skirmishing occasionally with our Dragoons as they made a forward movement. But a fort and two strong redoubts were constructed, which commanded the bridge and were occupied by a body of the enemy. They were formed out of two convents, and were placed in the heart of the town. The 6th Division was ordered to invest them, and it was droll enough to see numbers of officers belonging to regiments in bivouac coming into the town for curiosity, to see how the investment went on. I, with many others, went into a belfry which quite commanded the works. The enemy fired a shot at the church, and said if people were allowed to go into the belfry they would blow it down.

Was in bivouac near Rio Seco, the whole army in June position, and the French under Marshal Marmont 18th concentrating his force in front of us. Very much exposed to the sun's rays and very little shade ; for miles all round scarcely a tree of any consequence to be seen. This was directly opposite in appearance to the country we had passed through between Rodrigo and Salamanca, which was a perfect picture of nature as portrayed in her loveliest attire ; woods, with rich and fertile meadows and rills intersecting them, having water of the clearest kind, and the most inviting shade on their banks. There is nothing in life half so pleasant to the tired soldier after marching all day under a moderate load for a good-sized donkey to find these comforts at the end of his journey.

Moved to the heights of Monte Rubio near the 19th village of La Lengua.

1812
June
23rd   The forts and redoubts were stormed, and the parties sent to perform this business were repulsed. General Bowes killed. The convent connected with the principal fort was set on fire with red-hot shot thrown into it and the places soon after surrendered.

24th   The enemy advanced some Dragoons on the left bank of the Tormes, and a skirmish took place with some of our Dragoons.

25th   The company I belonged to on piquet.

27th   The fort surrendered. I went into the town, and could not help feeling great pleasure that these poor people had a release from the French garrison, which the most sanguine of them fancied would never happen. They expressed their joy in a most frantic manner and praised their deliverers, as they called the English, and expressed their abhorrence of the French officers and soldiery. To amuse myself, I visited the cathedral, which is a handsome building, and possesses a good organ of large dimensions. This place is filled with churches, monasteries, and nunneries, that gives it a very priest-ridden appearance, and makes one sympathise with the unfortunate people of such a country who are, partly by coercion, but more through the tenets imbibed from their earliest years, the dupes of superstition and bigotry. They fancy it necessary towards their eternal salvation to aid in supporting these fat-sided and sleek-faced rascals, who, under the pretended semblance of soul-savers, congregate in large bodies, gourmandising the richest viands and drinking the best wine, and have frequently been known to live in every species of vice and idleness. Such men are decidedly drones in the industrious hive. I have often seen the poor

peasant handcuffed and taken from his little field and 1812
from the bosom of his family (probably in him they
lost their only support), called a *volunteer*, and
entered upon the book of a regiment. If he deserted
and was taken again, in all probability he would be
shot. Meanwhile the stoutest men in the country,
brought up in the service of the Church, were allowed
to live in idleness, although the country was filled
with their enemies, who were abusing the people and
oppressing them in the most flagitious manner, burning their towns for amusement—in fact, committing
every species of atrocity.

The army moved forward towards the Douro. June
As our movements had been confined between the 28th
northern frontier of Portugal and the banks of the
Guadiana for so long a time, it gave us great delight
to be entering the very heart of Spain to offer battle
to the French army ; each day seeing towns and
villages we had never entered before. Marched to
Castellanos de Moriscos and bivouacked.

Marched to Parada de Rubiales and bivouacked.   29th
Marched to Castrillo and bivouacked.   30th
Marched through Alaejos to Nava del Rey, in July
the town with the Division also. This was a very well 1st
built town with a handsome church. I had a good
billet and slept upon a comfortable mattress, which was
a luxury I had not had for many a day. My usual bed
was two blankets stitched together and made into the
shape of a sack, into which I crawled, and if I rolled
about, the clothes never left me until I took a fancy
to crawl out again ; my pillow a good sod and a
smooth stone, and if, before I lay down, I could
obtain some wild lavender, which generally was in

1812 plenty, I then had a splendid bed, exhaling the most agreeable perfumes, with the canopy of heaven over one's head.   This, to an astronomer, would have afforded an hour's amusement before he went to sleep, but as I am not a character of that description, I generally fell asleep, and that right soundly too.   Often, before daylight, I have been well soused with rain with many thousands more in the same predicament, and in spite of the elements, have not been much disturbed.   It is astonishing what habit will produce in a man of strong and robust health.

July   Marched to Rueda, and halted close to it ; made a
2nd lodgment in a shed with the officers of the company, horses, mules, servants, etc.   The country round abounds in corn and wine.   The latter is kept under ground in vast excavated cellars, with high chimneys above ground to ventilate them.   The casks containing this wine, which is white, and of a pleasant and agreeably sharp flavour, are of immense magnitude, and must have been introduced piece-meal and then afterwards formed ; they contain many thousand gallons.   The enemy retired before our advanced guard entered.

3rd   The Division moved opposite Tordesillas, upon the left bank of the Douro, the French army being in large force upon its right bank and in possession of the town.   This movement was supposed to be a feint.   Retired back to Rueda in the evening and bivouacked.

16th   Marched from the place about 9 P.M. and halted behind Castrejon.

18th   The enemy advanced at daylight in great force.

Lord Wellington reconnoitred the enemy's move- 1812
ments. Some French Dragoons dashed forward and,
being numerous, rather intimidated the small escort
with his Lordship. Marshal Beresford and some of
the staff soon rallied them, and they charged the
advanced men of the enemy and checked their
progress. The enemy had crossed the Douro by a
ford so rapidly that our piquets were obliged to retire
after exchanging a few shots. A partial cannonade
commenced upon our encampment. The whole
British army were in full retreat, the country
all round was one vast plain, and the soldiers were
moving across it in column of companies at quarter
distance, ready by regiments to form square if the
enemy's cavalry should charge ; the march was taken
up literally as coolly as if it had been a field day,
taking distant points to march upon, and avoiding the
villages in order not to lose time by passing through
them. Upon our right as we then faced, and
frequently not more than five hundred yards distant
from us, was a dense mass of Frenchmen moving in
the same order, horse, foot, and artillery. It was
quite ridiculous to see two hostile armies so close
without coming to blows, but the two chiefs were
trying to out-manœuvre each other the sequel will
show who succeeded.

Our brigade of Horse Artillery fired a few rounds
at the enemy. Some cavalry made a dash at them,
and for a moment had possession of their guns. In
passing a small river named the Guareña in order to get
possession of some heights that both armies were moving towards as the immediate bone of contention, the
enemy began to cannonade our columns, and towards

1812 evening, in the pursuit of the French Marshal's favourite object during this day to turn our left, they pressed too hard upon that part of our line.   Lord Wellington directed the 27th and 40th British Regiments to receive their attack, and then charge them, which was done handsomely, and their career terminated for the night, leaving us upon the high ground we wished to occupy.   My servant brought up my baggage, but a fine young mule, with a canteen and a variety of comforts that could not be replaced in a hurry, was lost to me for ever.   A stallion had broken my mule's thigh on the line of march.   There was no time to lose, so the man was obliged to unloose the halter from the one that he led and move on.   This

July was a sad grievance.

19th   Lord Wellington reconnoitred the enemy, and found the French in great force and seemingly upon the move.   For annoyance, the enemy threw a few shot and shell at our columns.   One shot knocked off the head of a Rifle Man who had just joined us for the first time.   Things of this kind seem droll.   Why this poor fellow's head should have been singled out amongst many thousand others and given the preference to, I cannot say.   Remained here for the night.

20th   At daylight the enemy was entirely gone.   Lord Wellington found that Marmont had marched to his right with great rapidity.   Our army was immediately upon the march.   Halted near a village of which I do not know the name.

21st   Marched with the dawn and continued till 2 P.M. Halted near Villamorisco.   A little before dark forded the river Tormes above Salamanca.   The river was very much swollen from the rain, which 1812 made it very deep. Everybody got wet up to near their shoulders in crossing. Luckily we got over before the rain, which immediately afterwards began to fall in torrents. The night became excessively dark, the whole army groping their way, up to their knees in mud, to the different bivouacs. The lightning became very vivid; some of the flashes ran whizzing along the men's arms in an extraordinary manner and really checked the march for some time most strangely. The thunder was louder than I ever heard before, excepting at Almeida. Numbers of horses belonging to the French and English had broken loose from their pickets from terror, and were galloping about most furiously, and some of them exchanged masters. The rain continued until nearly daylight, when it abated.

BATTLE OF SALAMANCA

At daylight the enemy's columns were moving July rapidly upon our right flank, and from the orders to 22nd send the baggage to the rear as soon as possible, we made up our minds to abandon Salamanca, although we felt sorry for such an event. However, before long our gallant Chief found he had got Marmont into a trap at last, and immediately knew how to take advantage of it. A brisk cannonade commenced on both sides, and about 11 o'clock A.M. the columns on our right moved to the attack.

The high ground and tops or elevated points were crowded with Frenchmen, and in the afternoon these hills, the Arapiles, were lost and won often, but

1812 ultimately the French were completely driven off them. About five o'clock the Light Division were ordered to move forward. We had remained idle spectators, only keeping the right of the French line in check. We soon came in contact with the enemy, and very shortly drove him from the position. An odd circumstance happened ; I saw a partridge running on the ground between the contending lines. I ran, at the impulse of the moment, after it, caught it, and put the bird into my haversack, which afterwards afforded me a savoury supper. The French were routed at all points, and darkness came on, which enabled many to escape that would otherwise have fallen into our hands. Some accidents happened to officers of ours, who were at the heads of our columns, coming in contact unexpectedly in the dark. Marshal Marmont was wounded in the action and was very near falling into our hands. The pursuit was continued through a wooded country until eleven o'clock at night, when we bivouacked near the village of Huerta.

July 23rd Moved forward at daylight after the French. A Brigade of Heavy German cavalry, commanded by Major-General Bock, that had only recently joined our army from England, was in advance of the Light Division, and came up with the French rear-guard. The officer commanding the latter formed three squares. The Germans made a most brilliant and dashing charge at two squares, and succeeded in breaking them, slaughtering numbers. The French had 1500 killed and taken. One of the squares was formed at an elbow in the road, where it wound upward towards much higher ground, and this, very likely, saved it. General Foy, who commanded the

rear-guard, was in this square. We were hurried for- 1812
ward as quickly as possible, but the business was most
effectually done just as we arrived. A great number
of Germans and their horses were dead close to the
squares. I saw a very affecting scene : a Hussar
officer came up to see his brother he had not met
for six years. He found him stretched a lifeless corpse
with his sword grasped and fixed in his saddle ;
his horse, having been killed at the same moment
with its rider, was lying on its side with the legs
stretched out in the attitude of galloping. The poor
fellow threw his arms round his lifeless brother. I
could bear no more, and so moved on, and was again
in pursuit of the enemy, which was the only way
to get quit of gloomy reflections. Bivouacked near a
village.

Marched to Flores de Avila. Passed on this day July
through a large town named Peñaranda. 24th

Halted. 25th

Marched to Aldea Seca. 26th

To Montijo del Viejo. 27th

To Pedrajo de Portello. 28th

To Olmedo, a curious town with the remains of a 29th
Moorish castle. Close to the place was interred the
body of General Férey. He was the officer who
ordered the night attack at Barba del Puerco in 1810.
How extraordinary are the changes produced by war !
Only two years before he had 10,000 veteran soldiers
under his command. He was then actively employed
against us, and now humbled to the dust, and I
standing by his grave gazing at his mutilated carcase.
The Spaniards had dug him up directly after the
French left the town and just before we entered. He

1812 had been buried with great honour, and a canopy of laurels, which had been placed over his grave, was torn down, his body exhumed, and his head severed from it.   It was a noble head, with a fine expressive countenance and a pair of large moustaches.   I could not help observing, "Well, you must have been a brave soldier, although our deadly foe.   You shall be replaced by an enemy where your friends interred you, to rest in peace."   The remains were then in a most decent manner returned to the grave, and the Spaniards made acquainted with the horror and disgust we felt at their inhuman conduct towards a dead soldier.   The laurel was replaced, and we begged it might be allowed to remain, which I have no reason to doubt was complied with.

July   Forded the Duero.   Encamped upon the right bank 30th about six miles from Valladolid.

CHAPTER X

Journal—1st–31st August 1812

The Light Division march on Madrid—Bivouac in the park of
the Escorial—A wild-boar hunt—Visit to the mausoleum
in the Escorial and the public buildings in Madrid—King
Joseph's quarters—Joy of the inhabitants at the arrival of
Lord Wellington's army—The French in the Buen Retiro
surrender—Bull-fight in honour of the British army.

LETTER No. XVI

To his Parents, from Madrid, dated 8th September
1812

Narrates the loss of his horse and mule, and discomfort and hardships resulting therefrom—Unable to remit any more money
in consequence, until after Christmas—Joseph to join the
Rifles—Intends to make him study—Sends his picture to
sister Ann and remittance of £22 to his parents.

Journal—1st September–31st December 1812

In cantonments near Madrid—News of brother Joseph being ill
—Visit to Alcala—News of the failure of the assault on
Burgos—The British army forced to retire from Madrid—

Letter No. XVII

*To his Parents, from Alameda, Spain, dated
12th December 1812*

Letter No. XVIII

*To his Father, from Alameda, Spain, dated
29th December 1812*

Journal—1st–31st August 1812

Marched to Tudela de Duero.

Visited Valladolid, a gloomy, sombre-looking 2nd
town. Returned to camp and marched to Aldea
Mayor. Recrossed the Duero.

Marched early and bivouacked in a wood near 6th
Mata de Cuellar.

Marched and bivouacked on the right bank of 7th
the Piron.

At daylight marched, and passed through Carbon- 8th
nero. The women in this part of Spain had
tremendous pigtails, which produced much joking
amongst the soldiers as they went along. Bivouacked
in a wood near the Rio Eresma.

Marched through Madrona and bivouacked in a 9th
wood near Palacio del Rio Frio.

Marched and bivouacked near Otero and Madrona. 10th
Segovia is about 1¼ leagues from the latter place, which
I could not visit, being on duty.

Passed through the Puerto de Guerto de Guada- 11th
rama—these mountains separate New from Old Castile
—and bivouacked in the park of the Escorial. The
men of the Division had only just got off their knapsacks when two large wild boars were started from
a thicket. They were so alarmed at the sight of
so many men that they literally ran directly amongst
them, and tumbled over numbers of them, but after
receiving a cut or a stab from a hundred bayonets
or swords, they fell covered with wounds, and in
five minutes their carcases were divided and distributed.

1812 Halted.
Aug.
12th   Marched to Las Rozas. Two days back, some
13th Portuguese cavalry and two guns were in advance from
here when the French Dragoons made a dash at the
Portuguese, who did not show fight, but set off. The
guns in consequence fell into the enemy's possession
before any British could be brought up.

14th   The enemy had moved away. Marched to Villa-
verde, three miles from Madrid. In the afternoon I
went into the city. The public buildings are really
splendid, and in general the streets spacious and houses
well built. No abominable dunghills in every direction,
like Lisbon, which is a great comfort.

20th   Marched to Getafe, eight miles from Madrid.
Nothing could exceed the frantic joy expressed by
the people of all classes on Lord Wellington's entering Madrid. Ladies threw down their most valuable
veils and shawls for his horse to pass over ; they got
hold of his legs as he sat on horseback and kissed
them. The French had left a garrison in a place which
had formerly been a palace and also a china factory,
called the Buen Retiro. The place was enclosed
with a deep ditch and stockade. It had plenty of
cannon for the use of the fort. It was closely invested, and the men on the third day had orders to
storm it. They were formed upon the glacis ready
to be slipped at the place, when the Governor begged
to be allowed to remove his movables and baggage,
as well as the men and officers, which terms were
granted and they became prisoners of war. The
mob wanted to be allowed to stab them as they
passed out of it, but we got the prisoners as fast as
possible with some difficulty out of the town.

Lord Wellington left the Light Division in and about Madrid, as well as the 2nd Division, and proceeded with the remainder of his army to Burgos, which place he invested. 1812

A bull-fight was given in honour of Lord Wellington's entering Madrid. I was present at it. The bulls were most tremendous animals. The men that attacked them displayed the greatest intrepidity and courage. The poor horses suffered the most. Aug. 31st

Letter No. XVI

Madrid, 8th September 1812.

My dear Parents—I received the letter with the bill enclosed. I am very sorry you have had so much trouble. I assure you it annoyed me exceedingly. I wrote to the merchant who sent me the bill. He was very much surprised at the circumstance—at least he told me so. I expect daily another bill for the same amount. I then will directly transmit it. I have experienced within these three months back some unpleasant losses. One day my horse took it into his head to fight. He was kicked upon the thigh, and being upon the march, he died. By him I lost one hundred dollars. A fine mule broke his leg two days before the battle of Arapiles,[1] at the time we were retiring. Away went baggage and mule. I luckily had the company's money and the best part of my baggage in or near Salamanca upon another animal. By that means the better part was preserved.

[1] Salamanca.—Ed.

At times like these a soldier can ill spare his little comforts, marching the whole day, probably exposed to a burning sun, and very often halting just to get a little of anything and then away again. I lost also a skin containing 100 pints of wine, which I could ill afford. All these misfortunes coming at once, played the devil with me. However, I took up my pipe and thought to myself that things might have been worse. This is the way I generally reason myself into a good humour, and the life of a soldier is well calculated to make a man bear up against misfortunes and smile at difficulties that other men would never get the better of.

I fully meant to have remitted you some money, but my losses disarranged my intentions. I shall be obliged to defer it until Christmas, when I shall have at the least twenty pounds for you, and, believe me, my heart never feels lighter than when it is in my power to render a service to my dear parents.

I often think when I look back upon the hairbreadth escapes that I have had so many times over and over again, how kind the Almighty has been towards me. I hope still to live to see you all enjoy happiness. However, should fortune not be so propitious to my wishes, depend upon it, my exit will be that of a soldier.

Joseph obtained a commission in the 23rd Fusiliers. I directly lost no time in applying to my Colonel to have him transferred into my regiment, which Lord Wellington sanctioned. It was instantly done. I had satisfied myself Joe would have got his appointment in the 34th Regiment, and from motives of delicacy I did not interfere with him, or he might have been with me two months before. However, we cannot help it. The difference will be a loss of 1812 £12 for fees of commission in both regiments, which is not of much consequence.

The task of instructing Joe will be a pleasure to me as far as my humble abilities go. I know Maud has not paid that attention to him I could have wished. I wrote him several plans how to proceed, but instead of studying, they were playing, I suppose. However, that will not be the case with me. I shall make him keep my accounts, and set him systematically to work for some hours daily when we are not otherwise employed.

The duty of a soldier is (in this country) hard or extremely light. Under these circumstances if a person has no resource within himself, he will spend one-half his life in idleness. It is my greatest pleasure to spend one-half the day in study.

I hope Joseph will soon imbibe my principles. I have got everything necessary to equip him on his arrival. We have lost so many officers lately that clothes new from England are cheap enough.

I send Ann my picture. I assure her that it was not from vanity I sat for it, but to gratify her request. I might have had it done on a smaller scale for a locket, but it is a thing so ugly, I could not collect sufficient impudence to see myself displayed in a shining gold case. I have had some good jokes with some of my brother-officers about the picture. Some are very inquisitive to know who is to have it, as I now and then receive some nonsensical letters from Kent by officers from England. I have some fair friends there that write to me occasionally.

This little medal is a cross of the Second Order of

1812 the Legion of Honour. I got it at Redinha. Ann must keep it for me until I return. I prize it much, as the taking of it was attended with a story that modesty will not allow me to lay down in writing, as a soldier should be delicate in displaying or boasting of great deeds. This moment have received the bill from Lisbon amounting to £22 : 6 : 7, which I shall immediately send by the post this day ; so should this paper come to hand first, you may expect the letter daily. I send this by an officer coming to England, but I do not like to send the bill by him, as the gentleman might by accident be delayed upon the road.—Yours truly,   G. SIMMONS,
Lt., 95th Regiment.

Journal—*1st September*–*31st December* 1812

Sept. and Oct.   I visited Madrid occasionally, but was much in want of money, the army receiving pay irregularly, seldom more than a few dollars in advance when six months' pay was due to each individual. However, specie was very difficult to be obtained, so that was quite unavoidable.

I went one day to have some amusement in the town with a few friends, when I found a letter from my brother Joseph, who was ill at Salamanca, and, of course, in want of money. I put all I had, a gold piece, under a large seal, and sent him a letter, which he received quite opportunely. I slid away from my friends and went back to my quarters at Getafe. My friends wondered what had become of me, until I made them acquainted with my reasons for suddenly disappearing.

Marched to Ribas on 21st, and on 22nd to Vical- 1812
baro.   Oct.

Marched to the celebrated city of Alcala, and 21st
billeted in the College. The headmaster, a priest, 25th
appeared a miserable fellow, but by flattering his
nation, and paying him and the College some high
compliments, he gave me a little bread and some very
good wine. I never was so poor as at this moment,
little to eat and no money, or I would have seen the
priest far enough before I would have flattered him,
but being hungry and dry was my only excuse for
such conduct.

Marched to Arganda. Assembled in the dark and 27th
marched back to Alcala, which place we reached
after daylight.

Rested in the streets and under the piazzas. In 28th
the afternoon marched to Barajas.

Marched to near El Pardo, a short distance from 30th
Madrid.

Moved close to the city, and halted near to the 31st
Segovia Gate. Very much distressed at the wretchedness and deplorable state of mind displayed by great
multitudes of people, being aware that we were going
to leave them to their fates. The 2nd Division
joined the army here. My brother Maud came to
me, being very hungry. I luckily had just got a bag
of biscuits from a store. He loaded himself and went
back to his corps.

Our army now commenced its retreat in earnest
and marched to Las Rozas and bivouacked near the
river Guadiana.

I was truly glad to get away from this unfortunate Nov.
place, as we could not do the people any good, and 1st

1812 pity is at best (under the circumstances) a sorry way of showing good wishes. It would have delighted me, as well as thousands more, if our noble Commander could have risked a battle ; that was impossible. He was in full retreat from Burgos, having failed in an assault of it, owing to the guns used on this occasion being too light to make a sufficient breach in its walls, also a very powerful French army was ready to attack him under Marshal Soult, and a large force was moving upon Madrid to attack us.

Nov. 2nd   Marched to the camp of the Escorial.

3rd   Crossed the Sierra de Guadarama and bivouacked near Villacastin. General Hill took the command. My brother Joseph joined. He was in a very bad state of health. The 34th were encamped near us. I brought Maud to dine.

4th   Marched to near La Vega and bivouacked.

5th   Marched to near Fuente de Baños and bivouacked.

6th   Moved to the heights between Flores de Avila and Peñaranda.

7th   Marched and bivouacked a league from Alba de Tormes. Crossed the river at the bridge of Alba de Tormes and bivouacked in a wood near Calvarrasa de Arriba. The Division on retreat from Burgos joined us here and Lord Wellington took the command.

10th   Marched into Salamanca. In quarters. The troops placed in different large buildings. The Light Division put into the Irish College.

13th   In the evening, being orderly officer, I went at eight o'clock to see the lights out and that the men were present. I met Lieutenant Firman, who was upon the same duty for our 3rd Battalion. Finding

the stairs very slippery and the place very dark, I
observed, " If you will wait, I will go in search of a
candle," as I knew there were open spaces in the
balusters a person in the dark might walk through. I
left him, got a candle from a neighbouring house, and
returned. I went up three or four stairs, when I heard
a slip and in a moment, poor Firman fell through.
In his progress downwards his feet repeatedly
struck one side and his head the other. He came
with tremendous force to the bottom, which was a
flagged pavement in the cellar. I directly retraced
my steps and found him almost dashed to pieces, his
skull frightfully fractured and several ribs broken. I
had him removed to his billet. He remained for two
days in a state of insensibility and died. It was odd
enough that a soldier of the 43rd and his Portuguese
wife were sleeping together close to the place where
he fell and never were awakened by the noise until I
came to the place.

The army crossed the Tormes and took post Nov.
upon the heights of the Arapiles.   14th

In the evening the army began to retreat from 15th
Salamanca upon Ciudad Rodrigo. Weather very
bad and the roads excessively deep. My brother
exceedingly unwell, which caused me a deal of uneasiness and trouble besides having to attend to my duty.
The enemy moving upon our right flank in large bodies.

Marched and bivouacked in a wood near Cillero. 16th
Very ill off for provisions. My brother so ill that I
was obliged to give him my cloak to keep him warm.
I had given my mule up to him to ride, so that at
every step I was up to the knees in mud, and
frequently small rills, which it was necessary during

1812 the day's march to cross, became rivulets from the continued rain.

The Light Division, being the rear-guard upon this retreat, were the first under arms in the morning, and the last in bivouac at night, which was generally some time after dark. Our poor fellows lit fires, and then, being nearly starved, went about in search of something to eat. Some lean and half-starved bullocks were here and there lying dead in the mud in the deep parts of the road, yoked to carts laden with baggage. From these, the hungry soldiers sliced off a delightful repast, which was grilled, half-smoked, and half-roasted, and as tough as a shoe sole, but severe hardship and hunger made this an agreeable substitute for better food. Other soldiers would be groping about upon their hands and knees under a bastard description of oak and cork trees for acorns. These trees yield them in abundance, and at this time of year they are to be found in plenty. Although hard and bitter, still such food was found better than none. The country people send their pigs, marked, into the woods to fatten. They are half wild. Some soldiers could not resist shooting them, which caused Lord Wellington to punish with death two men to deter others from such a breach of military discipline.

COMBAT OF THE HUEBRA (SAN MUNOZ)

Nov. 17th   Fell in before day. The enemy began to press us. My battalion immediately took possession of the commanding ground on both sides of the road, and although the men were half-starved, cold, and wet, they one and all showed the greatest alacrity in 1812 obeying the command and were anxious to fight. The enemy were very superior in force, consequently the Division retired leisurely before their cavalry. Some French cavalry dashed across the road our baggage was upon, took some, and had momentary possession of Lieutenant Cameron, who commanded the baggage guard, when the head of the column made its appearance. The officer was let go. Rifle Men were sent into the wood near the road and fired a few shots, which made the Dragoons scamper off. These same fellows met with Sir Edward Paget and took him prisoner.

Numbers of men were left behind, and several died. The road was covered with carcases of all descriptions, and at every deep slough we found horses, mules, donkeys, and bullocks mingled together, some dead, others dying, all laden with baggage. It is a most disagreeable sight to a soldier to see everything going to rack and ruin without being able to prevent it. About mid-day the army descended from some very commanding ground and passed the river Huebra at San Munoz, which retarded the rear-guard for some time. Our company extended, and were the last to retire down the inclined plane towards the river Huebra, followed a short distance by the enemy's skirmishers. The high ground was covered with masses of infantry and cavalry, also many guns, which played upon us handsomely, which was fun for them, but death to us. The enemy got up guns and infantry, and as the Light Division descended to pass the ford, which was rapid and breast-high, their guns cannonaded us and killed several

17

1812 men and some officers. On getting through this
ford we faced about and formed column of battalions.
A little way from the ford I found my brother was
absent. Almost distracted, I observed him seated some
distance off on the wrong side of the river, and the mule
close beside him. I returned through the water with
all speed possible and seized hold of him and placed
him upon the mule, and uttering a few hearty
d—ns, brought him safely through, under the music
of shot and shell. I then made a bugler lead
the animal close by me, so that I could not lose
sight of him. The enemy now made a demonstration
and menaced an attack. A Brigade of Swiss wanted
to reconnoitre the river, opposite where the 52nd were
posted, but were put back handsomely. Captain
Dawson, a friend of mine, was killed.

Nov.   My brother passed a very bad night. I really did
18th not know what to do with him. The mule was so
much exhausted, it would not be able to go another
day's journey, and in that case he must be left to the
mercy of the captors. An hour before the day,
having fallen in, I was reflecting upon the gloomy
position before me. I was surprised in my reverie
by the sun beginning to shine upon us, which it had
not done before during this unlucky retreat, and soon
afterwards to learn that the French army had given up
the pursuit and was now in full retreat on Salamanca.
This was very good news. The day was very fine, but
the road extremely bad ; we were obliged to wade for
miles in slush and water, which made the feet extremely
tender. Also, not being able to see where to place them,
made one hit the stumps of small trees, which gave great
pain. I do not know when I suffered so much from

a day's march; it was a very long one. Bivouacked 1812 upon the side of a mountain near Santiespiritus.

Marched to near Ciudad Rodrigo and got fresh Nov. provisions in abundance. Bivouacked by the river- 19th side. The night frosty and clear.

At daylight jumped into the Agueda with some 20th of our officers, and found myself very comfortable after it, not having had my clothes off or a clean shirt on for some time.

The mule that brought my brother through the retreat died this morning; about 130 dollars lost for ever.

Villar del Puerco. Supplied ourselves from Rodrigo 25th with every comfort required and had our baggage and our company's mess as comfortable as ever. Lieutenants Pemberton, Haggup, my brother, and myself lived together and I resumed the office of caterer. On our arrival at the empty house given over for our occupation, we found three Dragoon officers had remained behind their men, and fully intended staying all night. Now in that case our animals would be badly put up and ourselves sorely inconvenienced by their laziness, as they ought to have marched with their men. I took upon myself to adopt a modest way to dislodge them, which was sanctioned by my companions. I ordered some men to cut a quantity of green timber and bring it into the room, as it was a cold winter's day. This I had placed upon the floor, and made a blazing fire; the smoke of course filled the room, and passed in volumes from every window. I then had a large cooking pot put upon the fire and some beef and vegetables put into it. I now asked the Dragoons if they would partake of our fare, saying in the most polite and pressing manner that we should be glad to share it with them.   I ordered more wood to be heaped on the fire, and lay down with my head upon a knapsack and smoked my pipe. Although I could bear a smoky fire as well as most folks, this was rather too powerful; still by lying down, the smoke did not affect my eyes half as much as the Dragoons'.   One moved into the yard, and the two others could stand it no longer and followed. They held a council of war, at which, I was informed by a mess-mate who had purposely placed himself to overhear their conversation and to report to me upon my success, the following remarks were made.   " Did you, pray, ever hear a fellow so gallows polite as that black-looking ruffian is ?   He bears fire like a sala-mander.   And how the fellow's dressed too."   " I join his mess," says another, " I'll see him d——d first." " I should expect to be poisoned if I did," the third observed.   " Besides," says the first, who commenced the oration upon my qualities, "we are nearly smoked and burnt in that d——d room already, and I now hear him roaring out for more firewood ; he will cer-tainly burn the house down before morning.   How the officers that are obliged to live with such a madman are to be pitied !   My eyes are quite inflamed.   I am determined this instant to follow the troop."   The others acquiesced, and their horses were ordered out and their baggage animals loaded.   I directed our servants to assist them, and expressed in the most polite manner my regret at not being honoured with their company at dinner, as it was now nearly ready— at least the soup was quite done.   They individually as politely refused my solicitations.   We parted in the most friendly manner. The fire was soon made 1812 more agreeable to our feelings, and we all enjoyed the joke very much.

Marched to Alameda. The people were glad to Nov. see us return. We had begun to look upon the 26th villages near the Agueda as our homes.

Formed a regimental mess ; we got wine from Lamego upon the Duero, and passed the winter very comfortably and happily, I not being the last to give my hairbreadth escapes in the manner in which soldiers that are real ones tell their stories. I am sorry to say these are often imagined impossibilities by other folks because they cannot comprehend that certain men may, from circumstances and habit, be made to do anything if their country requires their exertions.

LETTER No. XVII

ALAMEDA, SPAIN,
12th December 1812.

DEAR PARENTS—I sent you in September another bill directed from the neighbourhood of · Madrid, which I hope you have received, and also got the money. I am anxious to know when this letter came to hand. I beg you will directly inform me, as I begin to think and long for an answer. I have the second and third Bill of Exchange, which I hope will not be required. However, in case of accidents I shall take care of them. I fully expected to have had it in my power to have transmitted you some money immediately, but not having been paid up to the period I expected, I must reluctantly defer the pleasure for the present and put you off a little while longer.

1812 We flattered ourselves with the hopes of passing a pleasant winter in Madrid, but in consequence of the failure at Burgos, and the enemy receiving great reinforcements from France, besides concentrating the whole of their force in the country, we were obliged to retire before them.

Our noble Marquis of Wellington did everything that was possible to bring them to action when circumstances offered favourably, but the enemy, confident of success through the vast superiority of numbers and ten thousand effective cavalry, continually adopted the plan of moving on our flanks, which obliged us also to retire before them, not being able to oppose their course.

I will give you a specimen of our occasional hardships, though for my own part I am no croaker. Privations sometimes make you enjoy a comfortable quarter much more than if you had never felt them. About the 27th of October, we moved forward from our cantonments in and near Madrid in consequence of the enemy approaching and menacing this capital. Every one was rejoiced to move out to fight, thinking how comfortably the winter would be passed if wounded, having Madrid at our back.

On the 27th marched to Arganda, six leagues. The same night at eight o'clock moved back towards Alcala. Halted under the piazzas in the town, as the weather was very cold and rainy. Marching the whole night.

Moved towards Madrid on the 30th; the day very rainy; roads swimming with mud and water. Halted at nine o'clock at night in rear of Madrid upon the side of a hill. Extremely cold and windy; raining at intervals. Had some difficulty to find wood for a fire. 1812 Benumbed with cold and obliged to smoke my pipe and walk about, praying for a fine day to dry my clothes.

Moved at daylight on the 31st to the walls of Madrid. Halted and cooked upon the road. The people in the English interest very gloomy ; others flying from the town. The people in the French interest dressed up and delighted beyond measure. Maud visited me, and told me how wet and uncomfortable he was, not having been dry for four days. I asked him, "What of that ? Many thousands are in the same way." He then said, "I have had no bread or anything to eat these two days." I luckily had plenty, and gave him some. I was with him for ten minutes. I had not seen him since the storming of Badajoz. The Light Division now formed, as usual, the rear-guard. The other Divisions of the army walked generally near us, so daily I had the pleasure of seeing Maud. Towards night marched some distance ; passed the night in the fields. Joe joined me this evening, and Maud visited me. I had plenty of wine and a good dinner in my tent. Joe was wet through and very delicate, having left Salamanca before he had recovered. I had an opportunity of letting him have blankets. We moved on daily in this way, always in the fields until we arrived near Salamanca. Weather generally bad. Moved from the right to the left of this place daily.

On 14th November we were upon the old position in order of battle. The enemy made a flank movement in the night, and we were obliged to retire.

On the 15th we halted in a wood, having been marching the whole day ; continued rain. The

1812 country between Ciudad Rodrigo and Salamanca is a plain covered with woods, and in rainy weather the roads are intersected with rivulets, which makes them almost impassable.

Joe was so ill on the 16th I was obliged to walk the whole way, or he must have fallen into the enemy's hands. Bad weather and roads.

On the 17th the enemy attacked us in force, but we beat them off. Some of the enemy's cannon kept up a brisk fire upon a ford which we passed in good order, and luckily only a few of our men bit the ground. The enemy were checked here for the night. Occasionally some sharp skirmishing. Joe very unwell, though pleased with the fight. Under arms nearly all night. Very rainy and cold.

On the 18th the enemy, for want of provisions, could not push us ; we expected to have had a tough day's work, but *Johnny* did not press us much. In want of bread. Several men died this day from cold and wet. Horses and mules were lying dead in every direction, which shows plainly a man can bear hunger and being exposed to the inclemency of the weather for a much longer period than an animal. In this country I have seen the same thing often. Being upon the rear-guard exposes a person to a much longer period under arms, as he must endeavour to drive all before him, and very often to form up to repel an attack of the enemy. This day's march it is impossible to describe, wading up to the middle very often, and all day up to the knee in mud and water ; raining repeatedly. This night picked up a quantity of acorns and roasted them, which we were all very thankful for. Night excessively cold.

The enemy followed us on the 19th ; most of us 1812
walking barefooted, my shoes also having no bottoms,
as well as my friends' ; my legs and feet much frost-
bitten ; could hardly crawl. Halted near Ciudad
Rodrigo. Three days' bread served to us upon the
spot. I sent into the town for a pound of English
butter, only six shillings per pound, and some wine.
This day tolerably fine. After eating and drinking
most tremendously, in a moment you would see all
faces jovial and everything forgotten. We halted in
the fields near this town for a few days. I washed
myself in the river every day and bathed my feet with
cold water often. Thank God, I am as well as ever.
Joe, though he rode, still got worse. However, he has
had every attention paid him and is now quite well.
He eats and drinks like a farmer. I keep him five
hours a day at his studies, and I have no doubt he will
soon astonish you. I must say he implicitly obeys my
injunctions. He is now clear of the world, with everything comfortable. I have nothing more to do with
him but give my advice. I have since found it was
my interest got him into the 23rd Regiment, and not
the Colonel of Maud's regiment. I beg you will have
Charles well educated. I will then take him off your
hands at fifteen years old. Do not despair, though
you now are unfortunate. If I live and have any
luck in my profession I shall be able to support you.
I wish for no greater pleasure. Ann I am proud of.
I shall always adore her. She must bear up against
the misfortunes which at present cannot be resisted, in
hopes that a few years will put a period to them. We
cannot always be doomed to misery and misfortune.

I thank my dear mother for her kind remembrance

1812 of me.   Joe often tells me little anecdotes of your
fireside.   This winter we are settled in our old quarters
near the Agueda, and two or three leagues from Ciudad
Rodrigo.   I hope we shall get out several regiments
before spring, and commence again handsomely in the
New Year.   Joe joins me in best wishes for your
welfare.   Believe me, yours affectionately,

G. SIMMONS.

I sent a parcel for Ann with my picture.   Let me
know if the thing arrived.

I send this letter by a friend, free of expense to
England.   You will find under the seal a small gold
coin, value a dollar ; it will pay the postage.

Pay particular attention to the education of Charles
and Betsy.   Let me know how Charles's leg is.   By
no means use quackery with him.   Sea-bathing, plenty
of exercise, and clean linen will be most essential at all
times.

It is a great task imposed upon me—Joe's education.   However, he is exceedingly willing, which pleases
me, and he possesses no one vice.   He regularly
attends drill, and begins to move with the appearance
of a soldier.   He is very proud of his green clothes,
and is a very smart fellow.

He is already wonderfully improved ; he is two
inches taller than I.   Maud is about my size.   When
in England he was rather delicate in features ; you
would hardly know him, his complexion has changed
so much.   Exposure to all sorts of weather—in
summer roasted, in winter nearly frozen—soon
changes the appearance. Occasionally we get a
detachment from England.   They look as delicate as

women when they first join us compared to those 1812 hard-faced veterans of the regiment.

When Joe left his brother to join me we were marching upon Madrid. He travelled nearly 500 miles before he joined. He has some wonderful tales to tell about his different adventures. He was six months in joining me from the time of starting, in consequence of illness brought on by hardships from starvation.

In England you little know the hardships a soldier endures in this country.

LETTER No. XVIII

ALAMEDA, SPAIN,
29th December 1812.

MY DEAR FATHER—I received your letter dated the 4th December. It astonished me how you could have any trouble in getting the bill cashed if properly presented, as the merchant informed me he never before had any difficulty, and he has been in the habit of giving numbers to individuals.

I examined carefully that part of your letter where you state the likelihood of procuring me a company. My ideas upon the point in question are by no means sanguine. I am too well hackneyed in the ways of the world to for a moment imagine that a Member of Parliament would give me anything, or, in other words, ask for a company for a perfect stranger who had not given him the least assistance. You may say, that does not follow, he may wish to offer himself at some distant period, and may wish

1812 to make friends or make himself popular, but I should think there are numbers of people more deserving than myself. In this world, men generally (and particularly M.P.'s) have some great object in view before they will exert themselves very materially on behalf of others. Things of this kind daily stare one in the face. I remember Mr. Arden very well, but I believe he has got sons; consequently his first attempts will be to favour them, and there are very few in existence who may not be in want of Parliamentary aid at one time or other, therefore you will agree with me that it is not likely he would ask favours for a person he knows little about. This is my opinion. I wish I may be deceived most heartily. I think it was a wrong step letting him have my letter. The curious are very anxious to know particulars relating to the army in the Peninsula. If my letters are shown, and given into the hands of strangers, the contents may find their way into the public papers, which would be very unpleasant, and might prove very serious, as according to the old adage, "The truth is not to be spoken at all times." I must observe again you ought to be very cautious as to whom you give my letters. Mr. Arden may hand my letter about among his friends, who will comment upon it according as it strikes them, which is not pleasant. I hope it may not be the case, and I have a better opinion of him; at the same time, it is just as well not to put it in any one's power.

You make me laugh with the idea of an aide-de-camp being the high road to a Brigade-major's situa-

tion.   Aides-de-camp are generally chosen by 1812
general officers through relationship or family
connections or friends.   My ideas of the world since
I became a soldier are quite changed.   Campaigning
has inured me to hardship, and it is quite immaterial
to me whether I roll myself in my blanket and sleep
upon the ground or anywhere else.   There was a
time when wet clothes would have frightened me.
Here I have been wet through for weeks and slept in
the fields in winter, sometimes without a cloak,
enjoyed health, and been happy and proud of my
situation.

If there was any chance of success in procuring
me a company through the M.P., you should have
asked for only one thing at a time.   Any country is the
same to me, hot or cold ; I could always exchange,
after a little time, by giving a difference of one or
two hundred pounds, which then would not be an
object.   However, building castles in the air is not
exactly the thing, and really I do not expect any
promotion but through the common routine of
service, which, if I live, will be the case four years
hence.   I certainly applaud you for giving your vote
to Mr. Wharton.   I hope he will befriend you.   I am
afraid you have hit upon a wrong situation for yourself.   A barrack master has a great deal to do, and he
ought to be well acquainted with the mode of writing
returns in a military way.   It is a situation generally
filled by an old officer.   I think you would be much
more likely to succeed by requesting Mr. Wharton
to obtain for you anything more easily filled that
may strike you.   I am not well acquainted with what
is easy to obtain or what is not so, but in my opinion,

1812 a barrack master has much trouble and responsibility, and particularly if he is not a military man, he will find soldiers odd fellows to deal with. There are situations that would not be attended with great responsibility on your part, as at your time of life you must not think of learning a profession, but endeavour to procure something easy, attended with little trouble ; this is the kind of occupation I should point out to you. I am very well aware it would be productive of the most essential comfort.

We are in good cantonments, and have forgotten the hardships experienced upon the retreat. I hope the next campaign will be a brilliant one. The winter hangs heavy on my hands already, but I must wait patiently. I think next summer will terminate the career of the French in the Peninsula and allow us to move the theatre of war into some other quarter.

The successes of the Russians are great and glorious, and will be a means of rousing the Continental Powers from their lethargic state. It will show the world that a true spirit of patriotism will always overpower tyranny and oppression. Bravo, Russians! they are worthy of the country they inhabit, and their labours will be crowned with success. The man that would not be profuse of his life in defence of the place that gave him birth, deserves not the name.

I wrote by a friend. You would receive it from some place in England. I shall be able to send you some more money when I get hold of it, but have not been regularly paid, I cannot say since when. I had a letter from Maud, who tells me he is well

and gives me a long history of the three or four 1812
days after leaving me, which I joked him upon.   Joe
feeds uncommonly.   I allow him two bottles of good
wine each day.   He has entirely driven the ague
from its position through the able support of bark
wine, and I keep him daily employed at his book
or drill.   He feels some consequence in having been
in a fight since he joined.   I asked him at the time
how he liked the shot and shells.   He replied they
were ugly fellows, he did not like them much.   But
there are many things we do not like that we must
put up with.

Endeavour to get the letter back from Mr. A.,
as I do not like people to comment upon my sentiments ; it is too tender a point.   If I had thought
the letter might be read by any other person but
yourself, I should have been more cautious in speaking of myself ; some people might fancy I was a
swaggering fellow.   There are many things a man
may unbosom himself about to his family that he would
not think of doing to the public.   I am afraid, father,
you are very young in the ways of the world.   My
love to my dear mother, Ann, Charlie, and Betsy.
Be attentive to Charlie's education.   I have written
to Mrs. Wild about her son.—Yours,

G. SIMMONS,
Lt., 1st Batt., 95th Regt.

Do not write me upon that part of the letter you
fold down, as any person may read it, and do not
talk about me to people, as it will do you no good
and me harm.   My respects to my good friend
Whitaker.   If I might be allowed to judge with

1812 respect to his son, if he likes the life of a soldier, by all means let him go to the East Indies.

Do not talk to me about Spanish donkeys. It is really too ridiculous. You had better request me to send you a load of diamonds !

CAMPAIGN OF 1813

NAPOLEON's failure in Russia considerably altered the aspect of affairs in the Peninsula, since he once again drafted thousands of his best soldiers and officers to stiffen the new levies with which he strove to oppose his enemies in Germany. Notwithstanding this, he had still 230,000 men in the Peninsula, of which 120,000 were barring the northern route from Spain to France, with reserves at Bayonne. It was at this juncture, in May 1813, that Wellington ordered Graham to advance from Portugal through Tras os Montes to the Esla River with an army of 40,000 men, so as to turn the line of the Douro, whilst he himself, with 30,000, moved direct on the Tormes, with the object of forcing a passage at Salamanca, crossing the Douro, and joining hands with Graham. The Galicians under Castaños were now to meet him, and the three forces, amounting to 90,000 men, were then to advance on a broad front and force the French back on the Pyrenees. " A grand design and grandly executed " are the words of Napier.

King Joseph made desperate efforts to assemble his scattered forces, and after various changes of plans, fell back to the Ebro and took up a position behind the Zadorra River, covering Vitoria, where an immense amount of war material and treasure was collected.

Wellington, pushing forward without intermission, attacked the French on 21st June at Vitoria, and inflicted a most crushing defeat on them, capturing all their guns, stores, and treasure. The French army retreated to the shelter of the walls of Pamplona, King Joseph fleeing to France. The victorious advance of the allies had placed Foy and Clausel, on either flank, in danger of being cut off. The former, although roughly handled by Graham, made good his retreat to the Bidasoa ; the

18

1813 latter, pursued by Wellington himself, retreated to Zaragoza, and after destroying his guns and baggage, escaped with his force into France.

San Sebastian was now besieged by the allies, and on 24th July, an attempt was made to storm it, but was repulsed with heavy loss, and the siege perforce turned into a blockade. Soult had meanwhile been appointed to command the "Army of Spain," as it was now styled, King Joseph having been wise enough to voluntarily resign.

Now commenced the fighting which, under the name of "Pyrenees," is so well known. Combat succeeded combat with unceasing rapidity, commencing with that of Roncesvalles on 25th July. In nine days, in August, ten serious actions were fought, the allies losing some 7300 men, and the French about double that number.

The siege of San Sebastian was now resumed, and on 31st August it was stormed, but at the expense of appalling losses to those of the allies engaged. Meanwhile, Soult fought a battle on the Bidasoa with the covering force at San Marcial, and another at Vera.

After the fall of San Sebastian, there was a lull in the fighting for some weeks, and it was not till 6th October that the allies effected the passage of the Bidasoa, and on the following day fought the second combat of Vera, in which the Rifles took a leading part and lost over 200 officers and men, killed and wounded.

Soult now entrenched himself strongly on the line of the Nivelle, but on 10th November, the battle of the Nivelle was fought and Soult retreated behind the Nive. Wellington having been compelled to divide his wings by this river, Soult projected an attack on one of them with his whole force, the entrenched camp of Bayonne on the Nive assisting him in this enterprise. The battles and combats which ensued are commonly known as the battles in front of Bayonne, that of the 10th December being distinguished as the battle of the Nive, although they all took place in the same theatre of operations.

In the five days' fighting before Bayonne (9th to 13th December) the French lost 6000 men and the allies about 5000.

After some minor operations, hostilities ceased for a brief period on the 18th December, only to be renewed with redoubled energy within less than two months.

CHAPTER XI

Letter No. XIX

To his Father, from Alameda, dated 30th April 1813

More lectures to his father for showing his letters to people—
Good winter quarters—Five months without seeing the
face of a Frenchman—Hopes to see the Pyrenees before
September—Starting on target practice with his men.

Letter No. XX

*From Lieutenant Joseph Simmons to his Parents, from
Alameda, dated 5th May* 1813

Describes life in winter quarters—The regimental mess—
Weekly balls to the ladies—The retreat from Madrid.

Postscript by George Simmons

About to be reviewed by Lord Wellington—Expects to drive the
French out of Spain this campaign.

Journal—1st May–30th August 1813

The army formed into eight Divisions—The French army de-
pleted to obtain veterans for the campaign in Russia—The
British army in the highest order—Composition of the
Light Division—General advance of the army—The Horse

Guards and Oxford Blues join—Cavalry skirmish near Sala-
manca—The French retire—Advance resumed—The 10th
Hussars execute a brilliant charge near Morales—The
French retire from Burgos—The British army crosses the Ebro
—Fight at San Millan—The Rifles "make a sad example of
Johnny"—Salt springs at Salinas—The battle of Vitoria—
Dispositions of the French—All three battalions of the Rifles
sharply engaged—The French driven *into* the town, *through*
the town, and *out of* the town—A running fight for twenty
miles—Bivouac at nightfall—The pursuit renewed—Skirmish at Echarri Arinez—Skirmish near La Cuenca—
Splendid work by British Horse Artillery—The Rifle Men
capture the *last* gun of the French army—Sad spectacle of
wounded French Artillerymen—Arrive in front of Pampeluna
—The march to intercept General Clausel, who crosses the
Ebro and escapes—On fatigue getting fuel—Rencontre
with General Picton—"It's a d——d concern to have to
follow you"—General Alten to the rescue—A present of
a skin of wine—Blockade of Pamplona—Camp at the
foot of the Pyrenees—Magnificent scenery—The Rifles
drive the French from the heights of Santa Barbara—The
Bidasoa and the town of Vera—The Pass of Vera—Soult
captures the passes of Roncesvalles and Yanzi, and the Light
Division has to fall back—The attempt to storm San Sebastian fails—Marshal Soult retires—Forced march of the
Light Division—The fights at the bridge of Yanzi and at
Echalar.

LETTER No. XIX

ALAMEDA, SPAIN, 30*th April* 1813.

DEAR FATHER—I send you a bill upon Ireland
for twenty pounds English money. You must
separate it from this epistle, and give it into the
hands of any banker, who will be able directly to
procure you the money. I must, dear father, request that you will not in future show my letters to
the public. I find that the letter I wrote you respecting

the fight upon the Coa was read at the mess table of 1813 a Militia regiment and exposed to every one who chose to read it. How the devil it got there I cannot say. I can so far say that the officer is now present with this regiment who heard it read. You have no idea what material injury you may do me by such exposures.

I remember in this letter I said a great deal about my family concerns, which it is very wrong to publish to the world. If the young officer had been a quizzical fellow and thought of telling some tales to any other officers, it would have produced amusement, and, why then, what must have been the consequences? I should have instantly called him out, and the result either to one or the other must have proved serious. A soldier's honour is as sacred as a woman's virtue. I mention this, hoping it will deter you from doing so again, as you can form no idea what trifles lead to among soldiers.

Joe is going on remarkably well. He has had repeated attacks of ague through this winter. He is, however, much better, and will, I hope, stand the campaign well. I have provided him with a horse. He is very well acquainted with the first duties of a soldier. He is very much liked by the officers, which gives me much pleasure.

The army is in high health and spirits. In a few days we shall take the field. I am heartily tired of this idle life. We have been five months in snug winter quarters without seeing the face of a Frenchman —a thing which has never happened before. It is expected that our Division will be slipped at Burgos. If we are, I hope success may attend us. Those

1813 employed will have smart work.   However, bad as it may be, Badajoz, for a desperate business can never be rivalled.

The campaign bids fair to be most brilliant, as we shall have little more than equal numbers to contend against.   I hope to see the Pyrenees before September. The success of the noble Russians is wonderful.   I hope my dear mother is well.   I thank her for her kind remembrances of me.   I hope while I live I shall merit her affections.   Tell Ann in a few years more I have no doubt to make her comfortable and happy. Her fortune is at present hard, but she can look forward with confidence to seeing better times.   I am glad Charlie and Betsy are improving ; for God's sake, take care of Charlie's education.   Military drawing would be very useful.   As soon as you have received the money, write.   I shall send the second bill next week, so if you get this bill, burn the second after you receive the money.   I must end my letter, as the company are already mustering at my door for target practice, so I shall pass the remainder of the day in proving the abilities of my men in hitting a mark in order to do justice to our enemies when we meet with them.   I have had Joe very often at this work.   Adieu,   GEO. SIMMONS,
Lt., 95th Regiment.

LETTER No. XX

ALAMEDA, *May 5th* 1813.

DEAR PARENTS—Since our retreat from Madrid we have spent a very pleasant and comfortable winter. The village that we have been in all the winter is very

small, the houses bad, and the inhabitants poor, miser- 1813
able creatures. They have a fire on the ground, which
generally smokes so intolerably that we frequently are
obliged to go out of the house. As soon as an officer
gets into a house that is allotted to him, he must build
a chimney, as it has been very cold and rainy this
winter, particularly in this part of the country. When
we got a little settled in the village and found it was
likely we should stop some months in this place, we
established a regimental mess. There we had the
best of things that this part of the country could
produce ; it was a means of passing away the dreary
winter nights pleasantly. We usually gave a ball
once a week to the ladies of the village, who did us
the honour to attend it. If you saw them they would
astonish you. They dress in short brown jackets,
and petticoats of the same, very coarse, figured with
ridiculous patches of red cloth. These delicate ladies
feed so grossly and eat so much garlic, that it is
enough to suffocate a person being in the room with
twenty or thirty of them. I am only giving you a
description of the women in the villages on this
mountainous frontier. In large towns there are
beautiful women, and something like the English (but
not so fair), who dress splendidly in black satin. We
received a letter from Maud the other day. He is very
well. In his regiment they do not understand
carrying on the war so well as our officers. My
brother George gives him sometimes a little advice
how to live. When I joined my regiment at
Madrid I happened to meet with my brother Maud
before George. He told me he had had nothing to
eat for two or three days ; it had rained all that time.

1813 I had just received four days' rations. We went into an old house and cooked some mutton chops and drank my rations of rum. His Colonel gave him leave to go with me to find my brother George. As soon as we joined my brother, he gave us a good dinner and plenty of wine and took great care of me. My brother was well provided with blankets. I was then near dead with starvation. I had marched three days with very little to eat, and it was raining most of the time. He soon started the ague away from me, but being obliged to ride with my regiment and continually raining, brought on the ague again. Near the end of the retreat I was so bad that I could hardly bear to sit upon my horse with dysentery and ague, so that my brother had me, as well as his duty, to mind. If I had fallen to the rear I should have been taken by the French. One day in particular, when the enemy was firing at us very briskly, and having a river to cross, I was so ill that I could not make the horse travel. My brother returned to me and seized my horse by the bridle and forced him through the river nearly up to the waist ; at that time a cannon shot struck the water as we passed. I had to lie out all that night with only my brother's cloak over me. It rained most of the night. The reason of not having more was on account of the baggage being sent to the rear. We had nothing to eat but acorns for several days, as we were passing through a large wood. We are provided with everything for the ensuing campaign. We are all wishing to be on the move again. Desire my love to my aunt, uncle, sisters, and brother.—I remain, your affectionate son,

JOSEPH SIMMONS, Lieut., 95th Regt.

I desired Joe to write this letter. I think you 1813 will find he has much improved since he came under my tuition. As soon as you receive this letter, if you have not had the first, which I sent a week previous to this, you must present this bill for payment, observing the first having miscarried. I should hope you have received the first bill ; if so, destroy this one. Lord Wellington, our illustrious chief, will review us in a day or two, which he always does yearly, previous to commencing the campaign. I hope we shall finish the campaign by driving the French out of the country, and may our next year's fighting be either in Germany or Italy. I do not want to see England till I am a captain. Joe has grown much. He is rather delicate. If he does not become stout I shall send him to our depôt in England for a year or two. I hope he will be able to rough it with me, as I am convinced it will ultimately be more to his advantage.

Joe is here telling you a story of escaping from being a prisoner. There is a good deal of truth in it. However, I told him he should not talk nonsense about me. He will know better as he grows older.

I often pleasure myself with the idea that if anything happens to me, Joe will be a comfort to his family. I often talk to him upon the subject. I got a number of silver forks and spoons. They are so weighty, I shall be under the necessity of selling them. I bought them after the sacking of Rodrigo

1813 and Badajoz for a trifle from one of our men. I
meant them for Ann. However, she shall lose nothing
in the end. I shall purchase some little thing more
portable. God bless you.   G. S.

Journal—1st May–30th August 1813

CAMPAIGN OF 1813

May   Five thousand British troops having arrived at
Lisbon as a reinforcement to the army, the
Divisions were now formed into eight, as follows :—

> 1st Division commanded by Lieutenant-General Hon.
> W. Stewart.
>
> 2nd   „   „   „ Lieutenant - General   Sir
> Rowland Hill.
>
> 3rd   „   „   „ Lieutenant - General   Sir
> Thomas Picton.
>
> 4th   „   „   „ Lieutenant - General   Sir
> Lowry Cole.
>
> 5th   „   „   „ Lieutenant - General   Sir
> James Leith.
>
> 6th   „   „   „ Lieutenant - General   Sir
> Henry Clinton.
>
> 7th   „   „   „ Lieutenant - General Earl
> Dalhousie.

Light Division, Major - General Baron Charles
Alten ; the cavalry under Sir Stapleton Cotton ; the
Portuguese under Marshal Beresford. Sir Thomas
Graham was made his second-in-command after the
battle of Salamanca. The 2nd Division was detached in
Estremadura. Napoleon's gigantic designs against
Russia had caused the French armies in Spain to contri-
bute ten men per company from a number of regiments
for the purpose of having veteran soldiers mixed with

the new levies. The British and Portuguese armies 1813 were now fully equipped and in the highest order. The Light Division was assembled and reviewed upon the plains of Espeja by Lord Wellington, most of whom had seen several campaigns, and few of them but what could boast of having been wounded in their country's service, and who were also ready to receive more if required.

Part of the Light Division marched to the May ford of Marialba and crossed the Agueda near a 21st mill and then moved on to San Felices, and the remainder of the Division joined us. Bivouacked. The Division is divided into two Brigades, the first commanded by Major-General Sir James Kempt, and consists of the following :—1st Battalion 43rd ; five companies 3rd Battalion Rifles ; six companies 1st Battalion Rifles and 17th Portuguese Regiment of Line under Colonel Rolt ; 2nd Brigade commanded by Major-General Vandeleur ; 1st Battalion 52nd ; 1st and 3rd Portuguese Caçadores ; six companies 2nd Battalion Rifles. Major Ross's troop of Horse Artillery still attached to the Division.

At daylight, moved forward and passed Santi- 22nd espiritus and the river Yeltes to Martin del Rio, where we bivouacked. This river rises in the Sierra de França, connected with the Gata mountains, and falls into the Huebra. The whole army now advanced in a most efficient state, and under the most favourable circumstances we commenced the campaign of 1813.

Marched to San Munoz, upon the Huebra, and 23rd under very different feelings I now passed through the river at the same ford where the French

1813 had cannonaded us on the 17th of November last.

May 24th Halted and bivouacked. The Household Brigade joined us, viz. Horse Guards and Oxford Blues.

25th   Marched through Castro, crossing the Matilla rivulet, and bivouacked a little beyond the village of Robliza.

26th   Marched some distance upon the road to Salamanca and pitched our tents near a small stream called the Valmuza, as the enemy's rear-guard was in possession of Salamanca. About two hours after, moved forward to the ford of Villa Mayor, upon the left bank of the Tormes, about a league below the town. Pitched our tents. The other Divisions of the army made corresponding movements, and General Fane's Brigade of cavalry crossed the ford of Santa Marta and the Hussar Brigade moved towards the bridge.

The enemy left the place and halted upon the heights in its neighbourhood. Our cavalry charged the enemy and made some havoc. The Horse Artillery made good practice at the retiring columns. 200 prisoners and some baggage fell into our hands.

27th   The army halted, and the Spaniards had *Te Deums* sung in their churches for being again free from French persecution. I visited the town.

28th   Marched to near Aldea Nueva de Figueira. Encamped not far from General Hill's Division. Went to see my brother Maud in the 34th Regiment. Remained until dark. Having had an extra glass of wine, I had a better opinion of my knowledge of the road to our encampment than of any other person's, and in consequence I was travelling about the greater part of the night.

The Light Division marched early by the road to 1813
Toro, and halted for some time near Villa Buena to June
cook. Again proceeded close to the bridge over the 2nd
Douro at Toro and then halted. A principal arch
has been blown up. We passed over the chasm in the
bridge in Indian file by means of planks having been
laid over the broken arch. The guns and baggage
passed through a deep ford.

The 10th Hussars made a brilliant charge at
a body of cavalry near Morales and overturned a
number of them, bringing in 200 prisoners yesterday. About mid-day moved to Tejera Buena and
encamped.

The Light Division marched six leagues through 4th
a sterile country; the ground was composed of
quantities of chalk. Passed through La Mota
and encamped near the convent of La Espina, on
high ground, with a stream meandering along at
the base.

Marched and halted an hour near Castromonte, 5th
and afterwards moved to Villamadarra and encamped.

Marched to Ampudia. The country flat and 6th
has little appearance of fertility. The cottages not so
good as the peasantry have generally had on our line
of march.

Marched early this morning, preceded by the 7th
cavalry and Horse Artillery, to Palencia. The
infantry followed and encamped close to the walls of
the town, which encircled it. The people were
enraptured at the entrance of the English army, and
the same feeling appeared general amongst all
descriptions. We were informed that Joseph
Buonoparte reviewed his rear-guard yesterday and

1813 was within their city. This day's march has been
through a rich and very fertile country.

June   Marched through Fuente de Valdepero and
8th encamped near Monzon. The weather bad—more
like November than June. The villagers every-
where as we passed, hurried together; the men
greeted us with *Vivas* and the women danced,
some of them in the most ridiculous and droll
manner, to the great amusement of the soldiers, who
although labouring under a heavy load and marching
rapidly, often forgot their hardships and partook in
the general mirth and hilarity.

9th   The Division marched to Piña de Campos and
encamped near Rio Cieza.

10th   Crossed the stone bridge over the river and
passed through Piña and Fromista. Crossed the
Castilian Canal, which for a considerable distance is
raised above the level of the country, and encamped
upon the right bank of the Pisuerga River near
Santillana.

11th   Passed over the river by a good stone bridge of
seven arches and moved forward to Villasandino.
Encamped near it upon the river Brulles.

12th   Marched towards Burgos. Halted a short time at
Castrillo de Murcia to allow the cavalry to advance up
a plain. Made a demonstration by forming two lines
upon the heights over the Hormuza at Isar. Our
cavalry moved forward near Burgos. The Light
Division encamped in the evening at Hornilla, upon
the Hormuza River.

13th   Marched very early. A tremendous explosion
took place at six A.M., which we were satisfied was in
Burgos, and afforded us great delight. I, speaking

for myself, would much sooner have a fair field to 1813 fight on, rather than storm a town. I was convinced that the enemy had evacuated the place, which soon proved to be the case. The castle had been blown up, and some of the outworks destroyed. We passed through Argano to Tovar, where we encamped.

Marched through Quintana to Quintanajuar June and Poza. The Brigade encamped in a wood near 14th the two latter villages.

Marched through Villalta and El Almine, the 15th road now winding and descending for a considerable distance. Entered the vale of the Ebro, and crossed this famous river over a stone bridge named Puente-areñas. Our band struck up the "Downfall of Paris." We were much amused at their wit on the occasion, and we had it followed by a national tune or two to remind us of Old England and absent friends. Encamped close to the village of Areñas. The banks of the river here are low, and from its appearance it must rise and fall very considerably, as the country is mountainous.

The villages about here are very numerous. We 16th crossed the river Nela, and encamped at Medina de Pomar, on the river Trueba.

On piquet after a tedious march through a 17th mountainous country covered with majestic woods. The Division remained on the side of a steep hill overlooking the vale of Rosales.

Moved off at an early hour through magnificent 18th woods, preceded by a troop of the German Hussars, followed up closely by the 1st Battalion Rifles. The Hussars surprised and took the greater part of a piquet of French, and finding that a Division of infantry was

1813 in San Millan, we made our distributions to attack them. Our Battalion was conducted by Colonel Barnard through wooded steep ground beyond the left of the town, the rest of the Brigade being moved forward when we became engaged. We made a sad example of the enemy in a short time, and drove *Johnny* through Villa Nueva to Villa Naña. Several regiments had formed in column, but were completely cut off. Under cover of night they dispersed, and got away as they could. Many were made prisoners. Our 2nd Brigade took all the enemy's baggage. My friend Haggup was shot directly across his stomach. Our loss was trifling when compared with the enemy's. We encamped on the Jumiçillo, below Villa Nueva. This was the first day we had fired a shot since breaking up from our winter quarters.

June The captured animals and baggage were sold and
19th the amount distributed amongst the soldiers of the 2nd Brigade, although the 1st was the real cause of its being taken. Crossed the Cunilla at Villa Madera; passed through Salinas. The water, sparkling and running clear and beautiful, appeared very inviting. The day was hot, and as soon as the soldiers got near they dipped their tots and began to swig away. I was astonished to see the wry faces it produced, and the exclamations also. "The water is d——d salt here; we cannot be very far from the sea," a man close to me observed, which made me laugh. The earth abounds with salt in the vicinity of this place.

At Pobes we crossed the small river Bayas by a wooden bridge, and formed our encampment.

20th Halted. I went and dined with my brother in the 34th and returned to camp in the evening.

BATTLE OF VITORIA

The Light Division moved at daylight, and was 1813 joined on the march by the 4th Division. Passed June through Subijana de Morillo and other villages. 21st On arriving at some heights, the Division drew up. The enemy could be very distinctly observed in very large force also drawn up, with the right of his army resting upon the river Zadorra beyond the village of Abechucho, the centre upon some very commanding heights in front of Ariñez, and the left upon Subijana de Alva, having a body of men posted somewhat in advance, on very rugged and high ground named La Puebla. The river took a serpentine course along their position. As soon as General Hill opened the ball by attacking the enemy's right, we moved nearer the river with the 1st and 3rd Battalions. We now had a fine view of the centre on the heights of Najara, which was destined to be attacked by the Light, 3rd, 4th, and 7th Divisions. Three bridges (Tres Puentes) over this river were left undefended by the enemy, and under a sharp cannonade they were passed. We moved up the heights to the attack. *Johnny* was very soon put off them, and took shelter in Ariñez, which place he held very obstinately, but ultimately was driven from thence. To the right the mountains ran at right angles with our front. On their very top you could see the contending parties engaged; from thence as far as the eye could reach along the line to our left a continual tiralade going on, the enemy gradually retiring, and the British, Portuguese, and Spaniards moving close upon their heels. Our 3rd Battalion

19

1813 Rifles was then posted in the village of Villodas, which was directly under the heights.   The French occupied the houses near the bridge over the river, to prevent our advance there.   In the afternoon the enemy to our front began to make less opposition, and only seemed determined to get out of our clutches as fast as possible, but they had to march over a fine plain, which enabled us from time to time to press them confoundedly.   Towards evening, the road became covered with baggage of every description, artillery, caissons, and French carrying away their merchandise and plunder by all sorts of conveyances.   We were advancing rapidly.   Occasionally a Rifle Man would shoot a horse yoked to a gun.   This stopped the rest behind and blocked up the way.   Now and then a few soldiers would fire shots at us from among the baggage.   Night at last drew its sable curtain over the scene of slaughter and confusion, and afforded a fine opportunity to many to go in quest of plunder.   We had fought over twenty miles of ground.   I seated myself by a fire with the officers of the company, and was fortunate enough to get part of a ham and some claret which one of the soldiers had taken from a cart belonging to the enemy.   In a little time we had a variety of eatables brought by men of the company. I never ate with a better relish in my life.   I lay down by the fire in a French officer's cloak, which one of the men gave me ; he had that day shot its wearer. I awoke at daylight refreshed and in high spirits.

June   The Division fell in and moved by the Pamplona 22nd road (the only one left to retreat by) in pursuit of the enemy.   The French had lost yesterday about 10,000 men killed, wounded, and taken, besides 151 pieces of cannon, 415 caissons, and the military chest and the whole of their baggage. King Joseph was so hard pressed that he was compelled to leave his carriage, mount a horse, and gallop off. General Gazan's wife was taken, but sent back in her carriage under an escort this morning. Moved through Salvatierra, preceded by the 1st German Hussars, 14th Dragoons, and one troop of Horse Artillery. We followed the French, and found all the villages abandoned by the inhabitants. The Dragoons came up with the enemy's rear-guard and took fifty stragglers encamped near the village of Alvisera.

At daybreak again followed up the retreating French through Ciordia, passed the river Buranda into the province of Navarre. We found the enemy posted upon the river at a small village. The bridge, being of wood, was set on fire. Our Horse Artillery commenced playing upon the enemy's column, which soon after moved off. We forded the river and followed the enemy, pushing his rear-guard so fast that several bridges were not destroyed, so great was the hurry to get away. The French now hit upon another expedient to retard our pursuit—they set the villages on fire, but that made us push on the faster through them, and at Echarri Ariñez we skirmished with some Voltigeurs, but they soon went off. The enemy again drew up at La Cuenca. The Horse Artillery opened fire upon their columns, which caused them to retire through Huarte, our cavalry occupying the place. The Light Division encamped at La Cuenca, having moved five leagues. The weather very bad.

Moved off with the dawn. Cavalry, guns, 1st and

[margin: 1813]

[margin: June 23rd]

[margin: 24th]

1813 3rd Battalion Rifles soon came up with the enemy's rear-guard and attacked it. They fought for a while and retired as fast as possible to another position. We as rapidly followed, and again turned the rascals out of it. The roads, from the quantities of rain, were very bad indeed, frequently up to the knees. I never in my life saw our Horse Artillery do such wonders in crossing the country. They passed over ditches and through places that no one would credit or think possible ; the horses were noble animals and in the finest order. Towards the afternoon we got upon the high road, *camino real*, from Madrid to Pamplona. The *only gun* the enemy had brought from Vitoria was now turned against us. The enemy again formed up across the King's road, gave us a few discharges of grape and round shot. Some Rifle Men were ordered to move quickly upon the flank and attack it, the Horse Artillery giving the enemy a few rounds of shot and shrapnel from two guns. The Dragoons dashed forward. Poor *Johnny* in the hurry to get away overturned gun, horses, and all. The road had been raised 15 feet over a flat. The side was built up like a wall. It was just the worst place for miles that the animals and gun could have been trundled over. Elated with our success, I came up to the spot, but was sadly hurt at a melancholy spectacle. Five French soldiers, who a few moments before were in rude health, now lay with their limbs frightfully lacerated and broken, the fibres hanging in strings from dreadful wounds, the blood mixing with the mud which their limbs and bodies were lying in. I, with the assistance of some others, dragged them upon some dry ground.

I pitied them and gave them a little wine from my 1813
calabash. They seemed to wish to be shot; one in
particular requested it as a boon. The sight was
too much. I turned away from it with horror, and
if a tear fell, what then! May not a soldier be in
possession of as fine feelings as other men? I have
seen a half-starved soldier give his last crust to a
famishing infant.

Occupied the villages of Santa Barafra, Berioplaño,
and Aldava, close to and north of Pamplona.

The Light Division assembled upon the great June
road in conjunction with the other Divisions for the 25th
purpose of cutting off every communication with
Pamplona. The Light Division moved by a mountain
road a little way out of the range of the guns of the
fortress, and had a fine view of the village of Villaba,
on the Arga. Pamplona is a large strongly fortified
town, with a very important citadel of great strength;
it is the capital of Navarra, and situated in a highly
cultivated country, with villages innumerable in its
vicinity, nearly surrounded with mountains, which
appear in the distance, one higher than another, till lost
in the clouds. The scenery is beautifully romantic,
and, literally speaking, the land flows with milk and
honey.

Marched through Noain and near the aqueduct 26th
of Pamplona, a splendid pile composed of one hundred
fine stone arches. Moved forward and encamped
near a village at the junction of the main roads
leading from Tudela and Zaragoza. This was done
to intercept General Clausel, if possible, but without effect.

Marched near Barasoain, rested and cooked. 27th

1813 Moved forward by the Zidaco River, and crossed over it at Tafalla by a good stone bridge. Encamped near Olite.

June   Marched past Olite and turned off the Zaragoza
28th road and took that of San Martin. Crossed over an uncultivated plain of great extent and halted to cook near Murillo de Fruto, four and a half leagues, in a pine wood. Proceeded along the river Aragon, crossed it near Galipienzo by a bridge of stone. The road became extremely bad, resembling a goat track. The head of the column arrived near Caseda, four leagues more, at 11 P.M. A great part of the Division bivouacked upon the road-side owing to the darkness of the night and the harassing march. The object of this forced march was to cut off Clausel's Division, but this rapid movement had been anticipated, for, like a skilful fellow, he had crossed the Ebro at Tudela and then moved upon Zaragoza.

29th   Halted.

30th   Crossed the Aragon at Caseda and proceeded to Sanguessa ; encamped near it. I was sent for wood with a party of men, and as it is frequently a scarce article, the authorities ordered a house to be given up, which we very soon had level with the ground and every bit of wood selected from the rubbish. I was returning to camp when General Picton, who commanded the 3rd Division, and was coming to his encampment near us, said, "Well, sir, you have got wood enough for yours and my Division. I shall have it divided. Make your men throw it down. It is a d——d concern to have to follow. You sweep up everything before you." Luckily at this moment I

espied General Alten, who commanded the Light 1813
Division, and told him the orders I had received.
He was very much annoyed, and came up to remonstrate with Picton upon interfering with me in
the performance of my duty. I took advantage of
it, ordered the men to pick up their loads and be off.
Fighting is a very minor part of a soldier's duty ; he
must be a complete man of the world, and if he has
the smallest command, it requires much cleverness to
perform his duty as he ought to do. There are a
thousand annoyances thrown in his path which he
must be philosopher enough to laugh at.

Sanguessa is a very good Spanish town with a
castle of some strength. Mina, a most celebrated
guerilla chief, took it from the French. I was hunting about the town for good wine for our mess
when a respectable-looking man begged me to enter
his house, and cordially shaking me by the hand,
offered me some excellent wine. I asked him to sell
me a skinful, but he said, " I will not sell, but I will
give you one." My servant was directed to dismount
from the mule, and my skin, which was the skin of a
large buck, was soon filled, amounting at least to
seventy bottles of wine. I gave a respectable-looking
woman five dollars as a present. On my arrival in
the camp my friends were highly delighted with my
good luck in adding so much to our comforts.

Halted.   July 1st

Returned towards Pamplona and encamped near 2nd
Monreal.

This morning the Light Division assembled upon 3rd
the main road near Noain, and moved partly round
Villaba to a small village near Pamplona.

1813
July
4th
The Division sent out strong working parties to throw up works to cover our piquets before Pamplona, which was now rigorously blockaded. The 4th Division relieved us.

5th   The Light Division assembled from different villages at Sauroren, and proceeded up a narrow valley to the town of Ostiz, and encamped upon a rivulet.

6th   Marched up the stream to Lanz, which is situated at the foot of the celebrated Pyrenean Mountains. Encamped in a fine grove of chestnut trees. The hills, which are numerous and richly covered with sturdy old oak and other magnificent trees, with the mountains towering above them in every direction, the tops of which are buried in the clouds, gives a grandeur to the surrounding appearance that can only be felt by those on the spot.

7th   Marched by a most romantic road, and ascended hills, many of them covered with fine trees, oak, beech, and larch, and the ground covered with wild strawberries; the valleys delightfully irrigated, and abounding with fruits, corn, and oil. How soon these peaceful vales will be disturbed with the noisy din of war! Halted for three hours upon the side of a steep hill, and afterwards moved into San Esteven, a charming village, where we fared sumptuously. Major-General Skerrett took the command of our 2nd Brigade, as General Vandeleur was appointed to the cavalry. The Bidasoa rises in the Pyrenees near Elizondo, passing through this valley, and ultimately disembogues itself into the sea at Fuenterrabia, where it divides France from Spain.

Remained quiet here until the afternoon of the 1813
14th; moved out of the town and marched and July
encamped upon the heights above Sumbilla.   14th

The Division at daybreak moved down the Bidasoa 15th
by a mountain track, sometimes close to the river, at
other times winding along the side of the mountain a
considerable height from it.   On arriving at the bridge
of Lezaca we discovered the enemy's advanced post
upon the summit of a mountain.   Ordered immediately
to move up and dislodge the enemy, which was done
very leisurely, as the sides were very steep, and it was
necessary not to waste our strength and vigour, as we
might have occasion for it.   On arriving near the
top the French fired occasional shots at us, but
ultimately we got to the top, and soon made *Johnny*
scamper down the other side.   These heights, Santa
Barbara, are named after a convent, the ruins of which
still remain.   We now had a fine view of the enemy's
position on the Spanish side of the ridge of mountains
which separate France from Spain; at their base
stands the small town of Vera.   The Bidasoa makes
an abrupt turn close to this place and runs through
irregular and precipitous ground to the sea.   The
enemy were dislodged towards evening from Vera,
with the exception of a piquet posted near some out-
houses.   Our piquet occupied some houses in the
town.   The Division encamped upon the heights.
The enemy's piquet now occupied a strong commanding rocky projection, which was placed
immediately over Vera.   The enemy's sentry had a
bird's-eye view of all our movements.   Our piquet
was advanced to the extreme end of the place.   The
road which leads into France through Vera is called

1813 the Puerto de Vera. It is a very strong pass, and, from its formidable appearance, a few men ought to defend it. A Division of the French army have occupied the strong ground on each side of the pass, and are engaged in throwing up fieldworks to strengthen the position. Lord Wellington's quarters are at Ernani, near San Sebastian. The siege of the latter place was proceeding vigorously under General Sir T. Graham. We remained in our position, going on piquet in turn till the 25th.

July 25th   Marched through Lezaca and Yanzi; encamped on the heights near Sumbilla. Marshal Soult, who now commands the French army, collected a large force and attacked the passes of Roncesvalles and Maya, which were carried, and consequently caused us to retrograde, endeavouring to cover Pamplona, as it was easy to see that Soult wanted to drive the British army beyond that fortress. San Sebastian was attacked at dawn this morning by the 5th Division at two breaches. 500 men were killed and wounded, and the attempt to storm the town failed.

27th   Marched off in the dark and blundered along the whole night. Arrived at Zubieta after daylight, which was only two leagues and a half, the roads being very bad, and amongst rugged mountains.

28th   Encamped this morning, and continually heard a heavy cannonade and peals of musketry, indicating hard fighting upon our right.

29th   Marched to Saldeas at 9 o'clock P.M.

30th   Proceeded to Lecumberri, and afterwards moved into a wood, and encamped across the high road from Pamplona to Tolosa, about five leagues from both, supporting the left of General Hill's corps.

Marched to Loyza and encamped.

Soult having been worsted in all his attacks upon the British, was now in full retreat, having suffered very considerably in killed and wounded and prisoners. The Light Division made a forced march this day by Zubieta, along a mountain track on the left bank of the Bidasoa to the bridge of Yanzi (the distance about eight leagues), the greater part of the day under a burning sun, which sadly exhausted the men, but they cheered up on seeing the enemy, and made the attack with such real pluck that the latter was soon scampering across the bridge in the greatest hurry. This body of the enemy had merely occupied the bridge to protect the march of a column moving from Sumbilla. Our 1st and 3rd Battalions took possession of some houses near the bridge, and a tiralade was kept up until dark, the enemy's force being so formidable from the beginning, that it was not deemed advisable to push on. I lost this little affair by being ordered to remain at Loyza a sufficient time to try by court-martial, Sergeant Hayes. It came on dark before I got up to the Battalion. I got bewildered in the mountains and lost my way. The enemy's fires and ours appeared all round me before I gave up the attempt to find the Battalion, so I tied my horse to a tree, pulled him some leaves and loose grass, and lay down near him until daylight. My horse was ill, so the other two officers who had been on the court-martial were obliged to leave me before dark.

Joined my Battalion. The enemy had withdrawn during the night. Moved after them by the road to the pass of Vera, the 2nd Brigade by Yanzi and

1813 Lezaca. Encamped on our original ground and took up the line of piquets without firing a shot. The enemy remained upon a rocky steep connected with Puerto de Echellar. It was found necessary to dislodge this force from that place. In the afternoon the 1st Brigade was drawn up upon the heights of Santa Barbara, and the 1st and 3rd Battalions were sent up the face of a craggy steep, almost perpendicular. The enemy opened fire upon us. Captain Pemberton, who was with my brother and myself, received a severe wound, the ball passing directly under the ham. Several men were knocked over as we gradually approached the top. The enemy made a charge, but were soon stopped ; and, a fog coming on and we still advancing and firing upon them, they gave up the hill without fiercely contending for it. General Barnes's Brigade, 7th Division, in a spirited manner drove a large body of the enemy from very strong ground on our right, so that the pass of Echellar was in our possession. The 17th Portuguese occupied the heights for the night and we returned to our encampment near the Bidasoa and Vera. The partisan, General Longa, had remained on the left bank of this river during our absence, and had thrown up works with a *tête de pont.*

Aug.   The 7th Division took up the ground we yester-
3rd day deprived the enemy of, and we resumed our old position upon the heights of Santa Barbara. We remained quiet here till the end of the month, keeping a good look-out on each other.

On the 29th, in consequence of the failure of the attempt to storm San Sebastian, Lord Wellington paid the Light Division a high compliment by 1813 allowing a subaltern's party from each Battalion, total 250 men, to go as a storming party. My messmate Percival, a most worthy and brave fellow, being senior, took charge of the party from the 1st Battalion ; 2nd Lieutenant Hamilton also went under him.

The town was assaulted about mid-day on the 30th, Aug. and after considerable delay and very hard fighting 30th the breaches were entered, and the place fell into our hands, the principal part of the garrison having retreated into the castle, which completely commands the place.

CHAPTER XII

LETTER No. XXI

To his Parents, from Vera, Pyrenees, dated 30th August 1813

Description of his surroundings in the Pyrenees—Describes the advance from Alameda and gives extracts from his journal and details of fight at San Millan and battle of Vitoria— The pursuit—Pitiful state of the French wounded—They curse their Emperor—Fighting in the Pyrenees—Would come home when the army goes into winter quarters, but has no plain clothes—Affectionate messages to his family and anxiety to be of assistance to them.

Postscript, dated 4th September 1813

Describes the fighting on the occasion of the defence of the bridge of Vera (the morning after the preceding letter was written)—Heavy losses of the Rifles—Bewails being a junior Lieutenant — Brother Joseph posted to another company and "to start fair by himself."

Journal—31st August–31st December 1813

Soult makes a final attempt to relieve San Sebastian—Defence of the bridge of Vera—A night on outpost duty—Night attack by the French, who carry the bridge of Vera—

Death of Captain Cadoux of the Rifles—The "Volunteer"
and his experiences of campaigning—He returns to England
—The storming of San Sebastian—The "high compliment"
paid to the Rifles by Lord Wellington—Final warning to his
father not to show his letters about—The fortress stormed
—The Governor surrenders the castle—Simmons visits San
Sebastian and sees the wounded officers of the Rifles—
Forcing the Pass of Vera—The 3rd Battalion Rifles covers
the advance — Heavy fighting and losses — La Rhune
occupied—Extensive view from the mountains—French
territory in sight—Witnesses a naval engagement—The
French fortify Petite La Rhune—Fall of Pamplona—Lord
Wellington thereupon advances—Battle of the Nivelle—
Colonel Barnard severely wounded—Asks Simmons if he
can recover, and gets a reply—Simmons ordered to remain
and look after his Colonel, who recovers—More fighting
in the Pyrenees—Lieutenant Hopwood killed—End of the
year.

LETTER No. XXII

*To his Parents, from St. Jean de Luz, France, dated
7th December 1813*

The fighting in the Pyrenees in October and the French retirement across the frontier—Wellington's orders prior to the
battle of the Nivelle—How the Rifles spent the evening
before the fight—The battle of the Nivelle—The French
routed at all points and driven from their entrenchments
—Colonel Barnard's wound—Simmons placed in charge
of him and "bleeds him constantly"—Simmons dines
with Lord Wellington—Takes steps to make brother Joseph
more independent—Expectations of being able to assist his
family.

Postscript

British soldiers on good terms with the French population—
Contrasts their behaviour to that of the French soldiers in

Spain—The French now suffering for their misdeeds—
Probabilities of peace and determination to enlist in some
foreign army if England has no wars—Expectations of more
fighting in a few days.

Letter No. XXI

Bivouac near Vera on the frontiers of France,
Pyrenees, 30*th August* 1813.

Dear Parents—Your letter, bearing date 17th
July, I received during the advance, and at a time when
each day's march produced something amusing and
interesting.   I therefore delayed answering it until
this period, wishing to say much in a small compass.
I am now seated in a charming hut of my own
forming, with a crystal mountain stream running
at my feet, on every side tremendous mountains,
whose lofty summits embrace the clouds, their sides
covered with rich woods and fruit-trees; the
valleys exuberantly luxurious, abounding with fruits,
corn, and wine.   Such delightful scenery I never
before beheld.   In such a place, if it were not for
war—cruel war!—how happy the inhabitants might
live.   But, alas! those innocent dwellings are pillaged
and the poor distressed owners fled with their families
into the wild recesses in the mountains, in hopes
of sheltering themselves from their savage pursuers.
These bloodthirsty rascals often, when they cannot
find the plunder they expect, set fire to the houses
and burn whole villages.   Such wrongs call out for
vengeance, and ere long I hope the country that has
caused so much *innocent* blood to be spilt will feel in
the bosom of her own the effects of war.   I am sorry

to hear of the death of my aunt. I had pleased 1813
myself with the hopes of seeing her again. How
fleeting and delusive are all worldly views!

.   .   .   .   .   .

As the newspapers have given you accounts of
our battles, I will describe some of the occurrences
that took place. On the 21st of May we broke up
from our cantonment and the Division assembled
near Ciudad Rodrigo in high health, and upon the
next day we commenced our march upon Salamanca.
The French scampered off. Our Dragoons roughly
handled some of them. We then marched upon
Toro, on the river Douro. The enemy were here
outwitted by our great Lord's superior generalship—
outflanked and obliged to leave that position. Our
Hussars came up with some cavalry and sliced and
carved them genteelly. We were much astonished
that we had already passed over so great a tract of
country without once exchanging a shot. We now
moved upon the river Ebro, passing through the most
iron-bound country I had ever beheld, and as we
crossed the river the band played the "Downfall
of Paris," which made us laugh and afforded us
some amusement.

To digress a little from the subject, I must say
something of the fertility of the place by referring
back to my journal of the 15th of June. After a
long day's march, we crossed the Ebro at Puente-
areñas and bivouacked near the village named
Areñas. The river narrowed, but very rapid. Swam
the river with some of my friends. This fertile
valley is called Villacayo. The scenery on the banks
of the river was sublime, novel, and picturesque.

1813 On every side, rugged and steep mountains. Plenty of wine, fruits, and vegetables. This manœuvre of our great Commander, which the enemy had not calculated upon, put *Johnny* into much confusion. Our army now was daily concentrating, and at the same time moving upon Vitoria. On the 18th of June our Division made a rapid march to intercept a body of the enemy, and came pounce upon a Division. Our 1st and 3rd Battalions were ordered to march over some very steep hills covered with trees to attack them in the rear, at the same time sending two of our companies just to amuse them in the front, and with orders not to press upon the town until we fell upon the rear.

Poor Joe had recently had the ague and looked delicate. This morning, however, he felt a stomach for the fight. I told him to keep at my side and he would see what fine bloodhounds Rifle Men were. We soon gained the spot, and rushed upon them furiously, and though they gave us several discharges from a good-formed line, they were so staggered that one Brigade ran into the mountains, while the other retreated, throwing away everything. We chased them through several villages, in which they usually made a stand, to the no small terror of the inhabitants, as it astonished peaceable people to have the balls whistling about their ears. Our men were their own commissaries this day, having taken plenty of white bread and bacon. Being very hungry, I fed lustily. Joe could not partake of the repast, though he felt pleased with the day's amusement.

On 19th June, I visited Maud and dined with him. I had not seen him for some time. Joe quite well.

June 21st was a day which will be for ever 1813
memorable in the pages of history, for the gallantry
which was displayed by all is beyond my humble pen
to describe.   I assure you I feel proud at being able to
say I was there.   Fortune favoured me as well as Joe,
who was always at my side (as he belonged to the same
company) ; he behaved as brave as a lion.   I thank
Almighty God for His kindness and protection from
injury in the hour of danger.   It is exceedingly
lucky, three brothers in the same fight and none
touched, and how we have escaped so long astonishes
me.   As you have had the whole business in the
papers, it is needless to dwell upon this.   We fought
till dark, being heartily tired.   Having been marching and fighting without tasting anything since
two o'clock that morning, there was no wonder.
I fried some ham upon the point of my sword,
drank a good dose of *Johnny's* wine, and fell fast
asleep upon the spot, forgetting even my blankets,
and was lost to the cares of the world until daylight.
The men standing to their arms awoke me, when I
found myself wet through with the dew of the night.
What strange vicissitudes of life the soldier meets with !
Campaigning is the life for me.   I have never felt such
happiness since I became a soldier.   I often think
that to be living in England after this wild, romantic
existence would not give me half so much satisfaction.

We daily hung upon the enemy's rear — our
Division, some cavalry, and Light Artillery.   In
this way we annoyed them very seriously, making
many bite the ground and other poor wretches travel,
wounded and bleeding at every step, until nature
could do no more.   Being exhausted, they fell, cursing

1813 their Emperor with their last breath. Whenever these unfortunate wretches fell into our hands, as soon as they ascertained we were English they were satisfied, knowing well the nobleness of the soul which an Englishman possesses.

On 24th June we drove the enemy into and past Pamplona, and took their last gun. Since that period we have been marching and counter-marching in the Pyrenees, among and upon such mountain tracks as would astonish milch goats, much more animals with two legs, ill-calculated for travelling in such rugged places. Different parts of our army, according to circumstances, have frequently dislodged the enemy from the strongest places that Nature could in her vagaries have formed. Such a place as this we attacked on the 2nd of August (our 1st and 3rd Battalions were the only people in the fight), which was carried handsomely, and what pleased our fellows most was beating the enemy over their own boundaries and letting the French peasantry see their soldiers run away.

This day I lost a valuable young friend. He was in the same company, and badly wounded in the knee, which I am afraid will finish his career of glory. Thus, since we started, Joe and myself have not received a single scratch, while the other two officers are both wounded. However, it is all a lottery. Maud had escaped until the other day. He was lucky having a horse to stop the force, or the ball would have riddled him.

Our regiment has lost above twelve officers killed and wounded during this campaign (I mean the Battalion), which has been less than we ever before lost. We are now placed upon the French frontier 1813 in the Pyrenees. The enemy's army are opposite to us, upon a chain of mountains similar to those we occupy. Our sentries are within fifty yards of each other, and their main body opposite to where we are, about a mile off, so we can come to blows in half an hour whenever our great Commander may think fit to pit us, or in other words, slip us at them. Our cannon is now thundering at San Sebastian and Pamplona. Whether *Johnny* will again raise the siege of these places, a few days will determine. We shall be in hot water until these places fall.

I had a letter yesterday from Maud. He informs me that the wound he received is quite well, and he is ready for another affair. Joe is in high health. He is now very stout, and cultivating a pair of moustaches, which amuse me no little. I have been thinking of visiting you this winter after the campaign is over and we go into winter quarters. I could with a fair wind cross the Bay of Biscay in three or four days from this point. I could have leave when I choose. The expenses of travelling in England would fleece my pocket. There is also another consideration— plain clothes, which are very expensive, and I have nothing but my military attire, which would make the people gaze at me as upon a dancing bear. I must now conclude with my best wishes for your general happiness. My duty to my uncle, in which Joseph most heartily joins.—Yours ever,

GEO. SIMMONS,
Lt., 1st Batt., 95th Regt.

Be careful and seal your letters. The last was open.

1813   Deserters inform us Soult means to attack us again in two or three days. When we get into winter quarters in two months' time or so, you may leave a note at the post office to inform me where you live in Hull; direct "Mr. Simmons" upon it. I hope you will not mention my coming to any one, as I want no acquaintances. You need not leave a note if the postmaster or man can give me the information, as you then may say you expect a person to see you about the time I have mentioned. As worldly views are so fleeting and uncertain, it is better for you not to make too sure of my coming, as it will increase the disappointment if any unforeseen accident prevents me.

Sept. 4th.—I had finished my letter on the 30th. The next morning at daylight a column of the enemy were drawn up opposite us, amounting to 20,000. Away went our baggage and we to arms. About 9 o'clock A.M. they descended in three columns into the valley, covered by some artillery, crossed the roads under a smart fire from part of our 2nd Battalion, and disappointed us by moving off to their own right in the direction of San Sebastian. The Spaniards fought well. Our Battalion was marching all the day, occupying first one position and then another, but, to our annoyance, *Johnny* never came near us. Towards night it began to thunder and lighten horridly, and poured with torrents of rain. I was on piquet, and observed *Johnny* by the lightning's glare retracing his steps back in this horrid night. At 2 A.M. *Johnny* attacked a bridge where we had a piquet of Rifle Men, two companies, who fought so handsomely, that with this small number they 1813 checked them for an hour. A captain of ours, who stood upon the bridge rallying his men round him, fell like a soldier, covered with wounds.[1] Five officers of ours were wounded. This attack of Soult's was to relieve San Sebastian and Pamplona—a miserable attempt. The three British regiments in the Light Division gave a proportion of men and officers for a storming party to San Sebastian. I am told nothing could exceed the gallantry displayed by our brave fellows; every part was defended by art beyond conception. One officer of ours had four wounds, another was shot through the side, and all the officers of our Division that were there, excepting two, were killed or wounded. It is a melancholy thing to be a junior lieutenant in such times as these, because the senior claims the first offer. Whenever a party is detached upon such an occasion, our Boys are so proud of it that, according to seniority, they would not think of letting it pass them. When I am senior I hope to have my turn. The castle still holds out, but it must surrender in a few days, as the town has fallen.

My riding horse, which cost me twenty guineas, the blacksmith unluckily pricked in shoeing. The foot is very bad, so if the enemy attack us, I shall be under the necessity of shooting the animal. I am very unlucky with my animals, and no person can be more careful. I bought Joe a good pony. I have now got him a strong donkey to carry his equipage, so he is not dependent upon me. I have also got him removed to another company, as the more he is independent of me the better. I have now settled

[1] Captain Cadoux.

1813 everything for him to my wishes; he is free from debt, with five months' pay due to him. He now starts fair for himself. I shall always give him such advice as may serve him, and make him steer clear of those misfortunes that young men are liable to, particularly in the army, without a monitor. He has always behaved himself to my satisfaction, which makes me proud of him, and whatever I tell him he carefully obeys. The officers like him much, which is highly flattering to me; and, above all, he possesses that tender affection for his family which I admire above all his virtues.

Journal—31st August–31st December 1813

Aug.   Marshal Soult, finding that San Sebastian was
31st closely invested and the breaches practicable, was determined to make a desperate attempt to drive the British from their present position and raise the siege of that place. He concentrated a large force, which at daylight we found filing from a variety of defiles in the mountains and forming immediately above Vera. Seeing his troops assembled so clearly from our position produced a good deal of interest and not a few jokes amongst us.

The enemy soon began to move down the steep hill towards the river, and crossed at a ford below the bridge, having previously driven our piquets from the town. Some French moved forward to take possession of the bridge and were repulsed by two Rifle companies in good style. A stronger force was sent to the bridge, and the two companies occupied some houses and fired upon the enemy from them.

A few shot and shell were thrown to cover the 1813 advance of the French in passing the river. Being fired from a spot considerably above their heads, the artillery officer had not given sufficient elevation, and three or four shells burst amongst themselves and set them scampering about, much to our amusement, who were literally looking down upon them. The enemy's skirmishers moved up the heights to our left towards the high road through Irun to San Sebastian, followed by their columns.

Don Manuel Freyre, with his Spanish Division, fought very spiritedly in the town, and also upon the heights of San Marcial, when the French attempted to crown them. The Spaniards beat the enemy back. Lord Wellington was an eye-witness on this occasion and was highly pleased. Before dark, Marshal Soult was completely beaten in all his attacks as well as having gained no advantage by his manœuvres, having had to contend with his *master* in the art of war. The 1st Brigade, Light Division, marched from hill to hill and towards evening crowned the heights above Lezaca and remained there for the night. The day had been exceptionally hot, and our march up the sides of high mountains was trying to the soldiers. Just before dark I was placed with thirty men upon the side of a mountain. The night now set in very stormy and rainy ; we had great difficulty to keep our fire from going out. I sent some of them to the house of a Spaniard close by and got a large chest. I had it placed on end before the fire and sat in it. I was obliged to be very much upon my guard and the sentries very active, being close to the enemy. The rain ran down the sides of the

1813 mountains in torrents, and the thunder and lightning were very frequent. By the occasional glare which illumined the mountain above me, I saw the enemy in full retreat, no doubt much alarmed for fear of finding the river not fordable. Our Rifle Men still occupied the right bank of the river as far as keeping a double sentry close to it and the other piquets in loop-holed houses near.

Sept. 1st   About 2 o'clock A.M. the enemy, finding no possible way of retreating but over the bridge and through Vera, made a desperate attack with a most overwhelming force on the bridge, and carried it. Captain Cadoux brought his company to the bridge and tried to drive the enemy back, or prevent more from passing. They fought most heroically ; he soon fell, after having received several musket-balls in his breast. His Lieutenant, Llewellyn, had his jaw shattered. Several men were killed and wounded. They were obliged to retire a little distance, but kept up a fire as long as the enemy continued to file over the bridge. Returned and occupied our old encampment, and took up the line of piquets as before. Cold, wet, and hungry, my friend Cox and I lay down, joking about the adventures of the last day and night, and waiting the arrival of our baggage to get something to eat.

A gentleman named Dornford,[1] who had been

[1] Joseph Dornford was originally at Trinity College, Cambridge, which he left for the Peninsula. On returning home he entered at Wadham College, Oxford, and in 1816 was elected a Fellow of Oriel. After some years of College work he retired to a country living, first in Northamptonshire and afterwards in Devonshire.—See Rev. T. Mozley's *Reminiscences of Oriel College and the Oxford Movement*, ii. 55, 78.—ED.

educated for a parson, but took a chivalrous idea, when 1813 comfortably seated in his mother's parlour before a good fire reading the description of heroes and fighting men, that he had completely mistaken his profession, determined to become a volunteer, and obtained letters to Lord Wellington, little doubting that he must ultimately become a great man and a General. With this idea he presented himself as speedily as possible before the hero of Britain, who sent him to the Rifles, since with that corps he would have a bellyful of fighting. He was very anxious to commence his military career, but he expected that he should have an opportunity, like the great men of old, to commence with an oration and to lead the people, and that every one would admire him for his personal valour. But, alas ! he found that impossible. The men had plenty of leaders who understood their business and had for years been at this sort of work, which also gave them the benefit of experience. Also, from exposure to every description of hardship, their bodies had become proof against what ordinary men (who had not gone through the same ordeal) would sink under. " I am astonished," says he, drawing near to us, " how you can joke and pass off so lightly scenes of misery and woe such as we have gone through the last day and night. God knows how I repent ever turning soldier." He was a clever, gentlemanly young fellow, and we told him he certainly had mistaken his profession, and we advised him to give it up and return home. He thanked us for the advice and set off the same afternoon to Passages, and embarked for England soon after.[1]

[1] I have since heard that he made a most excellent divine and a most worthy member of society.—G. S.

I went to examine the bridge and river where the French had attempted to pass. A number of men had been drowned close to the bridge, and also at the places fordable previous to the rain. The wounded had been removed, but the dead were still laid about the bridge. Trout of a large size were feasting upon the Frenchmen's carcases in the water.

The town of San Sebastian was assaulted about mid-day on 31st August, and after considerable delay and very hard fighting the place fell into our hands. The principal part of the garrison retreated into the castle, which completely commands the place.

3rd The Governor made a proposal that if we would desist throwing shells into the castle he would surrender if not relieved in a fortnight. His proposal was not acceded to, and shells were thrown in with redoubled vigour until the morning of the 6th, 6th when the Governor, General Rey, gave up and surrendered with the remainder of his garrison as prisoners of war—1300 effective men, 500 sick and wounded. The loss in killed at the assaults and during the siege was 1200 men.

26th My poor friend Percival had been dreadfully wounded at the foot of one of the breaches, and in the evening he was carried away to a house in the neighbourhood. To-day I paid him a visit, and was greatly shocked at his emaciated frame. However, he ultimately got better, as well as Lieutenant Hamilton, who was also seriously wounded in two places. I went into San Sebastian and found everything very dilapidated. It had the appearance of being a place of some note, placed at the base of a bold promontory, on the top of which is a Moorish castle. The town is well

fortified, its walls being washed by the sea on both 1813
sides, and the part that it does not come in contact
with has strong works across.   Every description of
defence possible for a skilful man to resort to had
been made by the Governor.

Went to Passages, another seaport town.   The Sept.
rocky cliffs on the sea coast are very bold, and 27th
the gaping fissure through which ships enter the
harbour appears to have been caused some time or
other by an extraordinary convulsion of nature, the
sides at the entrance are so abrupt and steep.

I left my poor suffering friend and returned to my 28th
corps.   Found all quiet, and continued taking piquet
duties as they came round until the 7th of October.

Forcing the Pass of Vera

Lord Wellington was determined to advance the left Oct.
of his army.   General Graham was ordered forward 7th
and the Light Division was directed to clear the heights
in our front.   We formed close to the bottom of the
hills.   Our 3rd Battalion moved forward in skirmishing order up the side of the high hill which appears
to overhang Vera.   Nothing in the world could appear
more beautiful than their steady advance.   It was
more like a field-day's manœuvre than a fight; 15,000
or 20,000 soldiers had an opportunity of witnessing
their cool intrepidity.   The two Brigades now
advanced.   The 2nd Brigade, under the command of
Colonel Colborne, met with great obstacles in carrying a star redoubt, and the 2nd Caçadores and the
2nd Battalion of Rifle Men lost a number of men :
the Colonel of the Caçadores killed, Captain

1813 Gibbons, Lieutenants Hill and Campbell killed, five
officers wounded. The Spaniards under Longa did
not reach their ground in time to turn the flank of
the redoubt. The Light Division had innumerable
obstacles to encounter, redoubts and field-works on
every eminence presenting themselves to our view ;
but the steadiness and daring intrepidity of the men
eventually surmounted all obstacles, and the French
were driven into their own country, of which we now
had a fine view.

Captain Cox and myself, with about sixty men,
followed the enemy down into the valley through the
Pass of Vera. We took some prisoners and two
French horn-players, and, laughably enough, our men
requested them to play some French tunes. What
with alarm and fright, they made sad music of it. We
moved up to our encampment, and thus ended a day
of as pretty rifle practice as I had ever seen, and the
enemy driven from a position that had cost them much
labour and trouble in putting into a state of defence.

One particularly high mountain named La Rhune
Oct. was still in possession of the enemy, and from the
8th top the French were amusing themselves by firing
long shots at the Spaniards all day. In the evening
their force was withdrawn and this morning La Rhune
9th was occupied by the Light Division. A smaller mountain, from its similarity and position, was called Petite
La Rhune, and divided from it by a valley. Our
advanced piquets were now posted on one side upon
the slopes, and the French on the opposite side within
200 yards of us.

From these stupendous mountains we had a most
commanding view of a vast extent of highly

cultivated French territory, innumerable villages, and 1813
the town and port of St. Jean de Luz. We could
also see our cruisers sailing about near the French
coast, which gave us an additional interest in the view
before us.

This morning one of our ships was observed to Oct.
be chasing a brig of war, and got between her and 13th
the shore. We observed the batteries near the town
trying to aid the escape of the French ship, but without success. As the boats from the English went to
board her, the Frenchmen got into theirs and made
for the shore. Some English sailors went on board,
but soon left her. A short time after she was one
mass of fire and soon blew up. A dense smoke arose
from the spot, but in a moment there was not a
vestige that we could perceive remaining upon the
bosom of the ocean. It was a beautiful morning,
and some thousands of veteran Englishmen having a
bird's-eye view of the whole affair, took a lively
interest in the gallant manner our brave Tars performed their duty. How delighted the sailors
would have been if they had been aware that so many
of their countrymen were observing and applauding
them from the tops of the Pyrenees!

The enemy endeavouring to form a connecting 30th
chain of breast-works along the line of their position,
and occasional strong redoubts at intervals supporting this line. The French officers would call out to
us and say, "You cannot remain in these bleak
mountains much longer. We suppose you will soon
retire into Spain for the winter?" Our answer was,
"Very likely we may, if we are so ordered." It
certainly was beginning to be exceedingly cold, with

1813 frequent storms of hail and rain. Our tents, from the tremendous gusts of winds which suddenly and frequently assailed them, were torn and often rendered useless. The Spaniards, and the Portuguese also, lost men from cold and severe weather. Strange to say, in this severe climate, exposed to every hardship, not a man was on the sick-list in our Battalion.

Nov. 1st Sir John Hope arrived from England about this time and took command of the left wing, as Sir Thomas Graham was so ill that he was obliged to go to England.

7th The enemy's position now had a very formidable appearance upon the summit of the ridge of Petite La Rhune. Where it was at all accessible, strong walls were built, with loop-holes to fire through. The ground was scarped, and at small distances along the front, strong redoubts were placed to strengthen more effectually their line of defence. Four French regiments were encamped upon Petite La Rhune ready to man the works at a moment. The roads through the mountains in our rear had been made and put in order by strong parties of soldiers so that cannon could be brought up with facility at any time.

8th Pamplona fell on the 31st of October, after being blockaded for about four months, the Governor, General Cassan, and 4000 men becoming prisoners of war. This circumstance enabled Lord Wellington to make a forward movement with his whole force. Officers commanding regiments in our Division received instructions at what points their regiments were to attack the enemy's works. At the same time the whole of the allied army was to co-operate with us and make a simultaneous attack upon the enemy's 1813 line of works, redoubts, etc.

After dark, the Light Division filed from the encampment behind La Rhune with the least possible noise and formed up into columns and lay down close behind our advanced piquet, which was partly across the deep valley that separated the French from us. Here we remain anxiously waiting until the day should dawn for the attack.

BATTLE OF THE NIVELLE

The happy moment came at last. The French Nov. piquet was seated around the fire, and with no 10th apprehension of what was going to take place. Some heavy cannon sounded the advance, and in a moment every one was in motion up the sides of this tremendous steep. Obstacles of an extraordinary nature were opposed to us, and the enemy kept up a very brisk fire from behind their walls, but nothing could impede the ardour of England's brave sons. The works were carried in every direction. Other works, more concentrated and filled with men, were now opened to our view and immediately attacked. Many gallant fellows fell to rise no more in this world. I saw some French officers standing upon their walls, and trying every means in their power to make their men remain. One young officer was doing prodigies of valour and would not leave the wall; he was shot, and came tumbling down. The French were driven from all their positions, and our army took up the line of the Nivelle. Colonel Barnard, towards the end of this day's fighting, received

1813 a musket-ball in his right breast, which made him tumble from his horse ; he fell upon the hilt of his sword and bruised his side very much. I was near him when he fell, and put my hand into his bosom to feel where the ball entered. I found his lungs had been wounded, as blood in quantities and air issued from the wound ; some blood was passing from his mouth also. He in a most collected manner said, "Do you think I am dying ? Did you ever see a man so wounded recover ?" I observed, "Your wound is a very bad one, but there have been many instances of men recovering from such wounds, and your pulse does not indicate immediate dissolution." "Thank you," he exclaimed, "you give me hopes. If any man can recover, I know I shall." He was immediately bled very largely and taken by four men in a blanket to a farmhouse. After all was over, Sir James Kempt, who commanded the Brigade, sent for me, and said it was his wish, as well as that of all the officers, that I should go to the Colonel and stay with him a few days. My brother Joseph had been in the day's fight. I was anxious to find him. He soon turned up, as lucky as myself, without a wound.

Nov. 13th I went to the house where the Colonel had been taken to and remained with him. Constructed a bearer, upon which the Colonel was placed and supported upon the shoulders of our band through the pass of Vera to that town. I remained with him night and day until every dangerous symptom was subdued, and having a good constitution, he speedily recovered, and on the 7th of December we rode to headquarters at St. Jean-de-Luz. Continued here till

24th December, when we joined the Battalion at the 1813 château of Arcangues. The companies occupied farmhouses in the vicinity. The French army were now in an entrenched camp under the walls of Bayonne, a strongly fortified town upon the confluence of the rivers Nive and Adour. The high road from Paris to Madrid passes through this town, and the road to St. Jean Pied-de-Port runs from it, and takes its course between the Adour and Nive. The by-roads in every direction are exceedingly bad, and more particularly at this time, as the rain had continued to fall in quantities for some time back. The Light Division had been occupied in fortifying the church and château of Arcangues, and field-works were thrown up in many other places. On the 10th, my friends informed me that Marshal Soult advanced with a large force by the high road from Bayonne and formed up near Bassussarry, which is directly opposite the church and château of Arcangues, and made an attack upon the left of our line. Lieutenant Hopwood and Sergeant Brotherwood were killed. A ball passed through both their heads, happening to be standing a little behind one another. They were both capital soldiers and were put in the same grave.

Marshal Soult made a number of attacks on different parts of our line, which in no one instance succeeded, and the loss to the enemy was very great. This Dec. night the regiments of Frankfort and Nassau, with 31st their commandant, Colonel Kruse, came over in a body. These regiments were very well-appointed and good-looking soldiers. They marched to Passages, and were shipped for their own country.

1813 Marshal Soult after this affair told his soldiers that a
hundred battles still awaited them.

The campaign of 1813 now terminated ; it certainly had been a most brilliant one indeed. I now
and then have mentioned officers of my corps that
were killed and wounded, but there were also many
that I have not in my hurry thought of.

LETTER No. XXII

SAINT JEAN-DE-LUZ, FRANCE,
7th December 1813.

MY DEAR PARENTS—As I informed you, some
unforeseen accident might prevent me having the
extreme felicity of paying you a visit this winter, so
things have turned out. However, when you are
acquainted with the circumstances you will rather
attribute it to good fortune than otherwise. To
begin my story. On the 7th of October a combined
attack of the whole army commenced upon the whole
line of the enemy's position. The papers have already
given you the particulars. The enemy were so
thunderstruck at the desperate bravery of our gallant
fellows, that they were driven from all their fortified
positions in succession, and when they had the
temerity to stand, the bayonet decided the business.
The enemy that day was sent scampering into his
own territory. Thus, using the words of Soult,
" The proud islanders overlooked the fine fertile
valleys of France."

The part of the line occupied by our Division was
on the top of an immense high chain of mountains.

In consequence of very bad weather, and being so 1813
elevated, we were exposed to continual hurricanes and
incessant snow, sleet, or rain.   Some men died from
the cold.   This respite gave the enemy time to
construct works, which he was incessantly labouring
at.   Our situation, as you may well conceive, was not
an enviable one.   We wished for the happy moment
to drive the enemy from his present position, in
order that we might have some warmer cantonments
for the winter.   Our noble chief soon gratified our
wishes, and gave out an order on the evening of the
9th of November : "To-morrow the army will
drive the French upon Bayonne and behind the
river Adour.   Light Division will get under arms
at 2 o'clock in the morning and march to the point
of attack, where the Division will form in three
columns of attack and remain until daylight, and
the signal to advance will be a salvo from thirty
pieces of cannon."   This order produced the greatest
joy.   We spent a jovial evening, singing and dancing
until 12 o'clock.   I then rolled myself up in my
blanket and slept until two, fell in, and marched to
the place appointed.   As soon as the day dawned the
long-wished signal was given.   No music is so delicious
to the ear of a soldier.   We moved forward under a
heavy fire from the enemy's works without ever exchanging a shot until we got up to them and scaled
the walls.   Then the work of death commenced.
Johnny was so paralysed at the cool bravery of the
British that he instantly became panic-struck and ran in
every direction.   Some few who had the temerity to
stand were instantly no more.   I saw some heroic
officers who tried to rally their men.   They fell like

1813 brave soldiers, covered with wounds and with glory. In this way we carried work after work which were apparently invulnerable. It was a beautiful sight to see 70,000 men or more moving in every direction. A continued roar of cannon and musketry, the smoke rising along the whole line. We marched and fought until about three o'clock in the afternoon, when we formed to attack the last body of troops opposed to us (I mean to our Division). The ground was at that place very strong. Just as our gallant Colonel Barnard was reconnoitring how to move to the best advantage, a musket-ball entered his right breast. He fell. I was near him, and got him put into a blanket and taken a few paces to the rear. He began to spit blood, the ball having passed through his lungs. He soon came to himself and said, " Simmons, you know my situation. Am I mortally wounded?" I felt the wound, and answered, "Colonel, it is useless to mince the matter; you are dangerously wounded, but not immediately mortally." "Well, Simmons," he replied, " be candid. I am not afraid to die." I answered, " I am candid." He said then, " I am satisfied." I was preparing to bleed him when two surgeons came up. I handed over my charge and ran back to my company, and had the honour of being at the finishing stroke.

As soon as the battle was done, Lieutenant-Colonel Gilmore and the surgeon came to me and requested me to go and take charge of the Colonel. I must tell you that Colonel Barnard for his great gallantry was made Prince of Wales's aide-de-camp. He is also a man of family and interest, and universally beloved by the regiment. I went to him and commenced as a surgeon. I bled him occasionally 1813 when the symptoms required it, and had the entire treatment of him. In ten days he began to recover, and has done so well that he is now out of danger. I daily wrote reports of him, which were shown at headquarters. Lord Wellington was particularly anxious about him. The most eminent surgeons in the army have paid me high compliments for my treatment, and the Colonel has not suffered any one to interfere with me.

Five days back we removed to this place, the headquarters of the army. I dined the other day with Lord Wellington, and have since dined at the tables of the first men of distinction in the army. I shall stay at this place for a fortnight, and then return to my regiment. To gain the friendship of a man of Colonel Barnard's ability, who will next year be a General Officer, will always be of use.

Joe is very well. He behaved himself most gallantly, I assure you. The regiment are very proud of him, and in my absence he is invited to dine out frequently. Joe sticks by me. I got him placed in another company, as the boy wanted me to take care of his money and concerns. As I am a bird of passage, I wished to teach him how to take care of himself, for fear he might be deprived of me one day or another ; he then would be at a loss. He lived away from me for a fortnight, that was, he paid to another mess, but whenever I had anything good I always found Joe present. I therefore told him he might live with me, but he should pay regularly and keep his own accounts, which he agreed to. Since I left the regiment

1813 he still lives with my captain, with whom he is a great favourite. I have a note from him daily about some nonsense or another. The last two fights cost us about four officers killed and wounded ; we have been very lucky in not having more. Joe is now at the top of the list, and will be a lieutenant in two or three months, which will give him ten dollars a month more. I gave him a horse to ride. He has another for his baggage. If .I have a fine jacket or anything *dressy*, he manages to make friends with my servant to use them. I have got the name of an old fellow. All the women say I am his father and laugh when I tell them he is my brother. I had almost forgot Maud. He is well, and I mean him to spend his Christmas with me if we are quiet. I anticipate the happiness we shall enjoy. If we could spend it under your humble roof, how much more happy we should be. However, you will have the satisfaction to know that your sons are moving in an honourable sphere of life, and their good fortune ought not to make them forget (though in a distant clime) those dear ties that can never be divided but by death. We are six months in arrear, and I have been at much expense this year. When I can raise a little money I shall send it. I hope my dear Ann is well, also Charlie and Betsy. When Charlie is fifteen I shall be able to provide for him. Three years more will give me a company. I then shall be able to maintain you handsomely. Something may turn out before. I do not like to build castles in the air. I hope my uncle is well. My best respects to him. It will give me pleasure in letting him read my letters, but do not make my affairs known to the world, I beg of you. Accept my

earnest prayers. I am, my dear parents, yours 1813
affectionately, GEO. SIMMONS.

If the weather becomes good, I think the army
will advance. The French people do not offer to
kill any British soldiers and we behave to the people
the same as if we were in England. The Spaniards
were sent back into their own country, as they began
plundering, which Lord Wellington would not allow.
It is much better policy to use the inhabitants well. If
you did otherwise, the whole country would be in
arms, and a soldier durst not go a hundred paces
from the battalion without being liable to be murdered
by some injured connection, whose misfortunes had
driven him to desperation. The French through
their horrid atrocities made themselves hated every-
where. This circumstance alone has been of great use
in making the nations, subjugated by these monsters,
throw off the yoke, or perish in the attempt.
Fortunately they are succeeding beyond human
calculation. The God of Battles is now inflicting this
just judgment upon the French. Write soon and
let me know how Charlie improves; Betsy also.
Educate them well, I beg of you.

As there is every likelihood of a peace taking
place, I shall endeavour (if such a circumstance should
happen) to get into the service of some country
allied with England after taking my pleasures in
England for some time, as I am determined to spend
my life and to advance myself, as a soldier. However,
there is time enough before this project need be
resorted to.

We expect another fight in a few days. I hope we

1813 shall soon be in possession of Bayonne. The foreign corps in the enemy's army, if they have an opportunity, will, I have no doubt, come over in bodies.

To be addressed, Lt. Simmons, 1st Batt., 95th Regt., Light Division, British Army, France.

CAMPAIGN OF 1814

Early in February 1814, Wellington, leaving a strong force to invest Bayonne, resumed the offensive, and having successfully passed a portion of his forces across the Adour and the Gaves, he fell upon Soult at Orthez and severely defeated him. Soult fell back slowly, but after a fight at Vic Bigorre it became clear to him that he must retreat on Toulouse.

Three miles from Tarbes he formed for battle once again, with Clausel in front of him, covering that town with Harispe's and Villatte's Divisions. Wellington, following up, launched the Light Division against the centre of the French position. The three Battalions of the Rifles who were in the van, made a violent attack on Harispe's Division and drove it from an exceptionally strong position without assistance.

Clausel made a skilful withdrawal upon Soult, and the latter retreated during the night.

Then ensued the operations on the Garronne which terminated in the battle of Toulouse, fought on 10th April. A few days later the news of the abdication of Napoleon arrived, and with it hostilities ceased, but not before the garrison of Bayonne had made a desperate sortie, in which many hundreds of lives were uselessly sacrificed.

There exists no more pathetic description of the treatment meted out by England to her soldiers, who had, by their gallantry and devotion, rescued Europe from the tyranny of Napoleon, than the words with which Napier brings to a close his stirring account of the long and bloody struggle in the Peninsula. ". . . The British infantry embarked at Bordeaux, some for America, some for England; the cavalry, marching through France, took shipping at Boulogne.

"Thus the war terminated, and with it, all remembrance of the veterans' services.

" Yet those veterans had won nineteen pitched battles and innumerable combats ; had made or sustained ten sieges and taken four great fortresses ; had twice expelled the French from Portugal, once from Spain ; had penetrated France, and killed, wounded, or captured 200,000 enemies, leaving of their own number 40,000 dead, whose bones whiten the plains and mountains of the Peninsula."

It was not till 1848, *thirty-four* years after the termination of the war, that the services of the few veterans who then survived was acknowledged by the issue of a medal !

CHAPTER XIII

Journal—12th January–21st March 1814

Is appointed to superintend the telegraph of the Light
Division—Visit from brother Maud—Commencement of
the campaign of 1814 —The 1st Battalion sent to St. Jean-
de-Luz for new clothing—Simmons joins the 2nd Battalion
—Bayonne invested—The 2nd and 3rd Battalions ford the
Gaves—Simmons and some of the 2nd Battalion occupy a
house and fire from the windows—Excitement of the lady
who owned it—The French peasantry are in great fear of
the English, but are soon reassured—Passage of the Gave de
Pau—Simmons puts his socks in his cap, as he is certain
the Rifles will be sent across the river—Three British
Divisions cross by a pontoon bridge.

Battle of Orthez

The 1st Battalion and the gallant 43rd Light Infantry not
present—The 52nd Light Infantry make "a beautiful
advance in the face of thousands"—The French driven off
the field—The French people treat the British soldiers as
friends—The 1st Battalion rejoins the army and Simmons
his Battalion—Sharp skirmish by 15th Hussars, supported
by some Rifle Men and two six-pounders with French
cavalry—Advance resumed.

The Action of Tarbes

The French occupy a strong position—The three Battalions of
Rifles ordered to dislodge them—The French fill a wood
with skirmishers, but are driven out—A very stiff fight—
Heavy losses—"Never saw Frenchmen so thick on the
ground"—Towards evening is severely wounded—Rescued
by his servant, Henry Short—Is moved into Tarbes—
Brother Maud hears he is wounded and searches for him all
night—Finds him and gets him a good billet—Battle of
Toulouse—"Is much hurt at not being there."

LETTER No. XXIII

*To his Parents, from Tarbes, France, dated
27th March 1814*

France a most delightful country—Detestation of the people
for Buonaparte—Their faith in the British—Description
of Soult's position at Tarbes—The eighteen companies of
Rifle Men (1st, 2nd, and 3rd Battalions of the 95th)
attack it and have some "fine rifle practice"—Is knocked
over at close of fight—Holds a medical examination of
himself, and finds his knee-pan is fractured—"Not for
Chelsea yet"—Hopes to get well and have another fight
with *Johnny*—"Our Boys got sadly mauled as usual."

Finished by Maud Simmons

Describes his brother George's wound and the life at Tarbes.

Journal—13th April–23rd July 1814

Is moved to Pau in a coach—Recovers and starts to rejoin—
Marches to Toulouse—Goes to the theatre with his two
brothers—Rejoins the 1st Battalion at Castel-sarrasin—
Pleasant life amongst the French—End of the war—

Orders to return to England—The Rifles give a ball—The Light Division bid farewell to their Portuguese comrades —Gets leave for England—Sails down the Garronne for Pauillac—Embarks on a transport—In collision—The voyage home—Lands at Portsmouth, takes the London coach, and arrives at the Old Slaughters Coffee House.

Journal—12th January–21st March 1814

This day I was appointed to superintend the tele-graph of the Light Division stationed near " Garat's house." [1] Had a log house formed to remain in. This post was near Arraunts. 1814 Jan 12th

My brother Maud paid me a visit. I gave him a good beaf-steak. The battalion he belonged to was returning from St. Jean-de-Luz with new clothes. One of his baggage animals lay down close to my post. I was obliged to send for a mule and take the half-starved devil in exchange. His servant seemed quite delighted when he had got his master's baggage upon my mule, and hurried away for fear I might change my mind. 15th

The 1st Battalion Rifles was placed in the 2nd Brigade, and the Brigade is now commanded by Colonel Barnard. The 2nd Battalion joined the other Brigade of the Light Division. 24th

Numbers of French families who had left their homes have returned, as they find the British soldiers only war with those who have arms in their hands, and not with the unfortunate inhabitants of the country.

The British army was again put in motion. The Feb. 16th

[1] The Château d'Urdanches near Arcangues was thus styled by the British, after its owner.

1814 Light Division moved to within a league and a half of Labastide-Clairence.

Feb. Marched near the town, and encamped near the
17th heights overlooking it.

18th   Put into houses, the weather being very cold and rainy, also changing into sleet and snow.

19th   The 1st Battalion Rifles with the 43rd Light Infantry marched to St. Jean-de-Luz for their clothing. I took the advantage of being on telegraph duty, and remained with the army.

21st   Marched to Isturits and joined Captain Duncan's company (2nd Battalion) until the return of the 1st Battalion.

22nd   Marched to St. Palais. The enemy had blown up the bridge over the Bidouze River. Sir John Hope with the 1st Division passed the Adour near its mouth and invested the citadel of Bayonne. A bridge was soon after constructed, and the town closely blockaded.

23rd   Marched to near La Chére and Charrette ; on piquet.

24th   Passed the Gave de Mauléon at a ford near the village of Nabas. Moved forward to the Gave d'Oleron. Found a squadron of French Dragoons drawn up on the opposite bank of the river. A neat little cottage close to the river had been built upon an eminence on its bank. I entered with some men and commenced firing from the chamber windows upon the French to cover the advance through the ford ; the river being nearly up to the men's shoulders, compelled them to link together by the arms to enable them to cross. Millar's and Duncan's companies were the first that crossed. The poor housekeeper, when my men began to fire from the 1814 windows, laughed and cried and jumped about in a most extraordinary manner, but still her curiosity led her to the window. I was afraid the foolish woman would be shot, and with little ceremony, assisted by one of the men, put her into a back room and bolted the door upon her. One bold fellow galloped forward to the ford. One of my Rifle Men from the window shot him off his horse in very pretty style. The ford was at Ville Nave.

Marched to near Oreon and encamped. I went into a respectable farmhouse on the roadside and found the people within in great confusion and some of the women in tears. It was very wet and cold, and my appearance was not much improved from having so recently waded up to my shoulders in the river. I sat down by the fire and asked for a little wine and something to eat. The people ran to get me some. A chubby, rosy-faced child, who appeared to be the only one of the family that did not look upon me with horror, came near. I took him up and began to kiss him. We were soon, as well as the whole family, great friends. These poor people expected that we should carry fire and sword amongst them. The French, I am sorry to say, did so in Spain and Portugal, and too often in their career committed atrocities that savages would shudder at.

Marched to near Orthez. The enemy blew up Feb. the stone bridge over the Gave de Pau on our approach. 25th The suburbs ran on both sides of the river, so that a sharp fire was kept up between the French and our Light troops. Towards evening, as a column of the enemy were entering Orthez, Lord Wellington ordered

1814 it to be cannonaded. Some French officers rode up and down their line of march to make the men move steadily along. The enemy appeared in great force, having concentrated large bodies near the town.

Feb. About 12 o'clock the Light Division was ordered
26th to move to the right of Orthez and pass a ford. I was so much impressed with the certainty of an attack being made that I pulled off my socks and put them into my cap to keep them dry. A large force of the enemy was formed up ready for us, with several pieces of cannon. When we were nearly within range, an order came to retire, and now a movement was made to the left of Orthez, so that by this feint the 3rd, 4th, and 7th Divisions had crossed the Gave de Pau by a pontoon bridge thrown over the river some distance to our left, and we were now moving to these Divisions. The Light troops skirmished with the enemy until dark. Encamped near Salles, close to the pontoon bridge.

BATTLE OF ORTHEZ

27th   The enemy were in position in great force, determined to wait our attack. We passed the river and moved forward. Unluckily our 1st Battalion and the gallant 43rd Light Infantry were away from the Light Division, so that during this action the Division was scarcely engaged, being only occasionally exposed to a cannonade, with the exception of the 52nd Light Infantry, who made a most beautiful advance in the face of thousands, and drove the enemy from their commanding position, which seemed to be the signal for the whole line to retire. Our columns followed until dark. The French appeared to me to have fought

this day better than usual. The loss was severe on 1814
both sides. Numbers of killed and wounded were
found upon the roads, and several of their soldiers
threw away their arms and put on farmers' clothing.
Encamped for the night near Bonne Garde.

Move forward to Duerse.   Feb.

Crossed the Adour at a very deep ford, and 28th
entered Mont de Marsan. The last of the enemy left March
it as we approached.   1st

I purchased a horse for twenty-five dollars, and
took him away to my billet. This place is large, and
abounds with wine and eatables of all descriptions.
The next morning the Frenchmen would not have
sold me the horse under a hundred dollars, so that I
was very lucky. It is quite droll to see the French
people treating us as if we were friends instead of
enemies. We certainly paid for everything, and now
it was found necessary to pay us regularly. A horse
of mine died here.

Marched to Bretagne. Bad weather.   2nd

Marched to Barcelonne, nine miles, and bivouacked 4th
near Aire. Frosty and cold.

At daylight marched to some straggling houses 10th
near Arblada. Snowy day.

Moved into a better house.   11th

My Battalion joined the army again. I left the 12th
2nd Battalion. I gave my friends an account of the
late operations. Took over the accounts of Captain
C. Smith's company.

The Light Division formed on the high road. 14th
An attack expected. Continued here the whole day.
At six o'clock marched back to quarters. Marshal
Soult menaced the 2nd Division. Nothing done.

1814
March
16th
A party of the 15th Hussars, supported by some Rifle Men and two six-pounders, attacked a party of French cavalry and cut them up in good style and took a number of prisoners. Strange enough, a French captain was desperately wounded close to his father's house, which house he had not seen for many years. He was taken into it, and died soon after.

17th   Marched to St. Simon. On piquet.

18th   The Division assembled at Ville St. Germain. Crossed the Arros at Task. The Division halted at Plaisance. Three companies of our battalion crossed the river, and took up their quarters in a small village. Close to the house that I, with the company, occupied, an inhabitant was murdered. I heard the shot fired just before I lay down, but had no idea that a human being had been deprived of his existence. We tried every means to find out the villain, but to no purpose. We collected and gave the widow a sum of money.

19th   Marched to near Auriébat. Continued there some hours. Moved to Aget and vicinity.

ACTION OF TARBES

20th   Marched through Rabastens to near Tarbes. The enemy were posted in very strong position on a chain of heights, and occupying the town of Tarbes. Our three battalions of Rifle Men were ordered to dislodge the enemy, which we went about at once. The front of the commanding ground was covered with wood. The enemy filled it with skirmishers, which we turned out, and then attacked their line. We were a considerable time in driving *Johnny* from all the strong ground whereon he was posted, but 1814 ultimately we succeeded. I never saw Frenchmen before so thick upon the ground; it was covered with dead bodies. Captain Duncan was killed; Lieutenant-Colonel Norcott, three captains, and five lieutenants wounded, and a number of our poor fellows bit the dust towards evening, after having passed through the day's fight. A Frenchman took a long shot at me; the ball fractured my right knee-pan and knocked me down as if I had been struck with a sledge-hammer. Some others, seeing me down, fired several shots at me. My noble servant, Henry Short, as soon as he observed me, came running to me, and, with an oath, observed, "You shall not hit him again but through my body," and deliberately placed himself in front of me. Colonel Barnard rode up, jumped off his horse, and showed me the greatest kindness.[1]

The following morning I was moved into Tarbes March in a cart. Part of my brother Maud's regiment 21st remained to guard the wounded. He was acting as Town Major. He was afraid I might be hurt, and before dark came to see me. Several soldiers told him I was wounded. He hunted about to find me the whole night, but without success, and quite in despair was returning into the town when I espied him. He soon got me a good billet. The battle of Toulouse took place soon after. I felt much hurt at not being there.

The fighting now terminated, and we lived upon the best terms possible with the French people.

[1] I suffered much from this wound until the bone united. I was put into a house for the night with many of my wounded comrades.—G. S.

LETTER No. XXIII

TARBES, FRANCE, 27*th March* 1814.

MY DEAR PARENTS—I received your letter at
Arraunts. As I had nothing worthy of your notice at
that time, I deferred writing until this period. The
remark in your letter pleased me. "You could
willingly forego the pleasure of seeing me, if it
was not compatible with my duty to leave my
regiment." It was a remark that showed a nobleness
of soul which every father of a soldier ought to
possess when duty and honour are the barriers. My
brother Maud's regiment casually passed my quarters
the day I received your letter. He was pleased with
it. He took a beef-steak and set off. Joe left the
regiment "on command" two months back to take
charge of all the convalescents belonging to the
Division in Spain. I have heard from him several
times. I have at last got him relieved, so he will
soon be again with his regiment.

I was appointed Director of the Light Division
Telegraph, for which I received a dollar per day for
some time. Colonel Barnard presented me with a
gold watch, which he purposely sent for to London.
France is a most delightful country and abounds with
everything. The people detest Buonaparte — all
but the officers of the army and those others who only
support him and his diabolical cause from interested
motives. The people are astonished at the liberality
of the English. We behave to them as if we were
at home, and, though fighting frequently with

Soult's army, in their towns the peaceable inhabitants
have more faith in us, generally speaking, than in their
own army. This is a happy way of making war,
for how many thousands of our brave fellows when
wounded and left on the ground would not otherwise
have been murdered by the injured peasantry. Instead
of that, they take the wounded to their houses, protect
and feed them. The army that is now opposed to
ours is Marshal Soult's. He is a persevering fellow.
Though thrashed every time we come in contact with
him, still he moves to another position, making it
as strong as possible, and waits till we move up and
thrash him out of it. The French army fought
very obstinately at the battle of Orthez, better than
usual, but every cock ought to fight better upon its
own dung-hill. After the business at Orthez our
army seldom could get a peep at *Johnny*. Though
we endeavoured to stick close to him, still he moved
off in the night. However, Soult began to pluck up
courage and get very bold, he having drawn us back
to the Pyrenees. His army was placed in position,
the left upon the base of the Pyrenees, the centre
covering the town of Tarbes (the high road to Toulouse passes through this place, and it is consequently
a place of importance to Soult) ; his right ran along
the high ridges of hills that rise abruptly from a fine
plain. There was a small river in front of the position, the hills occasionally patched with clumps of
brushwood and trees, which assisted the enemy much,
as he had an opportunity of hiding his columns.

Lord Wellington, with his usual coolness, took a
peep at the enemy's position (our columns were at
the same time concentrating) with the eye of an

1814 eagle, and ordered the different columns to advance to their different points. Our eighteen companies of Rifle Men attacked a steep hill, covered with wood, under a tremendous fire ; we soon hunted them out of it, and had fine rifle practice upon the plain. This day my usual good luck did not attend me, for near the close of the day about ninety men threw themselves behind a ditch and kept up a running fire. We were moving upon it to dislodge them when a musket-ball struck me upon the knee, forced into the wound my trousers and drawers, and glanced off. My fighting was finished. I fell, and seeing my knee bloody, I began to think I should soon be without a leg. However, on examination, after collecting myself a little, I found the joint had not received material injury, only the knee-pan, which is fractured, so that I shall not enlist for Chelsea yet. I hope in two months to be on the march with my regiment. I had the pleasure to see the enemy beaten at all points before I left the field of battle, which was great consolation. On the 21st I was moved on a waggon into this town. The first person that saluted me was Maud. Judge how delighted I was. He had got me a comfortable quarter. I had nothing to do but enter it. I have kept my bed until to-day. I have managed to get up and sit by the fire with my leg supported upon pillows. The pleasure I feel in having done my duty more than doubly repays me for the pain I suffer. If I am rendered incapable of joining my regiment as soon as I could wish, I shall come home for a while, but on the other hand, if I soon get better, I must have another fight with *Johnny*. I had been collecting some money for you,

as my pay and other emoluments were very good, 1814
but this job has brought me back upon six shillings
and sixpence per day, and the money will only
support me with what I have saved. My brother
told me I ought to be very thankful I had it. I
assure you it is a great pleasure and a comfort to me
to have him here. Three companies of his regiment
have been left to protect us from any armed peasantry,
so I am safe enough. You will see by the *Gazette*
our boys got sadly mauled as usual. I am glad Joe
was not there as things have turned out. If I can
purchase a veil for Ann I will. God bless her. My
best love to dear mother. I am glad Charlie is so
stout. Betsy I have forgotten ; she was young when
I left home. My love to her. I am happy to hear
my uncle approves of my conduct. I am striving
always to deserve his esteem. Let him see my
letters, but again I caution you not to mention them
publicly on any account. Maud will finish. I am
tired. Sergeant Fairfoot is well and with the regiment, unless wounded on the 20th.

Finished by Maud Simmons

MY DEAR PARENTS—I am happy to say your
brave son is in a fair way of recovery, thank God !
He and I spend our days together very comfortably.
We have everything very cheap. Claret and Bordeaux
wines very good and cheap—about a shilling a bottle ;
every other thing in proportion. We are well out of
the fighting at present, confound it ! Left here as a
guard to take care of the sick and wounded in this
town. However, I am repaid for being out of the

1814 fight by being able now and then to drink George's allowance of wine as well as my own and talk over past times.

The lady with whom I live is a most respectable woman. She made me laugh heartily just as I finished this letter. She observed I was uneasy, and asked me the cause. I told her my leg was very cold. She immediately pulled off her flannel petticoat and wrapped my leg in it ; so much for French politeness. She has been showing me all her fine clothes and dressing herself in the most ludicrous manner. Of course I tell her she looks charming. I have now a dozen French books upon my table, and the good lady is determined to learn me the language. She has also got me a master, so I shall be a complete Frenchman in a little time by force. My time, as you may suppose, with the exception of ague by way of interlude, passes very comfortably. George, I can assure you, is a desperate fellow amongst the French boys, but I do not think he will see any more fighting. Soult's army is deserting in great numbers. I am adjutant here for the present, merely for amusement, as I have had the command of a company for nearly twelve months, and lost nearly two-thirds of my company when I was wounded. However, M. Français has been paid off all old scores lately. Joe is expected up here. This is a very fine town, and contains everything to make a man happy. I am delighted with it, and could spend my life here were there not such people in the world as dear father and mother and sisters. Peace must shortly bring us together, when I hope we shall all meet without the loss of legs or arms. I am advising George to go home, but he wishes to see more fighting.   If George 1814 gets his company before an old soldier like me, it will be strange.   I wish he may, for he deserves it.   Tell Ann I was inquiring the price of veils, and find them too dear as yet.   We may go on to Paris, and then we will have an opportunity to buy cheap.   Let my mother know I have a snuff-box for her, which French manners oblige me to keep filled, and I now and then take a pinch myself, which never fails to remind me of my dear mother.   George and I mess together for the first time since we came to the Continent, and live here like fighting-cocks.   I wish it was possible for you to come and spend a few days with us.   You would not be a little surprised to see how happy we live in an enemy's country, as they call it, but I think them friends.   The Dragoon is just going off, so excuse. My love to you all.   God bless and take you into His Holy Keeping.

M. SIMMONS,
Lieutenant, 34th Regiment.

Journal—13th April–23rd July 1814

Moved in a coach to Pau.   Got into a billet the April next day.   Went to the Mayor and got a superb one 13th upon M. Colombots.   The kindness I received from this gentleman and his charming lady will never be erased from my mind.   Passed my time pleasantly, visited the play, and attended their balls.   The ladies pretty and handsomely dressed.

On the 9th of May, with much reluctance, took my May departure from Pau.   Rode to Tarbes.   My former 9th landlady highly rejoiced to see me.

1814   Halted.

May   Moved forward to Rabastens, being crowded.
10th
11th   Moved on to Contal. The roads covered with
Spaniards returning from prison.

12th   Marched to Mirande.

13th   To Auch, a very fine and large town. Halted at the
inn and dined. Moved forward in the evening to a
country house near Aubliet; the countrymen very
civil.

14th   Marched through Gimont to L'île en Jourdain.
Tired of dining *à la mode Français*, so bought a fine
piece of veal on my way and had it roasted.

15th   Marched to the famous city of Toulouse, and met
my brother. The town well built, the entrance by
the west gate very pleasing. The bridge a very fine
one, composed of arches over the Garronne.

16th   Visited the position and redoubts carried on Easter
Sunday by the English. I arrived at Toulouse and
went to my brother's quarters, his battalion (the
2nd Battalion 34th Regiment) being in the town.
To my agreeable surprise I found my brother, the
Rifle Man, with him. We talked over battles together,
and in the evening we went to the play. Some whim
struck me, and I put on my brother's red jacket, and
he took mine. The Colonel said, "I think Simmons
looks very dark in the face to-night, much darker
than I ever saw him before." The officer laughed
and told him I was the Rifle Man, which afforded them
much amusement, and made me acquainted with a
person, who but for this freak I should not have
known.

19th   Marched through Castelnau to Grizolles. Dined
with Captain Eaton, 2nd Battalion.

Joined my Battalion at Castel-sarrasin once again, 1814
and found the officers living in the gayest manner May
possible. The people extremely kind to us. On the 20th
22nd passed the Garronne with a party of ladies and
gentlemen to dine and dance at Belpeart. Passed a
pleasant afternoon, the dinner *à la mode Français*.
Plenty of eatables, but no knives or salt.

On the 26th passed the ferry opposite Moissac 26th
and visited the town. The French officers were
jealous of the civility shown us by the people, and
requested we would not visit the town any more.

The order having arrived for the English army to 31st
leave the country, we gave a ball and supper to the
gentry, who were highly delighted with our generosity.

Marched from Castel-sarrasin, the people in tears June
at our departure, and hundreds followed us a great 1st
distance ; showed the greatest concern at leaving us.
Halted at Montech.

Passed the Garronne by two boats at a ferry and 2nd
billeted in the town of Bourret.

Halted. Visited Le Mas, situated on the left bank 3rd
of the Garronne. The country very well cultivated
and abounding with everything.

Marched to Beaumont. The people at my house 4th
very kind. The good lady very sad and in tears
in consequence of a tremendous hailstorm having
materially injured her young crop of corn.

Marched to Tournecoupe. Yesterday left a fine 5th
turkey behind ; a woeful mistake.

Marched to Lectoure. Billeted upon an apothecary. 6th

Marched to Condom. Very wet. The road 7th
extremely bad.

Halted. 8th

1814   Marched to Nérac.

June   People remarkably civil. A lady presented me
9th   with some good Bordeaux wine.

10th   Casteljaloux, an interesting place. The country
covered with woods of pines, and the soil sandy. It
reminded me of some bivouac in Spain near Madrid.

11th   Bazas. The Portuguese in our Division formed
into a Brigade. Colonel Cerquiero commanded it.
All the Portuguese boys and women, and Spanish
ones also, to leave us and to go home in charge of
this Brigade, in order to be able to draw rations on
the road to their different homes. These soldiers
had been in the Light Division for several years and
were brave fellows. The Portuguese regiments, viz.
1st and 3rd Caçadores and 17th Portuguese regiment
of the line, formed in contiguous columns. The
52nd and 1st 95th were drawn up on each side of the
market-place and at 2 o'clock presented arms and
gave three cheers to the regiments as they filed through
us, which mark of our attention highly flattered the
Portuguese.

14th   Sailed down the Garronne from this place, the banks
covered with vineyards and highly cultivated villages ;
country houses innumerable. Arrived at the celebrated
mercantile city of Bordeaux about 9 o'clock A.M.
Found my brother, who happened to have got there
before me. Dined with him. Visited the theatre,
and also the small one (Gaieté).

15th   Marched at 4 A.M. Followed the regiment to the
camp near Blanquefort, about two leagues from
Bordeaux. Joe went to see his brother.

17th   Returned to the town.

19th   Camp.

Dined with Clerk, 66th regiment, at a small venta. 1814
Lambrecht not there.   June

Dined with Terry, 74th, and some others.   Drank 20th
to the memory of our brave fellows who fell at Vitoria. 21st
The men very jovial in camp.

Returned to Bordeaux.   22nd

Got leave for England.   23rd

Took leave of my brothers and sailed with Captain 24th
Kelly, 60th, and Lieutenant Dixon, from this place in a
boat about 5 o'clock.   Went on shore at an *auberge*.
Had a dinner.   Dixon and an officer of the 32nd fell
out.   Got into the boat at 10, rolled myself up in my
blanket, and did not wake until daylight, when the
boatmen informed me I had arrived at Pauillac.
Everything very expensive.   Got a billet upon M.
Mathier at Masset, two miles off.   Bad people.

Got an order to embark, hired a boat, and sailed 27th
at 1 A.M. for Verdon Roads.   Captain Kelly's servant
deserted and, by mistake, took away a bag of provisions.   The Garronne very wide and rough.   Never so
sick in my life.   Every wave ducked me and passed
over us.   Sailed among the vessels, and found the ship
had sailed the day before.   Returned to Pauillac.   Went
to my old billet.   Not well received.   Gave me a bed.
Had a good dinner and plenty of wine.

No ship for England.   The boatman wanted 100 28th
francs.   I offered him 40.   He refused.   Took him
before the Mayor and an officer of Marine.   Nothing
satisfactory.   Damned him and left him.

The boatman took 40 francs.   Major Lynche 30th
and Captain Dillon came into our quarters.   Dixon
played the flute, danced, and astonished the natives.   July

Got an order to embark on board the transport B.M. 1st

1814 A brig very much crowded and a very small cabin (name *Louisa*).

July   Went down the river. A signal made from a
2nd man-of-war to come near and put our people on board. Found it was a mistake.

3rd   Continued at anchor.

4th   Our Commodore on the *Zephyr* brig had the Blue Peter flying. Got under weigh at 8 o'clock A.M. Passed the Cordouan Lighthouse, situated about four miles from the shore. Captain Kelly, 60th ; Lieutenant Dalton, R.A.D., a curious fellow ; Lieutenant Dixon, and myself formed a mess. The wind now unfavourable daily.

10th   Our fresh provisions out ; the ship's beef not very good ; but the Captain did everything in his power to make us comfortable. Taken in tow frequently by the *Zephyr*.

12th   Becalmed when in tow. The *Zephyr* could not clear us, and stove in the quarter-gallery, giving the vessels a tremendous shock. Dalton, not having much faith in the vessel being able to put up with such rough usage, sprang out of bed and bellowed out, "Sinking, by G—!" He ran out of the cabin. Kelly and Dixon also turned out. I also made the best possible haste, being asleep, but started by the uproar on deck, where every one expected we should be stove in. I believe, from the good skill displayed in nautical affairs, the Captain cleared us. Dalton uttered some heavy "damns" against the *Zephyr* and took three or four stiff glasses of grog.

14th   Caught two sharks. The sailors persuaded me to try some. I was tempted, having been so long feeding on salt food. The flesh very disagreeable. In

the evening caught some mackerel, which was a great 1814
luxury. July

Entered the chops of the Channel. Soon had a view 17th
of the shores of Albion; a sight very gratifying
after the long absence.

Disembarked on the 22nd of July at Portsmouth. 22nd
My messmates dined with me at an inn. Took the
coach the same night for London.

Arrived in town. Went to Old Slaughters Coffee 23rd
House.

CAMPAIGN OF 1815

Napoleon, on his return from Elba in March 1815, finding that his overtures to the European Powers were without avail, and not daring to risk another defensive war, decided on assuming the offensive. For many reasons, the allied armies in Belgium offered him the most advantageous point to aim at, since, from their position and propinquity, they menaced Paris; also the Belgian nation was sympathetic to his cause, and if he could defeat the British and Prussians and possess himself of the Rhine frontier, he would be on the flank of the advancing hosts of Russia and Austria, and in the most favourable position for making peace on advantageous terms.

Having concentrated over 92,000 infantry, 22,000 cavalry, and 350 guns on the frontier, he suddenly broke in on 15th June, and the following day defeated the Prussians at Ligny with his main body, whilst his left wing, under Ney, fought an indecisive action with the British at Quatre Bras. After despatching Grouchy to pursue the Prussians, he turned with all his force on Wellington, who fell back to the position of Waterloo.

Here, on 18th June, the decisive battle was fought, the British and Hanoverians sustaining the repeated attacks of Napoleon throughout the day. The arrival of the Prussians on the right flank of the French during the afternoon greatly relieved the pressure on the British position, and towards evening the French, having been repulsed in all their attacks on Wellington, and being taken in flank by Blucher, were completely defeated and driven off the field of battle.

The Allies marched on Paris, which they entered on 7th July.

CHAPTER XIV

Journal—25th April–June 1815

The 1st Battalion embark at Dover for Ostend—Land at Ostend and proceed in barges to Bruges and Ghent—The Rifle officers call on Louis XVIII.—Reviewed by the Duke of Wellington—March to Brussels—Simmons is billeted upon Monsieur Overman.

LETTER No. XXIV

To his Parents from Brussels, dated 19th *May* 1815

Describes embarkation—Brother Joseph left in England as adjutant of the "four skeleton companies" at the depôt—The expenses of equipment for service—The voyage—Dreadfully sea-sick—Good quarters in Brussels—Many messages and good advice to his family.

*Journal—*15th–18th *June* 1815

The night of 15th June at Brussels—The call to arms—The Rifle Men march to Quatre Bras and get "a view of *Johnny*"—The British cavalry not yet arrived—The 42nd cut up by the French cavalry—The Rifles bivouac on the field of Quatre Bras—The morning of the 17th June—Breakfasts at a farm—The British Divisions

retire and are joined by the cavalry — The French
follow them up — Heavy rain and impassable condition
of the cultivated land — The 7th Hussars charge —
Also the Life Guards and Oxford Blues — The British
army reach Waterloo and take up a position there—Cannonading till dark—Bivouac on the field—The battle of
Waterloo—Dawn of the 18th June—The men clean their
arms and prepare for the contest—The French " form to
give battle "—No doubt now but that Napoleon himself
was there—Delight of the old Peninsular warriors at the
prospect of fighting under the Duke against Buonaparte—
The French artillery opens fire—Disposition of the Division under Sir Thomas Picton—The Rifles on the *chaussée*
by La Haye Sainte—Destructive fire from French guns—
The latter are advanced, and the French infantry columns
move to the attack—Terrible fire from the British Rifle
Men—The French column stopped—Simmons receives a
severe wound, and is dragged into the farm of Mont St. Jean.

LETTER No. XXV

*To his Parents, from Brussels, undated, but bearing
a postmark of 1st July 1815*

The march from Brussels to Quatre Bras—" A bloody and
obstinately contested battle "—The retirement to Waterloo—
The battle of Waterloo—The French cannonade—Advance
of "immense columns in imposing masses "—" Proud and
fierce appearance of the British "—Is wounded and trampled
on in the mud for some time—Finds himself in the farm of
Mont St. Jean—Mr. Robson, the assistant surgeon of the
Rifles, cuts a musket-ball out of his breast—Dreadful nature
of the wound—Sergeant Fairfoot endeavours to take him
to the rear—The French fire "riddling the house"—The
French press on, and the British have to fall back—Fairfoot
puts Simmons on a horse and he escapes—Terrible sufferings during the ride to Brussels—Reaches his billet at Monsieur Overman's at 10 P.M.—Is bled and has a quart of
blood taken from him—Followed by *five* more in the next

four days—Is going on well, but very weak—Sends money
to his parents—Expectations of a pension for his wound,
which will "make them comfortable."

Letter No. XXVI

To his Parents, from Brussels, dated 21st July 1815

Refers to his last letter as being written on 1st July—Has a severe
relapse two days after writing it—For seven days is in a
desperate condition with violent inflammation—Is bled
regularly two or three times a day—Followed by a stupor
of four days—The inflammation returns with more violence
—"The lancet was the only thing to save me"—Another
seven days of misery—Gets worse than ever, so sends for
the surgeon—Has "two large basins" of blood taken from his
arm—The surgeon is alarmed and does not like to try bleeding again—An eminent physician prescribes leeches—Thirty
are applied, followed by more, for three days—Suffers
great torture—Robson tells him he cannot live—Distress
of his poor little nurse (Mademoiselle Overman)—"Death
has no pangs for me"—The thoughts of his family too
much for him—Lies in a stupor for three days—Nature
effects a cure—Monsieur Overman's kindness, and devotion
of his "dear little nurse"—Is dreadfully emaciated, but
"sound at heart"—Makes arrangements for paying for
Ann's schooling—"The next letter will be from Paris."

Letter No. XXVII

To his Parents, from Brussels, dated
18th September 1815

Is able to walk about—First attempts to do so—Detailed account
of the scene in Mont St. Jean—Sergeant Fairfoot although
wounded, tries to put Simmons on a horse, but the latter
faints—The French cannon-balls and shells riddling the
farm—The surgeon's opinion of the wound and inutility of

moving him—Desperate onslaught of the French—All who
could crawl leave the barn—The dying Rifle officer—
Sergeant Fairfoot returns and lifts Simmons on to a horse,
also the other officer—Sends money to his parents—Paris
"a sink of iniquity"—Fears it may corrupt the morals of
the Rifle Men—Brother Joseph has more good advice—A
celebrated surgeon inspects Simmons's wound—"The next
letter will be from London."

CONCLUSION

Journal—25th April–June 1815

**1815
April
25th** Embarked at Dover at seven o'clock in the
evening ; after passing the pier the wind was not very
favourable.   Arrived at Ostend on the 27th at daylight and disembarked from on board the *Winsley-dale*
packet.   Embarked again on board Dutch schuyts
with six companies of the 1st Battalion, consisting of
ninety-two men per company.   The boats were drawn
by horses.   Arrived at Bruges before dark.   Our
boats halted for the night in the environs of the town.
It being dark, had no opportunity of seeing the
place.

28th Sailed at 4 A.M.   The country flat, but highly
cultivated and abounding with everything.   The people
dirty, and had not the appearance of being a healthy
peasantry.   The country in every direction intersected with dykes and canals.   Arrived at Ghent
about 3 o'clock P.M.   Got billets in the third
section.   My billet upon Mr. Barth, sugar merchant,
Quai de la Grue, No. 29.   The people very civil and
hospitable, every one making the same observation.
The houses very good and the town well supplied

with vegetables and fish. In fact, it abounded with 1815 everything. Rhenish wine, 2s. 3d. per bottle, of most excellent quality.

Paid a visit with all our officers to Lewis (Louis) April XVIII., who was flattered by the compliment. 30th The public buildings very good; the churches decorated in the Roman Catholic style. The statues in some of the churches are masterpieces of Art, and strike an attentive observer with astonishment at the natural appearance of the figures.

Reviewed by the Duke of Wellington, who was May pleased to express his satisfaction at our appearance. 7th In the evening went to the play. The house neither handsome nor well lit up.

Marched to Alost; it being filled with Lewis's 10th people, we went into the village of Wella.

Halted. 11th

At 3 A.M. marched to Bruxelles. Arrived about 12th 11 A.M. After much trouble got a billet upon the house of Mr. Overman, Rue du l'Etoile, No. 119. His family consisted of Monsieurs Jack, Albert, Edward, Gustavus, Mademoiselle Julia, Harriott, Ulalia, Mademoiselle Bolinus, Madame Notter, M. Lusmar. Continued here very comfortable until 15th June.

LETTER No. XXIV

BRUXELLES, 19th May 1815.

DEAR PARENTS—On the 27th of April five companies of the 1st Battalion embarked on board packet boats at Dover. As the senior officers of each rank

1815 had the refusal of going, the juniors were under
the necessity of staying at home, which was a very
great mortification to Joseph.   However, if we commence hostilities he will soon be wanted to fill the
place of some unlucky fellow that may bite the
dust.

Four skeleton companies remained behind. Joseph
was made adjutant of the depôt. He will have to
drill the recruits and young officers. He takes a
delight in his duty, and I have no doubt he will fill
the situation with credit.   It is highly flattering to
my feelings to see him pitched upon for a situation
of such responsibility by the commanding officer.
When I embarked it was nearly dark.   Our Boys had
been stationed some time at Dover, and the people
came in crowds to see us off, cheered us, and wished
us success.   It was at the same place that in 1809 I
embarked with as fine a regiment as ever left England.
Joseph was very sorry to part from me.   I wanted
him to come on board and sup, but he would take
nothing, and said, "I must leave you." He assured me
that through life he would always be a friend to you,
and if anything happened to me he would endeavour
to become your protector and tread in my steps.   I
have no doubt of him ; he is everything that I could
wish.   The moment at parting proved his heart, and
makes me daily bless the Almighty for putting it in
my power to serve him.

I think soon he will be able to send you some
money.   I was put to much expense in providing the
necessary articles for service.   I managed to buy a
baggage horse, which cost 15 guineas, and 3 guineas
for embarking.   I shall have £20 in July, but that is

some time to look forward to. When I get it I will 1815 transmit the money. I have not yet got a riding horse, but I must buy one ; my legs will never carry me through a long campaign. After a day's march I am lame. If I get hit again they must promote me or recommend me for Chelsea.

I was dreadfully sick all the way to Ostend. My throat swelled with vomiting to such a degree that I could scarcely speak for a week after. I saw very little of Ostend. We embarked upon the canal and arrived at Bruges in the evening. The next morning we moved forward to Ghent, a very fine town, the people remarkably civil, provisions and wine very cheap. Louis XVIII. is at this place. Our officers paid him a visit on the 13th. We marched to this town, which is very large. I have a room in a garden. The officers who mess with me prefer dining at my house, as I have the use of a delightful summer-house. At present we are enjoying ourselves. Rumour says Buonaparte is concentrating his forces, and means to attack us very soon ; for my part, I do not care how soon. I hope I shall see Paris before the summer is over, in a whole skin.

I hope my sister still continues to apply diligently to her studies. If she cannot pay Mrs. Sterling exactly as she could wish, I will be bound to pay the money for her. Do not let that damp her ardour or give uneasiness. I would rather sell anything I have got than suffer any of them being neglected on so essential a point as education.

I hope Charles is going on well, and Betsy also. If they endeavour to become clever I shall bring them some pretty things when I return.

1815   I suppose Joseph sent the parcel after I left England. I have not written to him yet.

Let me know Charlie's age and his height, as I want to ascertain when he will be able to commence his military career. I wish he was big enough. However, we must wait patiently.

I regret much having lost my old servant. His time of service was out previous to my leaving England. I was this morning obliged to turn off[1] some of our men for drunkenness. Liquor is so cheap here, the people give them it. My cook spoiled my dinner yesterday. I had friends dining, which made it more provoking. I am, as caterer to a mess, something like the father of a family. I always fed the officers in whatever company I belonged to. Major Beckwith is still with the company. He will go upon the staff very soon. On my own account I regret his leaving ; he is the most worthy of men. I am led to expect something handsome when the prize money for Spain is paid. It is expected to be paid soon. I hope it may. I shall empower Joseph to receive it, 'and send it to you.—Yours ever sincerely,

GEO. SIMMONS.

Direct, 1st Battalion, 95th Regiment, British Army, Netherlands.

Journal—15th–18th June 1815

June   At 11 o'clock P.M., when in bed, my servant came
15th to rouse me, saying the assembly was sounding. I directly dressed myself and went to our alarm post. Our Division (the 5th) formed in column of regi-

---

[1] *I.e.*, to "tell off" or punish.—ED.

ments near the park and waited for orders.   We had 1815
many vague reports in circulation about the French.

At daylight we marched through the Port de June
Namur. Numbers of people came to see us leave 16th
the town. We marched through Waterloo and halted.
I lay down for an hour. The Duke of Wellington
passed with his staff. The Division fell in and
moved forward to Quatre Bras, where we had a
view of *Johnny*.

The enemy commenced a cannonade, and our
regiment filed through high corn to the left. Four
companies were sent to drive *Johnny* from some
fields intersected with thick hedges and also ditches,
which we effected.

On this day our cavalry had not arrived, which
gave the enemy a decided advantage, and made us
keep nearer each other than otherwise would have
been necessary. The Cuirassiers charged the 42nd
and cut through them, but on recovering themselves
they formed a square, and the Cuirassiers paid dear
in turn for their temerity.

Until dark we had very sharp fighting.[1]

A man of ours was left near the French. When
it fell dark I went with three men to fetch him
away.   Both the poor fellow's legs were broken.
I deposited him in a house and joined my regiment.
Our Division formed in column of companies at
wheeling distance, the officers on the left of their
respective companies.   In this way we lay down.   I

---

[1] Marshal Ney says in a report that Buonaparte had taken
away his reserve, or he would have annihilated us.   In this fight
he must have had three to one, with the advantage of cavalry.
—G. S.

1815 pulled a greatcoat off a Cuirassier who was dead, and covered myself, which made me sleep well till one hour before daylight.

June   The piquets began to fire. We directly stood to
17th our arms. As soon as the day cleared we commenced firing at each other merely for amusement. I got a fire kindled, and purchased from a farmer, ham, etc. I made a good breakfast. This man's house contained upwards of fifty wounded French. Our men gave them water. About 11 A.M. the 5th and 3rd Divisions who had fought the day before, being the only part of the army engaged, retired. We soon were joined by the cavalry. The enemy followed close after us. The rain began to fall in torrents. The country being in a high state of cultivation, covered with corn, and the ground remarkably soft, the cavalry could scarcely raise a canter, the animals sank so deep. The 7th Hussars charged, but were sadly mauled. The Life Guards and Oxford Blues made some very fine charges, and literally preserved the 7th from being cut to pieces. About 3 o'clock in the afternoon the whole army moved into position in front of Waterloo. The enemy in parties re-connoitred, and was amused with the music of our cannon till dark. The night was very bad. The field where we were was all mud. I got a bundle of straw to lie upon, and I smeared an old blanket with thick clayey mud, and covered myself with the blanket, which prevented the rain from passing through, and kept me tolerably warm.

18th   At daylight the weather cleared. The men commenced cleaning their arms and preparing for the tremendous contest. We were soon convinced the

French were forming to give us battle, and had no 1815
doubt but Napoleon himself was there. Many old
warriors who had fought for years in the Peninsula
were proud of being pitted with our gallant chief
against Buonaparte and the flower of France. About
11 o'clock in the morning the enemy commenced a
heavy cannonade upon our line, which was spiritedly
returned from us. The 2nd Brigade of our Division
occupied the extreme left of the line, the 1st 95th were
upon the *chaussée* to Charleroi from Bruxelles ; 32nd,
79th, and 28th on the left, under the command of Sir
J. Kempt ; Sir D. Park commanded the 2nd Brigade ;
Sir Thos. Picton commanded this Division. Our
Brigade formed column and, from being much exposed to the enemy's guns, suffered severely. About
1 o'clock the enemy's guns were moved nearer. We
knew the attack must soon commence, and under
cover of their guns, four columns now made their
appearance, amounting to 20,000 men. They moved
steadily towards us. We formed a sort of line and
commenced a terrible fire upon them, which was
returned very spiritedly, they advancing at the same
time within a few yards. I had an impression I should
not be touched, and was laughing and joking with a
young officer about half-past four in the afternoon.
At this time I was a little in front of our line, and
hearing the word charge, I looked back at our line,
and received a ball, which broke two of my ribs near
the backbone, went through my liver, and lodged in
my breast. I fell senseless in the mud, and some
minutes after found our fellows and the enemy hotly
engaged near me. Their skirmishers were beaten
back and the column stopped. Two men dragged

1815 me away to the farm of Mont St. Jean, a little to the rear, where Mr. Robson extracted a musket-ball from my breast.

[Waterloo Journal ends. The preceding was apparently written in Brussels between 1st and 3rd July 1815.]

Letter No. XXV

[Undated but bearing post-mark of 1st July.]

BRUXELLES, 1815.

MY DEAR PARENTS—Through the blessings of Almighty God I am at last able to give you some account of myself, which I never expected to be able to do in this world. On the 16th of June, after passing a long tranquillity at this place, our Division marched at 4 o'clock in the morning. We moved forward 20 miles and gave the French battle. A more bloody or obstinately contested thing had seldom or never been seen. This convinced me that the French would fight for Buonaparte. The darkness of the night only separated us.

The following day was passed principally in reconnoitring and squibbing at one another; nothing done of consequence. Towards noon retired to a position. Our cavalry and the French had some charging and sabring each other. The rain fell in torrents, and continued raining all the night.

On the 18th the French seemed to be very busy moving immense columns opposite us preparatory to an attack. About noon they commenced a cannonade, from, I daresay, 150 pieces of cannon, which was very soon answered by us. Immense columns in imposing 1815 masses now moved towards us. If you could have seen the proud and fierce appearance of the British at that tremendous moment, there was not one eye but gleamed with joy. The onset was terrible. After four hours' exposure to it I received the dangerous wound which laid me amongst many others in the mud. Most of the men with me were killed, so it was some time before any officer noticed me, and not until I had been trampled over many times. The next place I found myself in was where the men and officers had been collected for the surgeon. A good surgeon, a friend of mine, instantly came to examine my wound. My breast was dreadfully swelled. He made a deep cut under the right pap, and dislodged from the breast-bone a musket-ball. I was suffocating with the injury my lungs had sustained. He took a quart of blood from my arm. I now began to feel my miseries. Sergeant Fairfoot was also here wounded in the arm. He got me everything he could, and said he would go and knock some French prisoner off his horse for me in order to get me off. The balls were riddling the house we were in. He got me a horse. They tried to lift me upon it, but I fainted ; some other officer took it. In consequence of a movement the French made with all their forces, our people were obliged to retire. If I stayed I must be a prisoner, and being a prisoner was the same as being lost. Poor Fairfoot was in great agitation. He came with another horse. I remember some Life Guardsmen helped me on. Oh what I suffered! I had to ride twelve miles. I forgot to tell you the ball went through my ribs, and

1815 also through my body. The motion of the horse made the blood pump out, and the bones cut the flesh to a jelly. I made my way to the house I had been billeted on—very respectable people. I arrived about 10 o'clock on that doleful night. The whole family came out to receive me. The good man and his wife were extremely grieved. I had everything possible got for me, a surgeon sent for, a quart of blood taken from me, wrapped up in poultices, and a most excellent nurse. In four days I had six quarts of blood taken from me, the inflammation ran so high in my lungs. At present everything is going on well. I am so weak, if I lift my head from the pillow I faint. I have sent you a five-pound note. This business has bothered me, but I shall get a year's pay, and most likely a pension, which will enable me to make you comfortable. My love to you all. Remember me kindly to my uncle. It distresses me that I cannot send Ann the sum she wants. She shall have it soon. A number of our officers are wounded in the town. Poor Lister was killed the first day. He was wounded in the stomach, and died a few hours after. We have so many applications for commissions in this regiment that it would be impossible to do anything in the way that Ann wishes. The only plan I can advise is, should there be a turning out into the line, to volunteer into any regiment the colonel may wish.

I am not allowed any person to help me, so I know nothing, and for God's sake do not talk about me or show this.

[The above bears no signature.]

LETTER No. XXVI

BRUXELLES, 21st July 1815.

DEAR PARENTS—I wrote you on the 1st of July. 1815
Enclosed in the letter was a £5 Bank of England
note, which at the time I could ill spare, but was
afraid you were much in want of money. If
you directed your letter to me, 1st Battalion, 95th
Regiment, wounded, Bruxelles, Netherlands, the letter
would have come to hand. I am afraid you directed
it some other way.

On the 3rd I was attacked with convulsions, and
at night with vomiting. Afterwards I lay in a state
of insensibility until the morning, when a violent
inflammation had taken place in my body. I was
bled three times, which gave me temporary ease. In
this way I went on for seven days, bled regularly
two or three times a day. I felt better, but continued in a stupor for four days, when the inflammation recommenced with far more violence than ever.
The lancet was the only thing to save me, so I was
bled again very largely. My liver now was much
swollen, and consequently my body was a good deal
enlarged. I had always an intolerable burning pain
in the liver. I never slept—often in dread of suffo-
cation. Bleeding was the only remedy for it. In this
way I went on for seven days more, when one evening, the pain being very violent, I sent for my surgeon
to bleed me. He took two large basins from my
arm. The pain abated much. I requested a little
more might be taken, but I suddenly fainted. It
was about half an hour before I could be brought to

24

1815 life. This alarmed my friend so much that he did not like to try bleeding again. He went and brought an eminent physician to see me, who recommended leeches. I had thirty immediately provided and applied to my sides. The next day, I had twenty-five more on the same spot, and the day after, twenty-five more. The last application of them was horrible. My side was inflamed and nearly raw from the biting of the others. I got fresh leeches every time ; they bit directly. I was in the greatest state of debility when the last were put on the raw part ; all taking hold at once made me entirely mad with anguish. I kicked, roared, and swore, and tried to drag them off, but my hands were held. Such torture I never experienced. As soon as they came off I ordered my servant to kill them, as well as about fifty more I had in the house. My dear friend who had attended me so kindly through this doleful scene came to see me. It was then one o'clock in the morning. "I am sorry they have tormented you with leeches, as they are of no use. Are you resigned ? You cannot live,"—this, poor fellow, with tears trickling down his cheeks ; on seeing which my poor little nurse, knowing so well the meaning, sobbed aloud. I answered, "Death has no pangs for me," but, alas ! at that moment my poor family appeared before my eyes. I thought you would have no provision. My heart seemed fit to break. I told Robson[1] the only uneasiness I felt was for my family. He endeavoured to console me. He went away, not expecting to see me again. In the morning he found me in a state of stupor, in which state I continued for three days,

---

[1] James Robson, the regimental Assistant-Surgeon.

to the astonishment of all. I suddenly found my 1815
body very wet, and called my nurse, who was astonished to find me speak. The bed-clothes being
turned down, there I was deluged in matter. The
plaster was taken off the wound, when the matter
flowed forth as from a fountain. I was immediately
rational and my body began to decrease. I knew in
a moment my life was saved. My surgeon came and
jumped for joy at my good fortune. The whole
family in my house came too. The kindness and
delight which Mr. Overman showed was beyond
everything. Every night before he went to bed he
came to me ; sometimes I was insensible. He regularly went into his study and prayed for me every
night. He is a very good man, a Protestant, and
speaks English well. My dear little nurse has never
been ten minutes from me since I came to the house.
When I was in that dangerous state I often fainted in
the night. She had in a moment a strong spirit at
my nose to revive me. For ten nights together she
never went to bed, but laid her head on my pillow.
I now must finish with observing that I am with the
best people in the world. The ball passed through
my liver. . . . I am dreadfully emaciated, but I am
sound at heart. I eat roast meat daily. In consequence of this discharge, I am obliged to eat very
largely. I daresay in three weeks I shall be able to
get out of bed. My spine is cut through at the hips.
My backbone hurts me sadly. I was afraid of my
shoulders, but I feed so well and drink such good
wine that I must put flesh on my bones. I bless
Almighty God for His mercy to me, for restoring
me as it were to life in so wonderful a manner. I

1815 wish the Frenchman had not hit me quite so hard. I am afraid it will take many years off my life and make an old man of me. I have got the ball, and shall make Ann a present of it. Joe passed by the place, but did not come. I suppose he has not heard I was worse. However, it is as well, as he would be hurt to see me in this emaciated state after writing and telling him I was out of danger. Ann must be much in want of money to pay for schooling. Now the only thing I can advise you to do is to draw the £20 out of Mr. Boyse's hands and pay it. I shall not be fit to travel for two months to come, and I can get no money until I arrive at my regiment. After I have been a little time at the regiment I shall go to London and get a year's pay. I shall send you £100, and the £17 will pay my expenses back to France. It is likely that we may stay in France a long time, which will be very lucky, as I shall get wine good and cheap—in fact, everything else in proportion. One year from the day I was wounded being passed, I mean again to go to London and apply for the pension, which, if I am lucky enough to procure, you will never again be in want of money.

My dear Ann I hope continues diligently her pursuit after knowledge ; Betsy also. Charles I expect delights in his studies. If he means me to be his friend, it is the only way to acquire my friendship.

.   .   .   .   .   .

My uncle will, I am sure, be very happy to hear that I am in the land of the living. My best regards to him. You will think me a strange fellow to write so much, but I write perfectly at my ease. I have

plenty of books, and amuse myself all day very 1815
agreeably, and knowing the danger of offering to
stir, I am quite happy.   Adieu.   God preserve you
all in His holy keeping,   G. SIMMONS.

The next letter I hope will be from Paris.   Write
soon.

LETTER No. XXVII

BRUSSELS, 12*th September* 1815.

MY DEAR PARENTS—I am now, thank God, able
to enjoy myself once more.   My health is nearly as
good as ever.   I increase in strength daily.   The
felicity I feel at being capable to walk about is
hardly to be described.   My legs swelled very much
when I first arose out of bed.   For some days I was
often obliged to be carried back and rubbed with hot
flannel for hours together.   I was afraid of becoming dropsical, but these bad symptoms have
entirely left me.   On Sunday, being the birthday of
my worthy landlord, we were very gay.   After a
splendid dinner I was gallant enough to walk with
the ladies into the country nearly a mile, where we
had cakes, etc., at a house, and then returned back.
Two young ladies supported me, which amused the
people that passed.   I have invitations to dine out
almost every day, but as I must live very steadily,
I often refuse.   The more I know of the good family
i live with the better I like them.   If I happen to
mention my thoughts of returning to England, they
are all melancholy, and request me not to think of it.
Their fine children, as soon as they get up, come
into my bedroom to kiss me and wish me good

1815 morning. A little girl often puts me in mind of my dear Betsy ; she always calls me her uncle.

I shall be able to return to England in a month if I continue going on well. The violent spasms that often seized me have entirely disappeared ; sometimes they came on when eating or drinking, and obstructed my throat in such a manner that I could not swallow. At first when I got into the garden I was so delighted with the scenery that I fancied I could walk in the presence of several ladies who came to pay an afternoon visit. I attempted it, and fell to the ground in fits. I certainly was out of my senses at the time. I alarmed the good folks, so that they all went home. I continued in convulsions all the night. This circumstance made me keep my bed a fortnight longer. I forgot to mention a circumstance which deserved my notice. Sergeant Fairfoot was wounded through the arm, and also through the hand, on the 16th. When I was carried off the field of battle and deposited in a stable upon straw, he came near me and expressed much concern. He supported me while the surgeon cut into my breast and dislodged the ball, which, being flat and terribly jagged, required some time. Every five minutes the cannon-shot from the enemy and shells were passing through this house, which made it a very dangerous place. Fairfoot was very anxious to get me away. He went in search of a horse, and returned with a Frenchman's, and tried to put me on it, but I fainted, and was carried back to my straw. When I came to myself, I heard the surgeons say, " What is the use of torturing him ? he cannot live the night ; he is better where he is than to die on horseback." This admoni-

tion made Fairfoot desist, but he got me water and 1815
behaved very kind. The enemy made a very
desperate attack, and it was thought this place would
in a few minutes be between the fire of the parties ;
under such circumstances we should be either burnt
or shot. Everybody that could crawl left the place.
I asked the hospital sergeant, who was the last man
there, if we were to be left ? He durst not answer me.
A gallant young friend of mine, who was badly
wounded and dying, crawled near me and said,
" George, do not swear at the fellow ; we shall soon
be happy ; we have behaved like Englishmen." At
this moment Fairfoot entered, and a Rifle Man who
gallantly exposed himself to carry me off the field.
Fairfoot said, "We must not, nor shall not · be
murdered, but there is no time to spare." A Life
Guardsman and he put me on the horse. I was
held on by the legs. Fairfoot also got my friend
away, but he died the same night, being a delicate
young man.[1] I stated this affair to my Colonel, and
all the officers know how much Sergeant Fairfoot
merits my praise.[2] If I can do him a service he may
always command me ; his character as a brave soldier
stands with the first in the regiment. You may tell
this to his father. I hear from Joe frequently. He is
well. Never mention me in conversation anywhere,

[1] Lieutenant Elliott D. Johnston of the Rifles was being conducted on horseback towards the village of Waterloo by two
Rifle Men when a French cannon-ball, of which there were
many bounding along the road, struck him and killed him on
the spot. This was evidently unknown to Simmons when he
wrote this letter. It is hardly to be wondered at that this
" delicate young man " died.—ED.

[2] Sergeant Fairfoot had been with him throughout the six

1815 as I do not want to be known at Hull. My side
continues very numb still, but time will, I hope,
render it better.   I am anxious to come to England
for the purpose of procuring the year's pay, which I
shall send you—at least one hundred pounds.   One
year after, I shall present myself at the Medical
Board for the pension, and if I get it, which there is
every likelihood of, why then, I shall laugh at my
wounds ; for to protect and support those that are
dear to me, my sufferings will be highly recompensed.
I enclose a five-pound note, which I hope will reach
you safely.   When I landed I bought a horse, which
cost me nineteen pounds ; now that I want to sell it, I
cannot get £10 (ten pounds) for it.   I have sent the
animal to my brother.   He has one already of mine.
If there is any likelihood of staying long in this
country, I shall return.   My horses, in that case, will be
ready for me, and otherwise I have ordered them to
sell them.   I wish our brave fellows were away from
Paris.   It is a horrible sink of iniquity, and I am
afraid will corrupt the morals of the thoughtless.

I have given advice to Joe, but I am convinced
that he will not run into extremes or extravagance.
I had some very good accounts of him from the
depôt before he came out.   I have shown myself to
several surgeons.   A celebrated one from Edinburgh

campaigns in the Peninsula, and is mentioned by Simmons as
having been present at the fight at the bridge of Barba del
Puerco in March 1810. He was subsequently made Quartermaster of the 2nd Battalion, and died in 1838 at Galway, in
the cathedral of which town there is a tablet "inscribed by his
brother officers to record his good and gallant services as a Rifle
Man in the Peninsula, France, and the Netherlands."—ED.

saw me and asked me all the particulars. My case 1815 will be published among many others. The next letter will be most likely from London. You need not answer this.—Yours,

GEO. SIMMONS, Lieut.

CONCLUSION

LITTLE more remains to be said about the career of George Simmons. He remained at Brussels for several weeks after the last letter here published was written, and was then well enough to travel to England, where he landed on 28th October 1815. He was sufficiently recovered of his severe wounds to start to rejoin his regiment on 1st January 1816, and served with the British army of occupation in France for nearly three years, returning to England with the 1st Battalion in November 1818. It was after the battle of Waterloo, on 23rd February 1816, that the 95th Rifles were, in the words of the *Gazette*, "by command of the Prince Regent, in the name and on the behalf of His Majesty," ordered to be "taken out of the numbered regiments of the line and styled THE RIFLE BRIGADE"; in those days a unique honour.

Simmons makes no mention of the return of the regiment to England beyond noting the date of their arrival at Dover. Sir John Kincaid, however, in his usual vivacious style, gives the following account of the officers commanding companies on the day of inspection after their return. "Beckwith with a cork leg; Pemberton and Manners each with a shot in the knee, making them as stiff as the other's tree one ; Loftus Gray with a gash in the lip and minus a portion of one heel, which made him march to the tune of dot and go one ; Smith with a shot in the ankle ; Eeles minus a thumb ; Johnston, in addition to other shot-holes, with a stiff elbow, which deprived him of the power of disturbing his friends as a scratcher of Scotch reels on the violin ; Percival with a shot through his lungs ; Hope with a grape-shot lacerated leg, and George Simmons with his riddled body held together by a pair of stays, for his was no holy day waist which naturally required such an appendage lest the burst of a sigh should snap it asunder, but one that appertained to a figure framed in nature's fittest mould to ' brave the battle and the breeze ! ' "

Simmons subsequently served at home until July 1825, when he accompanied the Battalion to Nova Scotia. On 17th April 1828 he was promoted Captain, at which time he had close on nineteen years' service. In 1834 he married in Jersey a daughter of Sir Thomas le Breton. In 1836 he returned to England with the 1st Battalion ; ten years later he obtained his majority, and in 1845 retired from the service after thirty-six years' service. Some three years later he was, in common with the other survivors of the Peninsular War, granted the "General Service Medal." He died on 4th March 1858, aged seventy-two.

"Brother Joseph" exchanged to the 41st Regiment, and served with it in the Burmese War of 1824, where he greatly distinguished himself at the storming of several stockades. He served also throughout the campaign of 1842 in Afghanistan, rose to the rank of Lieutenant-Colonel, and was granted a C.B. He lived to a great age, dying in 1882.

"Brother Maud" served in India with the 34th Regiment, and died at Madras of cholera some time after 1816.

"My dear Ann" died unmarried.

APPENDIX I

THE following letter has been selected out of many written to George Simmons by his old Peninsula comrades, since it is of especial interest. Sir Harry Smith served as a Lieutenant with Simmons throughout the Peninsular War, and was wounded with him at the Combat of the Coa in 1810. His wife, Lady Smith, whom he alludes to as "Juana" and "Juanita," was a Spanish lady whom he first met under most romantic circumstances the day after the storming of Badajoz. Sir John Kincaid in his *Random Shots of a Rifle Man*, describes this meeting and its consequences.

Letter from General Sir Harry Smith after the Victory of Aliwal

SIMLA, *16th June* 1846.

MY DEAR OLD COMRADE, GEORGE SIMMONS—On the 13th of May I received yours of the 15th of March, and on the 15th of June, yours of the 13th April.

You know me well, George, and therefore know nothing can make me a vain ass, but when I tell you I have received since the battle of Aliwal upwards of 150 letters of heartfelt gratification conveying to me theirs and your participation in every feeling of success which Almighty God has so guided me to, then, George, my heart expresses its fulness through the eyes by tears of gratitude and reciprocal affection. From every old friend—I have several still left to us—from every old comrade of the Light and 4th Division, have I received every expression of their approbation, their happiness in my having realised their often-expressed anticipations.

Your old friend possesses the good sense which you so kindly give him credit for, keeps pace with his delight in all the congratulations of our friends. Then, George, comes the *encomium* of THE DUKE.

Dear old master! if I have done that which meets *your* approbation, then is the cup of glory full indeed, for it is to your example I have desired to apply any share of the ability bestowed upon me.

I have had too from him the kindest of messages, and to his old friend Juanita, as he still calls her. George, my fight of Aliwal was really beautiful, and now I cannot say I wish on that day I had done this or that, but what I give myself any credit for was on the 21st of January, when the enemy, with his army of 24,000 men and 50 guns, so ably, energetically, and secretly anticipated my move to effect a junction with the corps at Loodiana, and nothing but pluck, Light Division experience, and inflexible adherence to purpose, brought me to the desired field of Aliwal. I lost some of my baggage, but should not have done that if my orders had been obeyed, but *Finis coronat opus.* I have had a letter from Joe, who tells me your happiness was such that your nerves so thrilled through your desperate old wounds as to make you quite ill.

Dear George, we little thought at Belem, when hopping about there, I should become a master of that art we were both " gurning " under, or a swimming master, with pupils in Sutledge!

I certainly hurried the rogues over the river a little unceremoniously, and the credit you all give me is not thrown away, I do assure you. I am appointed to a Divisional command, and must leave these hills at rather a bad season of the year, viz. the rainy. Between the alternations of a fiery sun and torrents of rain, some 600 miles, Juana will go, through not staying here as I advised her. I begin to long to get once more to my native land. Mine has been an awful banishment. I do so long to seize by the hand all those old friends who have so adhered to me notwithstanding my absence, and who thus so kindly feel *my* success and honour *their own*. If anything could make a man an ass *this* ought.

Juana sends her love, and you and your good wife I pray accept mine.—Your old friend HARRY SMITH.

Our old, dear, and mutual friends, Sirs Kempt, Barnard, and Lord FitzRoy Somerset, have written in most enthusiastic terms. Oh! such a noble son of Lord F.'s was killed close to me.[1] George, the hand of Almighty God has shielded me; all my staff were killed or wounded, and not I, or even a horse of mine, has *been touched*. I never dismounted, and I never in my life so exposed myself.

[1] Major Arthur FitzRoy Somerset, Grenadier Guards. He was the eldest son of Lord FitzRoy Somerset (afterwards Lord Raglan), and was serving in India as Military Secretary to the Commander-in-Chief, General Sir Henry Hardinge. He was killed at the battle of Ferozeshah on 21st December 1845, upon which occasion Sir Harry Smith commanded a Division under General Sir Hugh Gough (afterwards Lord Gough). The battle of Aliwal, at which Sir Harry Smith commanded, was fought on 28th January 1846.—ED.

APPENDIX II

MEDICAL CERTIFICATES

BRUSSELS, *2nd September* 1815.

I DO hereby certify that Lieutenant Geo. Simmons of the 1st Battalion, 95th Regiment, was dangerously wounded on the 18th of June 1815 in the Battle of Waterloo. A musket-ball entered the right side near the spine, fractured the 9th and 10th ribs, passed through the liver; I extracted it from the breast near the lower end of the sternum.

He experienced a high state of inflammation from the nature of the wound.

A formation of matter took place in the liver, and was discharged by the wound where the ball was extracted.

JAMES ROBSON, Assistant Surgeon,
1st Battalion, 95th Regiment.

I CERTIFY that Lieutenant Simmons, 1st Battalion, Rifle Brigade (late 95th), received a severe wound from a musket-ball in the thigh in action with the enemy at the Battle of Almeida, in Portugal, on the 24th of July 1810. He suffered much from the injury to the bone, and a consequent confinement of near twelve months.

He even at this period, if he uses much exercise, complains of pain and lameness. Also a spent ball on the leg.

I also certify that Lieutenant Simmons received a wound in the right knee from a musket-ball, in action with the enemy at the Battle of Tarbes, in France, on the 20th of March 1814. He suffered most severely from violent inflammation. There is still an enlargement of the knee, attended with pain in using much exercise in consequence of the ball having fractured the patella in its course.

I further certify that Lieutenant Simmons received an alarming wound from a musket-ball in the side, in action with the enemy at the Battle of Waterloo on the 18th of June 1815. The ball entered his right side, and was extracted from the breast.

In its course it fractured two ribs and wounded the liver. He suffered severely from suppuration of that viscus, as well as from a profuse discharge from the wound of his breast. He complains of spasmodic attacks of his side and pain shooting towards the right shoulder, with pain of the breast and difficulty of breathing, particularly in moist weather. His digestion is also much impaired. With a view to moderate these distressing symptoms and prevent their more frequent recurrence, he is under the necessity of using stays in order to give support to the body, and also to adopt the most abstemious plan of diet, with almost a total abstinence from wine and fermented liquors.

> JOSEPH BURKE, Surgeon,
> 1st Battalion, Rifle Brigade.

BOILIEU EN ARTOIS,
FRANCE, 24th October 1816.

This certificate I gave to Sir James M'Gregor, with the following one from our friend Lindsay.—G. S.

CAMBRAI, 1st November 1816.

I HEREBY certify that Lieutenant Simmons, 1st Battalion of the Rifle Brigade (late 95th Regiment), received a severe gun-shot wound at the Battle of Waterloo. The ball entered the right side, and having in its course passed through the liver and fractured two ribs, was extracted from the breast. This officer suffered considerably from the succeeding inflammation and suppuration, as also from the effects of the large and repeated bleedings which it was necessary to have recourse to in order to moderate the inflammation and fever.

He is still very liable to frequent spasmodic attacks in the side and pain in the shoulder. The powers of digestion are considerably impaired, and his breathing is rendered difficult by using any exertion.

Mr. Simmons is under the necessity of wearing stays in order to give support to his body, otherwise he would be unable to enjoy the exercise of walking or riding.

OWEN LINDSAY,
Staff Surgeon, 1st Division.